The Art of Active Dramaturgy

Transforming Critical Thought
into Dramatic Action

D1596169

The Art of Active Dramaturgy

Transforming Critical Thought
into Dramatic Action

Lenora Inez Brown

Focus *an imprint of*
Hackett Publishing Company, Inc.
Indianapolis/Cambridge

The Art of Active Dramaturgy
Transforming Critical Thought into Dramatic Action
Copyright 2011 © Lenora Inez Brown

Cover images © istockphoto/plainview, © istockphoto/DSG pro
Cover design: Kathy Squires

ISBN 10: 1-58510-351-9
ISBN 13: 978-1-58510-351-5

Previously published by Focus Publishing/R. Pullins Company

Focus an imprint of
  Hackett Publishing Company
P.O. Box 44937
Indianapolis, Indiana 46244-0937

www.hackettpublishing.com

19 18 17 16 15   2 3 4 5 6

Table of Contents

For my parents Beatrice and Leon, whose generosity,
support, and love knows no bounds.
I love you.

Acknowledgements

I started this book in 2006 at the suggestion of a playwright and friend. In truth, she encouraged me to consider a way to discuss dramaturgy so that collaborators and especially writers might become better prepared to embrace the dramaturg's contribution throughout the development and rehearsal process.

The task seemed somewhat daunting. Dramaturgy tends to resist any and all attempts to define it. If you ask a hundred dramaturgs what a dramaturg does you will receive 100 different answers. These many definitions make understanding dramaturgy as challenging as shoveling snow with a teaspoon after a blizzard; a seemingly never ending task.

I attempted to answer what a dramaturg does by exploring the approach the dramaturg takes and the mindset we try to teach dramaturgs and their collaborators rather than define dramaturgy by various tasks.

My parents Beatrice and Leon supported me throughout this endeavor—as they have throughout my life. They have always supported my choice to pursue a life and career in the arts, and for that I will be forever grateful. My sister Elizabeth was always there with words of encouragement, and my brother Warren gave me full access to his quiet house as deadlines loomed; his wife Pam and their daughter Poplar lent their support, too. My aunt Dr. Yvette Jackson and uncle Howard Gollub read the occasional draft—even on family vacations—and offered advice that greatly informed the final version.

From the first day I began this project, I could turn to my cheerleaders Sarah L. Myers, Karen Zacarìas, Tanya Palmer, and Paul Selfa, especially when the words wouldn't come and the task seemed overwhelming. Karen Girolami Callam, Jonathan Dorf, Bruce Ostler, Kae Koger, and Jayne Benjulian were tireless readers, whose comments proved invaluable.

My many students at DePaul also helped shape this work, in particular: Caitlin Hansen, Evan Fillon, Matt Didier, Summer Sparacin, Dee Demons, Elizabeth Schmeski, John Rooney, Kelly Kerwin, Jessica Galli,

Alexis Links, and Leslie Cunningham. A special thanks goes to Nate Speare for reading chapters during his summer vacation.

I would also like to thank the dramaturgy students at the University of Oklahoma, Carnegie Mellon, the University of Puget Sound, the University of Texas at Austin, University of Massachusetts at Amherst, and MFA playwrights at Hollins University for allowing me to share and develop my ideas with them. A special thanks to Kae Koger, Geoff Proehl, Michael M. Chemers, Suzan Zeder, Harley Erdman, and Todd Ristau for inviting me to their classes.

I visited the majority of these campuses while on leave from The Theatre School at DePaul University, and wrote the majority of the book during this time. I am forever grateful to The Theatre School for this time, and I thank Dean John Culbert, Dean Corrin, Rachel B. Shteir, Reginald Lawrence, and Heather Jagman for their supporting me during my leave. I am also grateful for the encouragement of my fellow Old St. Patrick's Church choir members.

I would also like to thank my publisher, Ron Pullins for his unwavering belief in this project.

This book would not exist without the many experiences I have had working as a dramaturg on set texts and new works. I would like to thank Tazewell Thompson, Ricardo Khan, Chuck Smith, Scott Kanoff, Robert Blacker, Gregg Henry, Kim Peter Kovac, and Gary Garrison for providing many of these opportunities. I would also like to thank Mame Hunt, Liz Engleman, Megan Monahan, and many of my fellow dramaturgs for sharing their expertise with me over the years.

And last, but certainly not least, the many playwrights I've had the pleasure of collaborating with—without your words we would have nothing.

—L.I.B.

"You see, but you do not observe. The distinction is clear."

~ Sherlock Holmes
A Scandal in Bohemia

Introduction

When I first set out to pursue an advanced degree in theatre, I knew that I wanted to study dramatic texts and how to use research to enliven the rehearsal process, so I set out to apply for theatre history and criticism programs. One school on my list did not offer a degree in theatre history but something called dramaturgy. I had never heard the word, but chose to apply, was accepted, and began my journey with this little known artistic pursuit. I quickly discovered that I loved this active approach to theatre history, criticism, and production, because the goal was to influence and shape productions rather than produce scores of published papers. What I also learned was that as clear as this discipline was to me, most theatre artists were mystified by the practice of dramaturgy and seemed to think it defied definition. For whenever I or a fellow dramaturg began working on a production, we had to define dramaturgy and how we our approached it, as if there were no common philosophical truths and practices.

Releasing Your Inner Sleuth

In the first Sherlock Holmes mystery *A Scandal in Bohemia*, the great detective quizzes his longtime friend Dr. Watson about the stairs leading from the hall to the flat. Holmes contends that Watson cannot recall how many steps there are, even though he's climbed them hundreds of times, because the esteemed doctor has not observed them; Holmes knows the number because, "I have both seen and observed."(Doyle 162-163) Sherlock Holmes suggests that the key to effective sleuthing is to observe rather than to just see.

To see, as Holmes suggests, is to witness, to note, and experience passively. To observe is to engage with and analyze or consider what's before you, what transpires; to deduce and reason why based on facts. It is observation coupled with seeing that leads to unusual and exciting conclusions. Many dramaturgs and any truly creative theatre artist, in effect, behave like the great detective for they must both see *and* observe what happens in a text and on the stage.

That said, few are as gifted as the great and fictional Sherlock Holmes. Most of us are like Dr. Watson, more than able but content to, in effect, blindly walk the traditional paths. Holmes, however, observes *and* sees. He acknowledges the flight of stairs and then considers and poses questions encouraging him to contemplate each step individually, as part of the whole and as a collective unit. Holmes takes, in effect, a dramaturgical approach.

Unlike Sherlock Holmes, dramaturgs do not have all the answers and cannot tell an artist the solution to a creative mystery, how the play should end, or how a character should progress. A dramaturg does, however, use these observation skills and observed facts to inform their collaborations with artists and to foster a creative environment to discover unique, artistic solutions.

Critical Thinking and Dramaturgy

Whenever an artist poses a critical question while alone or in a room with others, a sort of dramaturgy occurs. Active dramaturgy, however, goes beyond the basic critical questions to include analysis designed to facilitate immediate or eventual artistic/creative application. An active dramaturg seeks ways to articulate heady ideas into active language—that is, language that a performer can easily use to shape an acting choice or a designer, a design choice.

It's worth noting that asking critical questions and offering criticism doesn't mean telling others what's wrong. Criticism isn't negative nor does it restrict creativity. Criticism provides a way to identify what works well and what can work better. Critical thinking implies assessing material by using experience, facts, and instinct in equal measure. Active dramaturgs rely upon criticism, critical analysis, and critical thinking to cultivate an environment for creative thinking that leads to solutions artistic teams and actors can use and *do* on stage. Probing the work by posing critical questions can provoke discussion, dynamic ideas, and rich solutions that liberate art and elevate it in unexpected ways.

When analyzing a text, the tendency to dissect it as a purely literary work exists. A dramaturgical approach, however, embraces a philosophy that believes dramatic/analytical interpretation will and must change from production to production. To generate the flexibility in thought needed to create a unique, production-specific vision, artists use a distinct process defined by questions that are informed by the patterns and rules established by the play's story. This outlook allows a dramaturg to construct a fluid game plan, a way of moving forward. A game plan is not governed by a rigid list of ideas to discuss and evaluate the artistic team against; rather, it is a collection of observations and ideas that informs and shapes a dramaturg's artistic voice. Throughout this book are examples and discussions of how to develop a game plan or engage artistic collaborators in conversation rather than step-by-step sets of directions. Active dramaturgy is about flexibility and using the basic or fundamental dramaturgical tools to their fullest.

The Fundamentals of Dramaturgy

Like acting, directing, design, and playwriting, dramaturgy has its unique set of basic skills that apply whether working on Euripides' *Medea* or Shakespeare's *Hamlet* or the newest draft of a world premiere. Unlike other theatrical professions, dramaturgy is one of the few (if only) disciplines every aspiring theatre professional can avoid studying. Most liberal arts theatre majors or undergraduate and graduate conservatories require introductory classes in performance, directing, and design. Yes, students must take theatre history as well, to comprehend theatre's evolution, especially as it pertains to dramatic writing. And yes, a dramaturg uses theatre history to inform an understanding of a text or presentational forms and patterns. But theatre history is not dramaturgy.

All artists call upon dramaturgical skills as they approach their work. However, many are unaware how much dramaturgical thinking they rely upon. And, if the artistic team includes a dramaturg, the team is often unaware how to best collaborate with dramaturgs because few know what a dramaturg actually is and what dramaturgs do. *The Art of Active Dramaturgy* offers the student and emerging dramaturg as well as experienced artistic collaborators ways to articulate, discuss and develop critical ideas or observations into dramatic action for the page and the stage. Providing artists with the necessary tools needed to isolate the elements of the project and separate them from personal bias or ego, ensures a healthy collaborative environment.

Dramaturgy depends upon a love and knowledge of many ideas beyond theatre and those that are sacred to the Dionysian art. The practical skills active dramaturgy calls upon are: analytical or visual or historical research; analytical or creative or critical writing; crafting questions for writers and other artistic collaborators to help every element of the project exceed expectation; engaging in flexible thinking, that is thinking that simultaneously focuses on the present moment and its impact on future moments or scenarios, many minutes ahead.

Like any pursuit, an expectation of proficiency and an accumulation of specific knowledge exists. Sports enthusiasts sum it up best; it's all about the fundamentals.

The Art of Active Dramaturgy outlines the analytical and critical fundamental elements a dramaturg needs to be active and effective in a rehearsal hall by taking the reader through every step of the dramaturgi-cal process for a set text first and then builds upon those ideas to ground the discussion for a new play. Throughout, the text addresses how the dra-maturg's skills and job requirements impact and inform the other artistic collaborators' processes (e.g., directors, designers, actors, writers).

When working on set texts—a text that has been published or produced and will not be rewritten, although cuts may be made, e.g. Shakespeare's *A Midsummer Night's Dream*—the dramaturg uses critical analysis to facilitate a collaborative process designed to make these texts fresh through cuts or translation. When working on new plays—a play that the writer is still rewriting or shaping—the dramaturg uses critical analysis to facilitate a collaborative process that respects the play's needs and the writer's goals to strengthen the play's story, characters, language, and themes.

What active dramaturgs *do* for any text, be it set or new, is articu-late how the play establishes its voice in ways that makes the intellectual ideas or themes that structure the dramatic work playable on stage. But an active dramaturg isn't a spokesperson for the play. The play speaks for it-self. Just as a director mines nuanced performances out of an actor and keeps the entire company within a single world, a dramaturg works to isolate the various patterns the play presents as aspects of its voice to help the entire artistic team develop their ideas more quickly and fully.

A Brief History of Dramaturgy

Who is responsible for dreaming up such a wide-reaching disci-pline? An 18th century German thinker and playwright named Gotthold Ephraim Lessing (1729–1781). Lessing began the dramaturgical art form with a collection of essays written between 1767 and 1769 titled *Hamburg Dramaturgy*. His weekly and then bi-monthly essays discussed the merits of Shakespeare's craft, Aristotle's vision, the troubles with French Neo-classicism, and the duty of emerging German writers to create dynamic work for the stage and dominate the French. (Schecter, *Dramaturgy in America* 18)

Lessing's compositions established him as the father of dramaturgy and German criticism which, along with his plays *Minna von Barnheim* and *Nathan the Wise*, guaranteed him a place in Western theatrical history.

Lessing also spelled the word dramaturg with 'e': dramaturge.

It wasn't until 1859, however, that the word dramaturg (note that it is spelled without an 'e') came into use according to the online version of the *Oxford English Dictionary*. And yet, the *OED* fails to include a separate entry for dramaturg. Here's the *OED* definition that introduces the spelling American disciples of Lessing prefer:

> *Dramaturge*: 1859 *Times* "Schiller was starving on a salary of 200 dollars per annum, which he received…for his services as "dramaturg" or literary manager.

The new spelling also indicates a pronunciation that embraces a final, hard 'g'. Unfortunately, Microsoft Word's spell-check, supported by the *Encarta World English Dictionary* doesn't agree, and doesn't recognize this legitimate spelling. Even *The New York Times*, which has fought to retain the 'e' in spite of numerous letters encouraging the opposite, has only recently seen fit to drop the 'e' in the listings if it mirrors how the program lists the credit.

The confusion surrounding the word isn't entirely baffling. The German word *dramaturgie* comes from the Greek *dramatourgia*, meaning "a dramatic composition" or "action of a play." Diehard linguists keep the 'tour' spelling and the soft 'g', but in doing so they inadvertently refer to dramaturgs as writers rather than artists who work *with* writers and other theatre artists. Adding fuel to the linguistic fire is that *dramaturge* is the French, Spanish, and Italian word for a dramaturg *and* playwright. Dramaturgs *may*, like Lessing, write plays, but in the United States when working with a writer—and *not* co-authoring—the dramaturg doesn't pen a single word. These varied spellings also continue the misconception that a drama*turg* is like a Hollywood script doctor who comes in and rewrites characters, passages or the entire story, suggesting another reason so many American dramaturgs vigorously lobby for dropping the 'e' after the 'g'.

Although there have been numerous unnamed dramaturgs throughout the rise of American theatre, credit for establishing the discipline in

America often goes to the critic and former dean of the Yale School of Drama Robert Brustein. In 1966, his first year as Dean of the Yale School of Drama and Artistic Director of The Yale Repertory Theatre, he officially introduced the Doctor of Fine Arts in dramaturgy and dramatic criticism degree. (Borreca, *Dramaturgy in American Theatre* 57) Brustein wrote that:

> "The new Drama School regime, however, was trying to improve the quality and aspiration of the profession rather than provide teachers for educational theatre, and this, we thought, meant trying to develop well-informed, intelligent drama critics. Thus as the same time we were professionalizing the training in acting and directing, we introduced a new program in Criticism and Dramatic Literature, offered in place of the old Directing/Playwriting DFA."
>
> (Brustein, *Dramaturgy in American Theatre* 34)

According to some of the earliest dramaturgy students, the Yale graduates who had yet to complete their doctorate had nothing but a Master's degree and were prevented from securing teaching positions, because in education an MA in theatre is not considered a terminal degree. To provide the appropriate terminal degree, Brustein and a number of Yale instructors devised the MFA in Dramaturgy and Dramatic Criticism in 1977.

Not too long after Yale established its program, the University of Massachusetts Amherst offered a dramaturgy degree and then the University of Iowa quickly followed suit. By 2006, the United States had 21 programs offering advanced degrees in dramaturgy and 38 offering undergraduate B.A. or BFA degrees; the United Kingdom, 16.

Dramaturgs have come a long, long way, and yet the question of *what it is that dramaturgs actually do* persists.

What is it about this discipline that isn't coming across? Why the confusion?

I think there are two reasons. The first is that every dramaturg offers a unique definition. The second is that many practicing dramaturgs define dramaturgy by describing a finite list of tasks. Yes, dramaturgs may translate texts, assemble Actor Packets, write program notes, critique plays, moderate post-play discussions, and develop plays with writers and directors. But this is the *doing of dramaturgy,* not a description of what goes into the dramaturgical art. Actors walk across the stage, invent interesting ticks and twitches, memorize lines, and occasionally sing songs; *what* they *do*, however, is embody and enliven fictitious characters. What active dramaturgs do is pose questions that activate the play's themes and other critical elements in ways that enrich the play's story and performance; dramaturgy facilitates the creative process.

Furthering the confusion are the many books that uphold the more parochial, literary definition for dramaturgy—exploring structure with an eye to understanding imagery or idea, not necessarily how to enliven or perform these dramatic elements.

The Art of Active Dramaturgy

Yes, dramaturgy is that oft misspelled, mispronounced word that means the study of dramatic structures. And yes, it has been difficult to define. But quite simply, production dramaturgy is the art of taking the critical thinking tools developed to dissect a dramatic text's structure or form and use this information to actively transform art (a production or a play) by posing questions that inspire creativity.

The Art of Active Dramaturgy is for the undergraduate or first year graduate student as well as anyone collaborating with a dramaturg on a production for a new play or set text, interested in how an artist approaches production dramaturgy. *Active Dramaturgy* is also for any creative thinker eager to conjure a unique theatrical world grounded in text. Some dramaturgy texts prescribe a series of tasks for the student dramaturg to follow or offer critical readings of specific plays or assemble commentaries on what was done during a particular rehearsal or development process to illustrate *what* dramaturgs contribute to the creative process. *The Art of Active Dramaturg*, however, presents and explores *why* and *how* an active dramaturg might approach and explore the fundamental elements and critical thought needed to shape the collaboration process be it academic or professional.

Although I graduated from Yale's dramaturgy program and the book is influenced by my graduate school experience, this book is not a summary of the so-called Yale Way. The *Art of Active Dramaturgy* is a distillation of what I've observed other dramaturgs do or heard other artists ask dramaturgs to do at Yale and beyond. *The Art of Active Dramaturgy* also offers ways to approach the hurdles students regularly encounter and the questions emerging dramaturgs commonly ask. The goal is to help all artists approach a new play with bravery and to discover ways to engage with older texts as if they were not hobbled by 450 years of scholarship.

The first three chapters introduce the most fundamental dramaturgical skills: how to read a play with a fresh eye the first, fifth, and one-hundredth time; how to analyze the text to discover innovative interpretations; how to form open questions and listen well. Emerging and student dramaturgs and artists who collaborate with dramaturgs, or wish to ground their artistic approach in the text may find these chapters particularly helpful in sharpening the dramaturg's basic and fundamental skill set. Throughout, the chapters begin with a discussion focused on dramaturgy for set texts, and then expand those ideas and applies them to the dramaturgical process for new plays.

Chapters four through seven focus on how to use these critical elements and advance these basic skills to forge a collaborative relationship. Sports enthusiasts would consider these chapters the fundamentals for creating a collaborative game plan. The chapters do not articulate a set-in-stone, step-by-step program, rather a philosophy and suggestions on how, when, and why an active dramaturg prepares or presents observations as possibilities. Emerging and student dramaturgs and artists who work with dramaturgs or use dramaturgical skills to fuel their art, may find these chapters improve their communication and collaborations.

Chapters three through seven also begin with a general overview of the chapter's thesis, and then present ways to address these challenges by focusing first on set texts, and then exploring the unique twists new play development presents. The premise is that basic skills are developed when working on set texts, and then improved and challenged when working on new plays.

Chapter eight looks at new-play development and audience talkbacks; and nine, the dramaturg's collaboration with marketing and education directors. These chapters are ideal for the dramaturg, playwright and director interested in new-play development and how to enhance audience engagement.

A Note About Adaptation and Translation

Dramaturgs play an active role in shaping the future of theatre within their country and the world. To do this many advocate for plays or playwrights and create more opportunities for productions by adapting and translating texts.

Many dramaturgy programs require their students to translate a play before graduating, and entire books could be written about how to adapt or translate a dramatic text. There are unique challenges to adapting or translating works; for example, when adapting a text a writer must consider how to activate the narrator's voice for the stage, and whether to faithfully recreate the book onstage, or look for ways to enliven the story for this new medium. Both adaptation and translation beg the dramaturgically-influenced question: should the work be set in its original era or updated through a change in time, place, or language style (i.e., slang)? Similarly, translators have the core text but must consider how to realize idiom, language style, and subtext or nuance in a language that may be more or less flexible than the original.

These are not small hurdles to clear, but in many ways they are the artistic questions any playwright confronts, and when the adaptation or translation materializes, the collaborators follow the development process for a new play.

The Active Approach

The Art of Active Dramaturgy outlines and defines *a* process, and *a* way of thinking and doing. But just as one must perform to become an actor, one must *do* dramaturgy to become an active dramaturg. One must discover how to finesse the fundamentals to be considered more than proficient. One must practice, practice, practice, if one aspires to become a dramaturg with the artistry and grace of an elite athlete.

Dramaturgy is a behind-the-scenes profession but, if done well, it can impact as many lives as those more visible theatre artists. The active and innovative dramaturg can identify the plays that will become the new classics that influence a generation of writers or transform how politicians see the world. The active and innovative dramaturg can compose essays that shift how an audience responds to language, casting choices, or subject matter. The active and innovative dramaturg can enhance a production's nuanced realization of theme and metaphor. The active and innovative dramaturg can motivate a playwright to make an astounding play exceptional. An active and innovative dramaturg achieves a palpable impact.

The first step is to know and understand the fundamentals. For that, read on.

The second, third, and fourth steps are to practice, practice, practice. And throughout the journey, strive to both see and observe.

Chapter I

Beginning the Dramaturgical Process: Letting Go of Bias

When Sherlock Holmes quizzed Dr. Watson in *Scandel in Bohemia* about the number of stairs leading to the Baker Street flat, Watson replied, "How many? I don't know." (Doyle, 162) Dr. Watson's pre-existing thoughts regarding his regular trip up and down the stairs—personal baggage and bias as well as the regularity of the event—prevented him from fully observing his surroundings; each time Watson climbed the stairs, he assumed he knew all he needed to know. As a result, Watson failed to enjoy the nuances of each step on every given day. His past experiences and bias prevented him from engaging fully with the task at hand.

Often when dramaturgs, emerging or experienced, approach a play for the first or fifth time, it's possible to behave a bit like Dr. Watson; the initial read (or re-read) is encumbered by personal baggage or bias inhibiting one's ability to fully engage with the story.

Why? Perhaps it's due to circumstance.

The first time many read *The Orestia* is typically in a college theatre appreciation class. *A Streetcar Named Desire* may have been assigned reading for a high school English class. Perhaps the extremely brief *Hamletmachine* or the surrealistically imagistic *Funnyhouse of a Negro* were required reading for a college seminar. What these first encounters have in common is that each was part of a mountain of homework that may have included an additional 200 pages of reading and a five-page paper to boot. The goal was to get through the play (and all remaining homework) quickly. Maybe the reading slowed enough so that the play revealed the writer's gifts with language and story, but odds are the first read was a wash. Once we leave school, this behavior might continue because, well, old habits die hard.

Not surprisingly, even less thought may go into re-reading a play once read or performed, be it in college or high school. Prior knowledge can color the experience and encourage the reader to be guided by assumptions, thereby causing the reader to automatically approach the assignment with an imperfect lens, one warped by memory.

Imagine a student who first read *Hamlet* in high school and then reads it for the second time in college. The second encounter for this imagined student might begin with the following assumption: this is the long and winding story of a young man who poses a lot of questions, has a strange and somewhat strained relationship with his girlfriend, his mother remarried a bit too quickly for his liking, and it's written in a language that is exhausting and arcane. Yes, this assumption allows the basic and partial set-up of the revenge tragedy to emerge. But what about the story as Shakespeare tells it? What about Laertes, Horatio, Claudius, or Osric's stories? It's important to apply the same level of care, openness, and attention to a script you are reading a second or third time as you do the first, for one simple reason: You know more now than you did then.

The trick to reading well and without bias, is to approach that initial read with an open mind or clean slate. The ability to let go of bias while reading, is central to any artist seeking to create original vision or work but crucial for the dramaturg to be effective no matter their experience level.

To Read with an Open Mind or Clean Slate...

When reading plays with the clean slate or an open mind, the chances of appreciating the play's individual merits, surprises, risks, and successes exponentially increase as do the odds of discovering new dramatic styles or ways to interpret text. An open-mind, clean-slate approach encourages reading without an agenda—the key to innovative thinking. This may be a simple concept to grasp, but requires some practice. All theatre artists can learn to read with a dramaturg's eye, and in doing so, improve the basic understanding of the play and in turn their artistry. To do so, follow eight easy steps.

Step #1: Know How You Read

When reading a play, some hear voices as they read (think: radio play), others see images (think: film or stage performance), and for others, it's a bit of both. Aural readers don't necessarily prefer language-based plays to the exclusion of image-filled dramas or vice versa. An aural prefer-ence simply indicates a tendency to focus less immediately on the visual elements, whereas visual readers may process the play's world through color, pattern and the character's physical language. Acknowledging an affinity for linguistic or visual imagery reveals a lot about the creative imagination—its influences, responses, and perceptions. If language usu-ally governs your reading, but while reading a play the visual elements grab you, there may be something extraordinary in this work. If, however, during the first read the play is neither easily heard nor visualized, this may reveal the challenges you and your creative team may have connect-ing to the piece. Understanding these preferences may also help shape the reflection process. Don't worry if you neither see nor hear a play. With experience reading complex and challenging plays, this skill will come. Eventually it may even be possible to both see and hear a play.

Step# 2: Know What Reading Environment You Prefer

Beginning to read or re-read a play starts with a simple question: Where to read and how much time to allot? Some dramaturgs create a reading environment by choosing a secluded or at least quiet room to facilitate a more true encounter with the play, others opt for a room filled with music, while others choose to read while traveling, noting that the better the play the easier it is to ignore the outside world. In the end, per-sonal preference wins out, but taking time to identify your ideal reading environment will make it easier for you to experience the play.

As varied as the opinions are regarding *where* to read a play, the general belief among dramaturgs regarding *time* is not: read the play in one sitting, this provides a truer sense of the play's flow, overall effect, and more closely resembles a theatrical performance.

To facilitate an uninterrupted read, avoid stopping to take notes; there's ample time for that later. Now is the time to get a sense of the play, its movement and flow. The urge to mentally flag patterns or moments when the piece fails to satisfy its set-up, pattern, or rules may arise, but resist the temptation to stop and mark the pages. Do not worry about writing the question down to avoid forgetting it. If the question raises con-cerns regarding the storytelling, it will reveal itself again if not repeatedly. Remember, the goal is to focus on experiencing the play's emotional ride.

More important, taking notes during the first read (or first re-read) can reveal how you, the reader, would like the story to progress. Active dramaturgs recognize that a playwright wrote the play and is ultimately responsible for articulating the play's voice. No one else. In addition, active dramaturgs understand that the play has its own voice and needs, which are established by the characters and a set of rules or patterns that govern the play's world. These ideas remain paramount for new play dramaturgy, but apply to set texts as well. So, read through to the end and enjoy the ride.

Step #3: Acknowledge Your Preconceptions and Biases

We all come to reading with baggage. We dislike the play because we remember not understanding the play in high school or think the play was great because the lead performer was cute, or, because the production bored us to tears, the play must be awful. To wipe away preconceptions, begin by acknowledging they exist. Don't dwell on them. In fact, allow them to float in and out until you complete the reading and begin the reflection process. Throughout the read, be open to noticing how the play differs from what you remember or the lore that surrounds the text. An open approach keeps assumptions from consciously informing and shaping any initial responses. The goal is to make this reading as fresh and new as possible; awareness helps the reader achieve this.

If it's easier, think of a play as a person. If you walk into a room and see a person with glasses and you've had a bad experience with a bespectacled person, it's possible to assume you would prefer to avoid the optically challenged. If, instead, you allowed yourself to be open to converse with someone wearing glasses, you might discover that by the conversation's end you had dropped your preconceptions. Had the encounter begun as effortlessly as it ended, imagine how much deeper the connection might have been.

To continue the metaphor, when looking at a play as a person, remember it's a person with a unique voice (look, style, shape, and language) that may not resemble its siblings, those plays written by the same playwright. Work to accept each play on its own terms.

Step# 3.5: The Caveat to Step #3

As important as it is to approach the play without expectation, you do, nevertheless, read with three expectations in mind. The first is the expectation to learn or discover the play's rules; the second, its world; and the third, its voice.

Step# 4: Reading to Discover the Play's Rules

Every play has a unique set of rules that are established by how time shapes the world, what events make the world work or throw it off balance, and how linguistic styles affect the piece's musicality. Actively looking for the play's rules rather than how a play conforms to preexisting styles and structures makes new discoveries possible. For example, Caryl Churchill ushered in a new era of depicting conversation on the page and radically reshaped the rules of language by using the virgule (/) to indicate over-lapping dialogue. Suzan-Lori Parks pushed the boundaries surrounding onstage silences and pauses with her distinct ideas governing silences and spells. Yes, Parks defines spells and silences in her essay "The Elements of Style," but before crafting that essay, a dramaturg read the work with-out this information and discovered the rules—and the play's power—by reading with an open mind.

It's tempting when reading a set text to assume the play's rules and the solutions based on previous knowledge and scholarship. New plays present a different challenge. The tendency is to relate the new play to known styles or genres (play, film, or book) and then evaluate the writing according to those previously established rules. What makes new plays new is their ability to reinvent the standards. Finding ways to remain open to different ways of telling a story, enables the discovery of new solutions to old questions.

The play's rules are unique and dictate the way events will and should unfold for that particular dramatic work. Reading to identify formula-ic structures such as the well-made play or five-act structure imposes a format to which the events must adhere, and may lead the reader to re-spond negatively if a writer violates those expectations. Reading with the understanding that form evolves in an organic way allows the play's unique qualities to be received more objectively, and perhaps, more positively. It often takes time for the rules to emerge, so patience while reading is key.

Although the first read introduces the play's rules, subsequent reads provide understanding and suggestions of how to evaluate the play ac-cording to its rules. Plays need not follow the rules consistently, for these deviations often lead to memorable, dramatic moments. However, every deviation must be grounded and governed by logic necessitated by the play; otherwise, the shift confuses the audience and remains dramatically ineffective. Excellent plays and playwrights present challenging scenes that purposefully violate expectation.

Once the play's been read in its entirety, active dramaturgs, and those who embrace dramaturgical thinking, take time to reflect and then analyze the play's themes, metaphors, story, and realization of character. In-depth contemplation often comes after the second or third read. The urge to consider the dramaturgical elements shouldn't stop your first reading, but should help focus subsequent reads and reflection.

Step #5: Reading to Discover the Rules of the Play's World

Contrary to expectation, the rules of the play are not the same as the rules of the world. The play's rules establish the way events unfold. The play's rules are related to plot, what happens in the story. While plot refers exclusively to events, the play's rules also includes the play's form.

The rules of the play's world govern *how* the world the characters inhabit regulates itself and, in production, often refer to production choices. Also, the rules of the play's world correspond to the dramatic story. The dramatic story informs how or why the plot unfolds or how the nuances or ideas enrich the plot and connect the events.

The play's world is a combination of the physical setting—for *Hamlet*; a castle in Denmark, for *A Doll's House*, a banker's home in Norway—and the emotional environment generated by the characters' interactions—in *Hamlet*, one public mourner amidst a seemingly remorseless court and in *A Doll's House*, one woman seeking a helping hand and rescue amidst a group who look to her for (and sometimes demand) aid and salvation. Each world is then governed by a set of rules.

In *Hamlet*, the world's rules create many of the play's obstacles. For example, a rule is that no one mourns as publicly as Hamlet does (he wears black when everyone else has cast off mourning colors). If everyone mourned as Hamlet wished, they too might scour the court for evidence of conspiracy. A production can reinforce or play against this rule to foster new interpretations.

Consider how a production's take on mourning could impact the closet scene between Hamlet and Gertrude (*Hamlet* 3.4). After watching Hamlet behave strangely and stab Polonius, Gertrude's lines indicate that she will do as Hamlet asks and distance herself from Claudius. If the production chooses to create a world where Gertrude and Claudius conspire and both proclaim Hamlet mad to help their case, the action might proceed differently. At first she appears willing to publicly mourn Old Hamlet's death to appease her son, and dons a black veil for the remainder of the production, but through physical behavior indicates that she stands with Claudius to the end. Or, the production could support the lines' surface meaning, and show Gertrude's anguish as she observes her son's madness, regrets her choices, and begins conspiring with her son against her new husband.

In *A Doll's House* the rules of the world require that the status quo changes drastically at regular intervals. Because each scene begins in the midst of a character's emotional turmoil without showing what perfection looked like, the text (and in performance the actors' behavior) must indicate what's changed and how. If such indications do not exist in the text (or production), two rationales are possible—what's occurring is normal or there's an inconsistency in the text (or production, if staged)—so the rules of the world demand that at some point we glimpse perfection. Perhaps the character of Dr. Rank could provide this, because his presence encourages a need for public artifice. In another production, the rules of the world may differ and Dr. Rank's presence could amplify what's troubling Nora, so that he chooses to extend himself, with warmth or malice or lust. No matter what the rules of the play demand, a production of *A Doll's House* must reflect throughout the specific choices that reinforce the protagonist's decline.

For another way to understand the plays rules vs. the play's world, consider Sarah L. Myers' award-winning play for young people *The Realm*. In *The Realm*, the world's rules emerge through specific character events, such as the moments when James, the male protagonist, loses his ability to use spoken language. As James forgets the words for objects and people, specific sounds replace language. James thinks he speaks intelligibly, because each sound has meaning to him; but the other characters hear a mish-mosh of sounds. However, as his situation worsens, even James forgets the specific sounds that replace particular words, except for one—Mother is always a heartbeat. This character detail does more than reveal aspects of James' character. The sound and stage direction unveil a rule that governs the world: any form of communication dies if an emotional bond ceases to exist.

When reading a new play, purposeful or accidental violations of the world's rules may occur, which the dramaturg and the playwright should discuss during a later meeting. Initially, however, simply read the text and know that later you will be able to reflect on these divergences. An occasional or even serious turn from the play's rules often appears in strong new plays. If, however, stiff, writerly language overwhelms these breaks in rules, an awkward, mechanical play can't be far behind. Remember, a great idea may fuel the story, but a great idea does not a drama make.

Step #6: Reading to Discover the Play's Voice

To find the play's voice in set or new texts, dramaturgs focus and reflect on the entire play and how the seven critical elements combine. These critical elements—story, time, character, language, image/metaphor, theme, and form or pattern—are a play's basic ingredients that combine to create a distinct work of art. Described another way, the play's voice is like a piano chord. Take, for example, the C Major chord. Three individual notes combine to form C Major. When played independently, each note has a distinct sound or aural character. When played together each note still exists but the ear registers one full, balanced sound. And much like music, the play's voice can exist in the mind's ear as a collection of sound, in the mind's eye as a collection of images, or as a combination of sound and image.

A writer's reputation or a play's storied past can influence the reading, and inhibit the play's true voice and world from emerging. Acknowledging that dramaturgs focus on time, structure, language, metaphor, themes, and the entire cast of characters, doesn't hinder the clean slate approach to reading; it merely sets some parameters to help the play's voice and world break free of years of criticism and scholarship.

All theatre artists read for the play's voice, but dramaturgs consider how to help the director, actors and designers realize these ideas in their work and facilitate their colleagues' process in ways that make an intangible idea active.

Early career dramaturgs and theatre artists may encounter difficulties when they fail to ground their comments and observations in these elements that shape production dramaturgy. If artists cannot separate personal bias or reaction from an observation grounded in the play's facts, confusion and poor communication follows. Focusing on these seven elements during a first read or when re-reading a play will foster a neutral approach and comments grounded in the powerful question: how does the play approach element X, Y, or Z?

Step#7: Read the Play

Step #8: Reflect on the Play, a Nine Part Process

This simple, often skipped step is the heart of excellent dramaturgy. The reflection process involves nine steps based on the elements that comprise the play's voice. Reflection leads to better understanding and, in turn, better questions. Chapter 2 will review the nine steps for the reflection process.

Final Thoughts

Reading often provides the first exposure to the play and its world. As when first meeting a person, make every effort to meet the work on its terms without bias. To do that, know your preferences and be aware of how you read and process a play.

Read the play the playwright wrote.

Chapter 2

Reflection: The Foundation of Active Dramaturgy

Reflection, an often-overlooked step, is especially useful for a dramaturg seeking to identify unique ways to make active contributions throughout the rehearsal process for either a set text or a new play. Reflection allows images, questions, and ideas to surface without needing to articulate ideas logically; it's a private endeavor.

On Reflection

Resist the initial urge to take copious notes or make intelligent critiques. Simply take time to consider how the critical elements combine to establish the play's overall style, impact, and rules. Using the critical elements to guide this process also eliminates the desire to connect a play to pre-established, formulaic structures, such as the well-made play, and frees the mind to recognize and embrace new forms as well as unique and innovative storytelling styles. Reflection also introduces a way to identify a play's patterns, strengths, or confusions without judgment. This important step presents a rare opportunity to connect more deeply to the play and discover its voice. Over time, this nine-part process develops instincts and provides for an incredibly active form of script analysis.

One: Reflect on Plot

It's tempting to begin reflecting on characters, creative language, and that amazing monologue somewhere near the play's end, but resist that urge and begin by asking the very simple question: What *happens*? The plot, the basic points that anchor the play's action or story, reveals what happens. To successfully identify challenges and anomalies later, begin to consider plot first and then work to define the plot in one or two sentences. Remember, plot focuses on the main events only and ignores story and the emotional color that makes every play unique.

A possible plot description for *A Doll's House* might read as follows:

> *A Doll's House* is a play about a woman at an emotional cross-roads. She has kept a secret from her husband and if it's revealed, she will lose everything. In the end, the secret is revealed, her husband does not support her, and she does the brave thing and leaves her home to begin a journey alone, as a free and independent woman.

This description does include what happens, but also includes descriptions that reveal an emotional bias. The paragraph also takes too long to get to the point. The phrase "A Doll's House *is a play about a woman at an emotional crossroads,*" leads the writer to compose a sentence that presents a clear point of view but not the play's facts. It tells us the woman is "*at an emotional crossroads*" and defines what or who the play is about, "*a woman.*" This description reveals additional bias, for it describes Nora's exit as a "*brave thing*" and her character as "*free and independent.*" Because of this biased plot description, the probable reality that Nora must contend with poverty and possibly prostitution (especially if the production were set in or around 1879) would not enter the conversation. A strong plot description makes room for the reality of a character's situation and choices, and creates more dramatic tension regardless of when the production is set.

A more successful plot description follows:

> Days before Christmas, a recently fired bank employee named Krogstad threatens to reveal the bank manager's wife's secret. The wife, Nora, schemes to prevent this from happening. In the end, Nora's husband Torvald learns the truth and does not respond as she hoped, which leads her to walk out on him and her children.

Hamlet, or any of Shakespeare's plays, presents a multitude of challenges, because the plot is complex and the number of characters great. But because plot is about what happens *in the play*, not necessarily what happens to each and every character, even a five-act play can be distilled to a few sentences.

A possible plot description for *Hamlet* might read:

This is a play about a young philosophy student who returns home to find his father dead and his mother married to his uncle. Convinced by a ghost that his father was murdered, Hamlet sets out to find proof and along the way manages to alienate everyone, including his girlfriend Ophelia. His mad antics lead him to murder Polonius, Laertes and Ophelia's father. During a climactic sword fight, Hamlet kills Laertes. His mother and uncle die, too. At the end, only Hamlet's nearly-silent friend Horatio remains to mourn the Danish prince and recount the tale to Fortinbras, who enters in the final lines to reclaim the kingdom.

This description includes a lot of unnecessary detail, a few crucial plot points, and implodes rather spectacularly at the end. For a play with as many sub-plots as *Hamlet*, a brief plot summary should focus on the primary events and, if possible, mention a second sub plot. The point of a plot description is to give the details briefly, while conveying as much detail as possible.

The above passage is also colored by personal response, making it an interpretation rather than a plot description. To begin with, Hamlet is described as a *"young philosophy student."* This fact helps us to understand character, but is it important to understanding the play's events? Yes, the Ghost visits Hamlet, but is Hamlet *"convinced"*? A production may choose to question whether the ghost was real or his words can be trusted, but this plot description limits exploration because it tells us his response. Describing Hamlet's behavior as *"mad antics"* again limits the possibilities. What if a production wishes to present Hamlet as sane and the other characters as those who say he's mad, to dissuade anyone from believing his claim that old Hamlet was murdered? In addition, many of the emotional qualifiers like *"manages to alienate everyone"* restrict the choices for interpretation, or set the dramaturg in opposition with the other artists who do not believe Hamlet is mad or alienates everyone. To describe Ophelia as *"his girlfriend Ophelia"* is to definitively answer a question that has plagued actors and scholars for centuries. Not knowing Ophelia's relationship to Hamlet provides a multitude of rich options; why close those avenues of exploration with a single word?

The above description begins to unravel as it attempts to include every character and his or her fate. The passage also ignores Fortinbras's storyline, making it seem unessential, when it's anything but.

The story of Shakespeare's *Hamlet* is complex, but a more successful plot description follows:

> Hamlet's father has died and his mother has remarried his uncle. Hamlet, the Prince of Denmark, looks for evidence to support his belief that something is amiss at the court following his father's death. By the play's end, the entire court—king, queen, and heir apparent—dies, as does the chief counselor Polonius and his entire family. Throughout, Fortinbras, the Prince of Norway, marches toward Elsinore to avenge his father's death and the loss of their land in Denmark.

Once a play's text is set, its plot rarely if ever changes. What changes from production to production is the artistic interpretation of the story, altering *how* the plot unfolds but not the actual events.

Two: Reflect on Story

If plot is the simplest description of *what* happens, story is the compilation of events that reveals *how* or *why* the plot unfolds as it does along with the ideas and nuances that enrich the plot.

Imagine the childhood nursery rhyme *Jack and Jill* as a play. The plot is what happens: two youths travel up a hill for water, and one seriously injures himself. The dramatic story would be how those events unfold:

> Jack and Jill set out on a quest up the great hill to find the water their village needs for the coming year. This honor goes to the village's two bravest and most inventive youths. Both must return, alive, without losing a drop, for water is so precious and extraordinary in this magical land that one pail can satisfy the population's needs for a year.

It is these narrative details, realized through theme, metaphor, language, and other critical elements, that combine to create a play. The story is how key events combine to form a world.

Two other important and interrelated questions that help active dramaturgs reflect and unlock the secrets that open set texts or identify exciting new plays are: *Does the story seem derivative,* or *Does it push the genre of story in new directions?* If the answer is no to the first and yes to the second, consider the play further.

For example, the number of family drama plays boggles the mind. Occasionally, however, one stands out, such as Suzan-Lori Parks' *Topdog/ Underdog.* This Pulitzer Prize-winning two-hander, or two-character play, explores the tempestuous and jealousy-laden relationship between two brothers, Lincoln and Booth. The plot can be described as: two brothers live together in a bed-sit and one is so jealous of the other that he eventually murders him. The story is made up of the events that show the younger brother, Booth, dreaming of castles in the air and having trouble putting foundations under them, and the elder brother, Lincoln, bearing the weight of behaving like the pragmatic and realistic elder sibling whose spirit is drained.

Parks elevates her African-American family drama and sets it apart by inserting sometimes subtle references to current social inequities among many ethnicities, while exploring the convoluted legacy of the Civil War within the black community. By focusing on the universal and bizarre love/hate relationship between siblings, Parks directs some of the focus away from the protagonists' ethnicity. Parks grounds the story in the characters' emotional life, which is informed by the perspectives of a particular ethnic experience that weaves its way through the drama. She doesn't imagine that this experience, a rivalry between brothers who work dead-end jobs and were abandoned by their parents, is unique to black people, because to some extent the play is about brothers first and African-American brothers second. And so, the play stands out among family dramas, among two-handers as well.

The active dramaturg's task is to notice how Parks tells this story and then to reflect on how she uses language, theme, and character to delve deeply into the strange bonds of siblings and their rivalries, and eventually to forge a connection to the larger society.

Three: Reflect on Time

Time, its march forward or progress backward, remains the play's most common way to organize story and plot. Reflecting on how time orders events and action helps reveal the play's voice and rules. Determining whether a drama unfolds in one day, over five years, or uses memories to drive the character's journey forward, can help the dramaturg organize the information needed to assist the artistic team to realize a dynamic production.

Reflecting on time may reveal another entirely different insight: that the play's action unfolds in a non-chronological manner. Most describe plays with scenes that skirt through time as non-linear. This term does the play a disservice. Non-linear suggests that events unfold without regard to dramatic build or action derived from cause and effect. Nothing could be further from the truth.

So-called non-linear plays remain hyper-aware of how events relate to and build upon each other. The intricately woven design is quite delicate, and yet the temptation to examine these events in isolation remains. Such analysis encourages the plays to be seen as wholly unusual or unproduceable. If, however, active dramaturgs take the lead in showing the piece as one where ideas build upon each other using tension, conflict, and release, it's easy to see that such plays exist as excellent examples of linear dramaturgy.

Because linearity definitely exists in all plays, even those that adhere to a funkier time clock, considering plays as following a *chronological* vs. *non-chronological* pattern proves more useful for active dramaturgs. Chronological suggests a play where the writer accounts for most forward progressions of time (for example, each season: fall, winter, spring, summer) versus the term non-chronological where the writer skips through time with reason but with no adherence to the conventional order of past – present – future.

Ibsen's *A Doll House* adheres to a strict chronological order, for throughout the play characters reveal plot points that relate to specific days and an ever-approaching deadline. The facts are firm: Nora must assist Krogstad by a certain time and day or Torvald will learn of Nora's deception. Should a production choose to emphasize time, the tension could increase considerably. Noticing how the critical element of time can inspire and shape the storytelling can lift a production from the expected to the innovative.

Kenneth Branagh's 1996 adaptation of *Hamlet* presents the Danish prince's story by emphasizing how much time passes between events. Old Hamlet's funeral and Gertrude's wedding take place during the height of winter, and Ophelia's death and Laertes' return in late winter/early spring when hats and coats are worn less. Using the seasons to frame the action reveals how long Hamlet mourns and the time he takes to plot and enact his revenge upon his Uncle Claudius. Branagh reinforces the idea that Hamlet's rash deed may have been bloody but took ages to plan.

Adrienne Kennedy's *Funnyhouse of a Negro* provides an example of a chronological play framing non-chronological moments. The progression follows Negro Sarah's response to outside noise (knocks from the landlady and her ex-boyfriend Robert) which is interrupted by scenes illuminating Negro Sarah's mental disintegration through moments featuring disembodied heads. That said, there is little sense of how time passes for the character and in turn us. The repetition and shifts of repeated passages fights the assumption that the order in which Kennedy sets the words down on paper follows a linear time progression for Negro Sarah. The play presents a snapshot of Negro Sarah's mind framed by the outside world—the landlady and Robert.

If Negro Sarah's been haunted by images of disembodied heads before the play's action begins, this isn't immediately (if ever) apparent. Were it not for the landlady and Robert's presence, the play's action might appear to take place in no time. Because the main character has little connection with the outside world, it is difficult to establish how much time passes between the interruptions the landlady's knocking provides. But at some point the play demands that characters and audience acknowledge time; otherwise, Negro Sarah's death will appear as nothing more than a figment of her imagination. Although the play's final speech calls the entire action of the play into question, everything up to that point must be believed to give the final line its full impact.

Sarah Kane's *4.48 psychosis* takes the idea of no time illustrated in *Funnyhouse* even further. Kane rids her play of characters who obviously engage in the real world. *4.48* forces the audience into an intentionally co-dependent relationship with the protagonist, for the audience is as isolated and unable to find rest as Kane's troubled voices.

Kane and Kennedy use time in their plays as flexible movements, compressing and elongating emotional moments and mental thoughts as their characters' needs change. Heiner Müeller also eschews a regulating timeframe in *Hamletmachine*. Müeller uses numbers to order his scenes. Although as much as Müller's scenes are numbered one through five (perhaps an homage to Shakespeare's five-act classic *Hamlet*), a dramaturg would note that he makes no attempt to document how much time, if any, passes between each. Artists applying these dramaturgical philosophies in the most adventurous way might understand through reflection that the need to present scene two following scene one exists only because Müller numbered the movements in this way. With a strong understanding of story and the play's rules and voice, the artistic team has space to generate its own unique 'why' that encourages the play's story and images to unfold in new and different ways, including interesting repetitions of certain moments.

Georg Büchner's *Woyzeck* is the most unique example of a non-chronological play. The story follows a low-level military servant named Woyzeck who is also the subject of a medical experiment. But because Büchner died before completing the play and early editors changed the order of scenes, each translation and subsequent production continues this practice by creating a unique vision of Woyzeck's experiences (world), and in turn the play's plot. Some productions begin with the experiment and chart Woyzeck's declining mental state as he follows a strict diet of peas; whereas, others highlight his love for Marie, which becomes twisted as his fear of infidelity and jealousy grows. Which situation influences the other—peas or thwarted love—depends on the passage of time, and creates the patterned progression. The active dramaturg helps influence the tale with adventurous and rigorous thinking governed by reflections on time and its impact on structure and character evolution.

Four: Reflect on Character

Because dramaturgs work to help theatre artists clarify the play's voice, an active dramaturg's allegiance lies with all characters, not just one. When reflecting on characters, dramaturgs generally consider each character's individual journey and how it connects to and propels the story forward. Noticing why each character enters the story or how the individual journey serves the story will inform the dramaturg's preparatory work. More important, dramaturgs work to notice when characters appear in a scene but remain silent. Dramaturgs articulate how this silence increases or decreases tension.

Some dramaturgs focus on whether the story evolves organically from characters. Others look for the play's form and patterns to shape character. In the end, both approaches arrive at the same question: Does the play tell an inherently coherent story with characters who interact in logical ways that adhere to the rules of the play? A blip in a character's voice (linguistic pattern) or action, informed by language or its absence, usually indicates where the play goes off track or a major shift occurs.

An initial reading (or re-reading) of Ibsen's *A Doll's House*, for example, reveals that Dr. Rank has only a few lines and a few key scenes with Nora. Upon reflection, a new observation emerges: he's actually present, witnessing the action more often than he speaks. While reflecting on what his presence adds to the scenes he witnesses, the active dramaturg may begin to see that he brings the outside world into Nora and Torvald's idyll without menace, and makes a triangle of power possible, all of which augment the scene's tension. Rank's physical presence also reminds the audience, and perhaps Nora, of her world's power structures and the impact, tension, and anxiety of secrets on her relationships. Rank's an intriguing, sometimes ambiguous character and therefore one of the theatre's most treasured. Taking the time to recall when he's present or where he seems to disappear, indicates places for the dramaturg to explore and focus on later.

During character reflection, try to avoid evaluating why a character behaves in a particular way. It's important to bring a sense of openness: a blank slate approach to reading applies to reflection as well. Discussions may reveal that the artistic team stumbled in the same places, and if they didn't, you may develop a keener eye or ear as they articulate how they tracked a character like Dr. Rank when you ignored or lost him. Just taking the time to reflect on your reactions will inform every subsequent read and discussion in amazing ways.

Five: Reflect on Language

How characters speak—with words that dance or move haltingly through a scene—determines the language of the play. Writers who disappear behind their character's true voice have mastered language. Those writers who insert themselves and use overly clever poetry or prose ignore both the play and characters' voices. Such conscious manipulation tends to produce flat, predictable prose. Yes, writers set the words on the page, but when the characters are true and clear, the writer's hand disappears revealing rich dialogue that drives the plot. Inventive language is the essence of all good plays.

Noticing how language shapes the play's world helps identify the play's strengths and the dramaturg's reflection process. Does dialect or slang convey aspects of character? Do the characters speak directly to one another or shroud their meanings so that the pauses or silences reveal their true aims and desires? Do metaphors shape the dialogue, or more lyrical poetic images? Each way of thinking and speaking has a rhythm that directs how to write and read language. The play's world or context will reveal whether the character speaks in fragments because he is shy, quick thinking, or stops in mid-thought

Other writers like Suzan-Lori Parks paint characters by placing words on the page in unique ways. In the play *In the Blood*, Parks indicates the word 'your' with either 'yr' or 'your'. Take a moment and think about how 'yr' sounds. What does the sound suggest about the person who uses it? Social status? Education level? Comfort with others? Now explore the word 'your' by asking the same questions. It's not surprising to learn that Hester, an illiterate, destitute mother of five in *In the Blood*, uses 'yr,' while the educated, more financially secure characters use 'your'.

Parks' abbreviation also indicates how words sound in the character's mouth. The use of 'yr' suggests a sound heavy on the 'y' and 'r' with less emphasis on the vowels; the ear might hear 'yer' rather than 'yuh-or'. Encountering writing that embraces dialect tells the dramaturg the writer hears language and character. Language may even be manipulated into an opera of sound, as in David Ives' *Philip Glass Buys a Loaf of Bread*. While reflecting and preparing to meet with the writer, the dramaturg might consider ways to discuss language in musical terms to create a common vocabulary with the writer.

For those characters who use less obviously voiced language, look at sentence structure for clues regarding character. Does the character use formal language laced with Britishisms? Do sentences begin with adverbs or adverbial phrases?

Sentence fragments peppered with dialect might give you a sense of a character's demeanor: I vant to see zhe menu (direct); or I'm gonna read this menu (casual); or Yo! where's the menu?! (impatient).

Also, look for moments when the language changes within character's dialogue, for these variations within language will reveal character quirks and may lead to previously unimagined directions the artistic team might explore. As simple as these questions may be, determining the nature of a play's language remains one of the most difficult aspects of dramaturgy. Reflecting on language gives the dramaturg an opportunity to consider how the writer approaches assembling words to create a dramatic world.

Six: Reflect on Metaphor and Imagery

Metaphors exist as ways to ground and discuss the ever-changing human experience. As a play uses metaphors to guide its journey through an idea, active dramaturgs use metaphors to direct their thoughts and analysis. Taking time to reflect on which metaphors and images jump to the fore and resonate below the surface helps dramaturgs identify the play's true voice.

Consider the imagined Jack and Jill play again. The pail of water holds great significance, for a single drop of water supports the community for a year. The images—a pail, a single drop of water, two chosen youths setting out on a journey—inform whether the world is a desert-like western outpost, or a futuristic city supported by technologies that can divide a single drop of water to supply millions. The metaphoric significance of the youths' journey in either environment (desert outpost or futuristic city) is similar: can the next generation successfully assume responsibility for the future and the lives of its people? Water, which is precious and required to sustain life, could represent the citizenry.

Whether the metaphors reveal themselves immediately or emerge slowly, they separate strong plays from good but dated plays. The specificity of Shakespeare's metaphors affords them, ironically, a fluidity that enables issues and circumstances to live grounded in a particular experience or era but also translate or connect to others. In *Hamlet*, for example, the young Dane makes many metaphoric references to prostitution and wanton women when discussing or speaking to Gertrude and Ophelia. Taken one way, Hamlet's comments reinforce his madness or skewed view of the court. Taken yet another way, the metaphors could establish Hamlet as abiding by a different code of conduct; he returns from Wittenberg a distinct outsider, changed and unwelcome.

Shakespeare uses muscular metaphors, which support anachronistic interpretations or concept-driven productions of his plays. Suzan-Lori Parks has a number of image and metaphor-infused plays like *Death of the Last Black Man in the Whole Entire World* or *The America Play*, which explore era-defined depictions and stereotypes of African Americans. Parks liberates these plays from becoming dated period pieces by employing a number of twists to the metaphors that extend the experiences of this specific ethnic group to the larger American, if not world, community. Parks' purposefully repetitious metaphors actually structure the play and illustrate the repeated mistreatment of African Americans and other ethnic groups who live outside what society defines as the mainstream, without demanding a monologue that precisely articulates a character's concern. For example, in *The America Play*, Parks plays with the language governing the phrase "the Great Hole of History". The linguistic pun triggers a metaphor for the many people and events American history often fails to include, the accomplishments of many ethnic groups (for example African-Americans, Puerto Rican Americans and Japanese-Americans), thus creating a great hole. A production might use this metaphor as an opportunity to present figures missing from the picture of history. One might hear the great WHOLE of history—as its entirety— rather than its absence, and the subsequent scene becomes an example of all that is crucial to a full understanding of history.

Because flexibility governs most metaphors, reading with an eye to how the current political or societal context pushes some metaphors to the fore and flattens others reveals clues to help reshape the play. But considering this question too soon can adversely affect a reading and lead a dramaturg to miss valuable signs needed to foster innovative interpretations or insights. In addition, certain lines will jump out or sound odd, perhaps even inappropriate, and an active dramaturg considers how these unusual moments might shape a contemporary production. It's the dramaturg's responsibility to shape the questions for discussion with the actors, the director, theatre, and subsequently the audience, that help the play retain or gain an undeniable connection to contemporary issues and ideals. But articulating the question comes later. For now, remarking on what might inspire the question should inform this initial encounter.

Seven: Reflect on Active Themes

Active themes are a dramaturg's lifeblood. Active themes connect language and metaphors to character and plots; they may also locate a play within a particular political or social framework. Themes are the big ideas that impact each character and the world of the play. Active themes are more than ideas or value statements, they provide a frame or impetus for choices that may be performed or realized on stage. An active theme may be expressed as a phrase or question, and should take the characters or production through the majority if not the entirety of the play's action. Whenever a dramaturg, or any theatre artist, becomes lost or unsure within a project, reconnecting with the play's themes will provide the necessary beacon and mooring to help them proceed.

Consider the imagined Jack and Jill play again. If the pair's journey serves as a metaphor for responsibility, it is possible to consider responsibility as a thematic idea. However, the term "responsibility" alone is not thematic, it is merely a word. To realize the theme as an active idea that the production and artistic team can pursue and stage, the theme must be connected to something a characters can do or someone the characters can affect. In other words, an active theme for the Jack and Jill play could be articulated as, "assuming responsibility for others". Another active theme could be "one's responsibility to guard nature's resources." Each of these thematic ideas lays the groundwork for conflict (will the youths prove to be responsible; will current populations conserve water) as well as how characters or audience might go about realizing this thematic idea (the youths or audience member will sacrifice comforts to secure the precious water). Active themes often extend beyond the play's world, presenting ways for a dramatic story to impact and transform actual, not just fictional, lives.

To go further, consider some basic themes in Strindberg's *Miss Julie*. The play focuses on two servants, the young lady of the house, and the sexual tensions that arise. The plot: during a Midsummer's Eve party, Miss

Julie and the head servant Jean begin to discuss, debate, and interact in a way that violates social norms governing their respective classes. They eventually plan to run away together. Unconvinced that Miss Julie will be faithful to him, Jean first kills Miss Julie's pet bird and then encourages his mistress to kill herself rather than be disowned by her father for ruining her reputation by sleeping with a servant. The possible story could be that a once strong and independent-thinking woman of means willingly sleeps with and plans to run away with a servant but, after realizing her mistake, abdicates her sense of self and looks to him for guidance. He exerts full control over her and pushes her to escape public ruin by killing herself.

Given this plot and story, the tensions created by wealth and social class or sexual liaisons could present a thematic idea. These ideas, however, do not immediately convey a sense of how to realize a character's journey or the play's story on stage. Yes, dramaturgs may first identify the thematic threads and look for ways to place them in relief against the dramatic action and current social structures, but then they need to reshape them into active themes.

A possible active theme rooted in the idea of wealth or social class could be articulated as "exploring how adherence to socio-economic class constructs encourages amoral behavior." In this instance "amoral" would be defined as murdering live creatures, or characters willing to tell lie upon lie. A possible active theme rooted in the idea of the tensions created by sexual liaisons might be "when class lines are crossed, how does the power dynamic or sense of loyalty change?"

In *Hamlet* a thematic idea might be loyalty and a possible active theme—the question the cast and artistic team might pursue—could be "how does one's memory or perception of a relationship inform one's sense of loyalty?"

In *Funnyhouse* race might be considered a thematic idea, and an active theme worded as "anyone regardless of race can admire Queen Victoria and Patrice Lumumba". But this is not a statement that can be realized on stage. In fact, race, like gender or mental illness, is not a strong thematic idea—all are merely topics. A better thematic idea for *Funnyhouse* might be colonization, a thematic idea that encompasses race and much more. An active theme might be "how exerting dominion over another influences behavior and perception".

Repeated images that evolve throughout the play first indicate metaphors and may eventually establish themes. An example of an image that transforms into a theme is the stage direction, "the digging of the great hole of history" from Suzan-Lori Parks' *The America Play*. In the play, characters actually dig and unearth a number of items, but the "great hole of history", is more than an open pit: it is literally a great absence in history. This physical and metaphorical image introduces the notion that people omitted from world history in general (and African Americans specifically from American history) will always dig to find their place within the great hole (and whole) society, and the history that historians created. As the story unfolds, the great hole of history refers to Lucy and Brazil's personal histories, and the absent husband/father, Foundling Father. And so, following the exploration of a single image and its metaphoric implications brings out thematic ideas of family loss, abandonment, and isolation and joins those of historical representation and exclusion. Noticing these indicators of active themes will influence a reading by pointing out new signposts, and may even shake up a traditional, staid interpretation of the play.

Considering themes in a vacuum, without an eye to production or performance, leads to literary analysis. Dramaturgs and those interested in developing a more dramaturgical approach to their craft, never cease to forget that plays are dynamic living pieces that truly come alive when performed, and that until production, plays live in a semi-conscious state. Active dramaturgs and theatre artists look for ways to enliven themes by directing their analysis with questions of *what* happens and *why*. Restricting analytical exploration to the quotidian fails to connect the dramaturg's discoveries to the creative imagination; the dramaturgs remain researchers. Research is necessary, but production dramaturgy goes beyond intellectual fascination and transforms those facts into active possibilities.

Eight: Reflect on Form or Pattern

Time, language, metaphor, character, and themes all combine to create a distinct pattern or form. By reflecting on these elements first and then considering the play's actual framework, active dramaturgs open themselves to discovering new patterns that frame the story; they allow the voice of the play to emerge and shape the frame, not vice versa. Many analytical texts use the term *structure*, which risks reinforcing old ideas. Writing plays by the numbers often produces uninspired, even turgid writing, just as analyzing a play according to specific, pre-determined formats can lead dramaturgs or theatre artists to miss exciting new works or new shifts in older, set texts. Liberating a text from the need to fulfill the requirements of the well-made play or two-act structure leads to exciting drama. When a writer remains true to the story and its needs, the structure will be organic and quite possibly unique. And so, using the term *form* to refer to how the critical elements of time, language, metaphor and theme combine to create pattern and order within a play's story allows the writer, active dramaturg and other artists to freely observe new twists within a set text and unique solutions when collaborating on a new play.

Nine: Reflect on Challenging Moments

The reflection process may reveal a challenging moment, a scene or event in the play with a less than immediately apparent solution. Or, there is a moment that doesn't make immediate sense. Sometimes these challenging moments emerge after the second or third read. Whenever the challenge manifests itself, a solution will emerge through reflection, analysis and focusing on the play's rules.

Active dramaturgs do access numerous sources and articles, and should spend their creative time contemplating the play's thematic nuances coupled with research. Even so, research and reflection do not guarantee a perfect solution to a challenging moment. There are no right answers in theatre; that's the beauty of the art. In the same vein, a dramaturg (or another collaborator) sometimes presents ideas that do not jibe with the artistic conversation. These observations are not wrong; they are simply not right for this particular production. Hearing the ideas with this truth in mind will improve the collaborative conversation.

Reflection encourages a clean slate approach, which is the dramaturg's ultimate goal: to encounter the play as the play wishes to be seen. Yes, a person is fallible, but entering the reflection process with greater self-awareness by acknowledging that you find it difficult to read comedies or you have a strong preference for political drama will improve your ability to read the play written, not the play you want to read. The more any artist reflects on the play and notices the play's twists and turns will make the reading process active and fresh; and the artist's insights more likely to be innovative and interesting. Risk-taking implies a willingness to be wrong.

Record Your Responses

After reflecting on the elements, begin to write your thoughts down. Initial responses to the play's use of story, plot, time, character, language, metaphor, all work to comprise the play's form, world and voice, and will inform the artist's dramaturgy and dramaturgical thinking. Subsequent readings will change those ideas and impressions, as they should. However, taking the time to craft a written response that follows a period of reflection develops an artistic memory. Over time it may be possible to remain in touch with these initial impressions, despite an increasing closeness with the text and production without committing ideas to paper, but the joy of tracking how ideas evolve makes the written record appealing.

In addition, these personal responses can help resurrect a play that has been ignored, and strengthen an artist's resolve when doubt begins to color the creative process.

Once the mulling draws to a close and the lists begin to emerge and coalesce into impressions, it's possible to see what appears as the heart of the play, which is where the artist's individual process begins.

Reading New Plays or Manuscripts

Dramaturgs who regularly read new scripts have one of the most exciting jobs in theatre. These artists often encounter a play before anyone else in the theatre or production company, and have the responsibility of recommending a play for further exploration or production. The dramaturg's job provides an opportunity to move a script ahead and connect possible directors with a specific play and writer. The dramaturg's impressions and responses may also create the zeitgeist for a play or writer within the college department, regional theatres, or the national community of literary managers and dramaturgs. Along with the responsibility of identifying strong work and unique voices, comes the responsibility to avoid shrouding the text in too much personal opinion. Inspiring someone else to read the text with few preconceived notions remains the ultimate goal. To meet those responsibilities well, apply the basic ideas regarding reading a play. However, unique challenges do arise with new plays or manuscripts, which this new play section addresses.

The Challenges of Reading a New Play

If a play is new, no (or very little) production history or reputation exists to consciously or subconsciously guide the reading. This makes rendering an opinion easy, right? Not necessarily. Dramaturgs and those who regularly read, evaluate, produce, and design original work do more than register opinions. These artists examine the work with an exacting analytical eye, largely because no one else has. The knowledge that the work has the potential to shape the future of the theatre adds to the responsibility.

Creating art is challenging; however, forging the vocabulary and tools to build something new is downright difficult. Supreme fun, but not easy.

The challenge to read with a blank slate remains.

What barriers exist? Perhaps the playwright's reputation rather than the play's lore or existing scholarship colors the reading. Or, an artistic director or dramaturg reads a script with the hope of establishing a relationship between the theatre and the writer. It's possible that artists are reading the play to find out if the theatre could support the writer for an extended period or become the writer's home (the place that regularly develops and produces that writer's work). The reading might become a search for work to include in the institution's new-play festival or play-development workshop process. When looking for work for these writer-driven events, the dramaturg's read might be distracted and shaped by questions like: *Is this play right for our festival?*; *Will the drama department lose its funding?*; *Can the theatre support this writer's style?*; *If the play makes it to a festival and the audience loves it, would we ever be able to afford a production?* Another barrier exists for freelance dramaturgs, who are often hired to work at festivals. They may also be looking for challenges to demonstrate their skill in hopes of securing regular work at the hiring institution. In essence, hypercritical thought runs the risk of encumbering any of these initial reads.

Yes, these crucial questions present high hurdles, but reading a new, never-before-produced play, perhaps a never-read manuscript, offers the best surprise any theatre artist can hope for: possibility and the opportunity to assist in realizing a vision for the first time. It's important to prepare for the experience so that you, the reader, can meet the play on its own terms, by using the techniques described earlier.

The Dramaturg's Concerns

To give a script a fair first read, dramaturgs should also take the time to acknowledge what's known about a writer as well as how the writer's other works impress or challenge them. Thoughts about the agent who submitted the work or the most recently read play can influence the reading, so taking time to separate the play from those thoughts will help ensure an open, clean-slate approach. These carried-over impressions may color a reading as much as the stories told about Tennessee Williams or his famous female character Blanche Dubois; acknowledging them will force objectivity if only because the reader stops to push aside all judgments as they arise.

Some dramaturgs try to accomplish this clean-slate perspective by approaching a new script as if it's a classic, meaning it's unalterable. Frankly, this tactic seems too heavy a burden to place on the writer and the script. To read a new script and expect a solid, well-developed text almost ensures the play will disappoint. However, choosing to engage with the script as nothing more than another play with clear, opaque, and challenging moments from the get-go allows the writer's gift and craft to emerge naturally. Ironically, theatre artists who re-envision classic texts often begin by approaching the classics as they would a new play, meaning they try to keep an open mind and ignore, for example, descriptions of previous productions.

When dramaturgs receive a new script, the agent or writer may include a *précis*, designed to entice and summarize if not sell the play. This summary may not accurately describe the play's actual story, but rather the story the writer or agent assumes the theatre wants to produce. Regardless, the dramaturg must read the new script without preconceptions to discover the story. After the reflection process, the agent or writer's summary may help the dramaturg assess whether the writer's intended story agrees with one the dramaturg read.

Reflection after reading a manuscript leads to more than the decision to recommend a play for production. If the writer's intended story doesn't connect with the submitted précis, the dramaturg may still want to meet the writer and recommend the script. Sometimes a strong voice emerges despite a vague story. The dramaturg may also wish to consider why the descriptions diverge and what to discuss with the writer should an opportunity arise.

Reflection and New Plays

The initial process for reflecting on a new play is no different than that used for a set text. This step prepares a dramaturg and the director for the initial conversation with the playwright. The difference lies in what to *do* with the ideas and thoughts this process generates. The thoughts and ideas should inspire a dramaturg to document what makes this play unique, fun and provocative, as well as what central ideas tie these observations together, rather than specific ideas of what to change or what doesn't work. During early meetings, the dramaturg (and sometimes the director) works to frame the discussion based on the playwright's comments and needs, but should be familiar with what the play offers before learning what the writer thinks the play articulates.

Reflect on Language and Voice of a New Play

Considering the writer's voice is often more important with a new play than a set text, because this may be the writer's first introduction to the theatre and a writer with little sense of story may exhibit a talent for sculpting silence with words or elevating the quotidian to the sublime. If the basic bones of the story exist and the playwright's linguistic style excels, pay attention. Story and form can be developed more easily than the ability to fashion words to form distinct dialects for each character and carve a world out of thin air. Spending extra time exploring how characters speak and how language defines circumstance will help identify the future's strongest playwrights.

Reflect on Symbols and Metaphors in a New Play

As when reading a set text, avoid taking time to write comments while reading. Don't hesitate, however, to make a few mental notes regarding what mysteries sculpt the play and which signposts map the world's secrets and solutions. Imagine you were one of the first to read Suzan-Lori Parks' manuscript of *The America Play*. It would be appropriate to remark upon that odd and multi-layered stage direction "the Great Hole of History", as it provokes a number of ideas and images. It's wonderfully ambiguous. Is "the hole" the missing stories of underrepresented people, or an ironic comment on the entirety of history? These thoughts and accompanying images enhance the reader's engagement with the play. In other words, don't be afraid to respond to ideas, but don't become too distracted by them either. If the image or idea appeared during a production we wouldn't (and couldn't) ask the actors to stop to honor our yen to contemplate, so why try when reading a play? Make a mental note and move on. The reflection period will provide ample opportunities for further exploration.

Reflect on Themes in New Plays

With any play, it's important to note what ideas or themes used to connect the characters and plots together. When reading a new play, it's possible that the themes do not always weave together perfectly. Rather than dismiss a play for this misstep, take time to identify well-integrated themes, ask how themes establish themselves and connect to the play's action. Do the themes inform design? Do themes intersect and shape character? If the writer has achieved clarity, and only a few themes fail to satisfy, keep an eye on this script and writer.

Reflect on Form or Pattern Within New Plays

When reading any play, scenic patterns (how scenes flow or are built) present clues to the dramaturg and director. When encountering a new play, those formed patterns help shape an impression of the writer's level of daring, especially if the language usage remains rather traditional with few metaphors or moments of poetic lyricism. One thing to look for is how the scenes build, which is not to be confused with the build of a scene.

The build of a scene relies on its emotional and cathartic arc, as well as the introduction of plot elements that direct the play's twists and turns. How scenes build refers to the writer's reliance on certain types of conventions. For example, does the action unfold through an exclusive use of two-person interior scenes (when it's not a two-character play) or do group scenes (three or more characters) enliven the work? Do scenes end neatly, and begin with a lot of exposition to catch the audience up, like a scene from a television drama interrupted by commercials? Or, do the scenes end in ways that introduce a question and propel the story (as well as the reader's curiosity) like any popular thriller minus the regular insertion of cliffhangers?

How scenes connect makes the difference between a traditional script and one that pushes the envelope. Pinter's *Betrayal*, for example, follows the traditional build of scenes, largely because the play's twist, moving backwards through time, requires significant attention. The audience must watch the current scene and apply those lessons to what was shown earlier. Not much different than most plays, except that here the cause is revealed *after* the result of the conflict, and the audience juggles the information differently. Adrienne Kennedy shares her protagonist's nightmare in *Funnyhouse of a Negro* with the audience by allowing images and scenes to dart in and out so that the scenes do not adhere to a traditional build; instead, they interrupt one another to mirror the protagonist's mental and emotional state.

There are, of course, a number of well-crafted plays that follow a predictable, by-the-numbers pattern. Neil Simon reigns as one of the best comedic craftsmen of the modern era. He forms his scenes so that characters enter at just the right moment to deliver information that redirects the comic play's action and heightens the tension. The jokes in his comedies jump off the page with the proverbial drummer's rim shot punctuating each humorous line. His plays are clear, funny and often touching, but few contain the level of mystery and questioning that theatergoers also crave. Because his scenarios develop into grand, modern farces, his work is prized. He pushes the expected comic form by mining it for all it's worth. In other words, tried and true can be spectacular in a new way.

Paying attention to how text appears on the page also indicates form. David Ives's one-act *Philip Glass Buys a Loaf of Bread* reads like the minimalist composer's music sounds—just as each note sounds separately, every letter for each word appears on a separate line so that the sound rings out separately. Letters repeat, shaping the sound of the play rather than character. Lines of dialogue visually overlap to show how Ives scores the language. Acknowledging the language's visual structure is as important and revealing as noting how Suzan-Lori Parks' spells and silences and unique spellings function in *In the Blood*.

Reflect on Challenging Moments Within New Plays

While reading, there may be scenes or moments in the play that appear a bit odd. Now, admittedly that word implies a judgment, which first reads should avoid, but if the word helps signal a moment or scene to return to rather than dismiss, it's worth using. A challenging moment or scene seems out of the ordinary, outside the order of the rules of the play. Choosing to consider the scene as unusual or unexpected prevents readers from initially judging the different moment as bad writing, a mistake, or something to fix. This mindset is crucial when reading new manuscripts. Marking an interesting and challenging moment allows a reader to move on and continue; the moment may be explained later.

It's tempting to rid plays of their challenging moments through cutting or directed rewrites, but dramaturgs and those who work on new plays resist the immediate urge to rid the play of its challenging moments, especially if the script is in development and rewrites are expected. Artists, and especially dramaturgs, aren't in the business of taming plays, merely enhancing the understanding of plays. Active dramaturgs look for ways to increase the team's ability to approach challenges so that the hurdles appear less high. The expectation for a solution lies with a number of people, not just the dramaturg. The active dramaturg's responsibility is to articulate what defines the challenge and to explore possible options.

A challenging moment or scene may also be one that strikes us as wholly plausible but difficult for many sensibilities to stomach. A crop of writers, led by Martin McDonagh and Neil LaBute, sometimes use an extreme level of brutality or emotional cruelty to enliven their plays and rouse their audiences. McDonagh's *Pillowman*, which premiered in

London in 2003 and played in New York in 2005, provoked controversy because of its violence. Violence shrouds much of the play, for a totalitarian political regime shapes the fictitious world in which the main character, Katurian, lives.

During an initial read, the cruelty may deter a reader, especially if the author isn't a known writer. The challenge is how much violence can or will a particular theatre support? Some believe that certain behavior exceeds the boundaries of live theatre. Film's inherent distance, in contrast, makes such brutish displays seem more possible and palatable, whereas the proximity of audience to actor in the theatre can make staging a horrific act too difficult to imagine. Of course, if everyone felt this way, *Pillowman* would have never been produced nor received a Broadway run. Those who first read and produced Martin McDonagh's manuscripts refused to judge the violence or assume an audience's tolerance level; instead these readers embraced the extreme behavior as a challenge rather than a precursor to negative critical response.

Final Thoughts

Each of the critical elements helps develop dramaturgical instincts but, like talent, instinct isn't taught, merely nurtured. Malcolm Gladwell writes at length in *Blink: The Power of Thinking Without Thinking* about fostering instinct, that unknown, intangible feeling that shapes opinions and actions. What emerges in *Blink* is the idea that years of experience will hone the ability to trust the innate sense of what works. Some of the experts profiled do teach others how to locate the signs that trigger instinctual responses, but ultimately Gladwell and his experts concede that cultivating awareness is the limit. But what a glorious limit. With strong basic skills and an education that introduces what to look out for and how to navigate the challenges, it's possible to groom basic instincts.

The same is true for dramaturgy and those artists who wish to deepen their dramaturgical sensibilities. It is possible to teach the skills needed to identify elements of production and dramatic writing in a way that grooms one's instinctive connection between the facts of the play and its emotional center. By learning to encounter new plays or set texts in general, dramaturgs come to understand how the basic elements shape dramas and learn how to identify how they work. This knowledge opens the channels needed to identify the logic governing the play's rules and to access the play's emotional core. All of these tools foster the growth of necessary dramaturgical instincts that help dramaturgs and others reach the goal of understanding rather than taming the play. If one's veteran status has led to creating more preconceptions than instincts of possibility, noting what shapes and informs those initial reads will loosen those muscles, just as it strengthens them for individuals just beginning to think like a dramaturg.

Chapter 3

The Dramaturg's Art: Posing Open Questions and Listening Well

The questions Sherlock Holmes asks sometimes befit a detective and at other times a cryptic seer. But when the story ends, it's clear the seemingly odd interrogatives revealed more information and helped solve the case. Yes, Holmes may know the culprit before he sets off, but more often than not he, like us, discovers the truth along the way. It is through these unusual, disarming questions that Holmes gets people to talk. He actively listens to the responses and uses them to form new insights based on previous observations to draw unique connections. An active dramaturg uses open questions to do the same.

Quite simply, an open question raises an idea, issue, or observation in a way that avoids prescribing the solution or revealing an agenda/personal bias. The open question ignites the conversation or sets the stage for a discussion to explore ideas raised by the text, and inspires expansive, creative thinking by framing the artists' conversation within firm yet flexible parameters.

All artists use open questions to identify dynamic ways to further the creative process. However, active dramaturgs rely on open questions more than their artistic colleagues, especially when collaborating with the director or the playwright. When active dramaturgs ask effective open questions, they help reconnect an artistic collaborator to her passion, which leads to a breakthrough and an eventual solution. By exploring how to craft and then pose open questions, many theatre artists can learn the heart of the dramaturg's art. Success depends on *how* one poses a question.

The open question is one of a number of possible critical questioning styles.

The Common Critical Questioning Styles

The Vague Question

The vague question is so wide-reaching that the respondent could choose to discuss anything, because the parameters are unclear or non-existent. An example of a vague critical question is: "So, what's happening in the first act?" Although commonly heard and used in a classroom to kick-start a discussion, this is less successful when developing a project. The responder could answer by describing character journeys, providing details for every interaction or moment, or choosing to reveal plot points.

The Closed Question

A closed question is focused and clear but has a simple finite answer such as "yes" or "no". An example of a closed question is: "Should this character initiate the argument in scene four?" The responder has no choice but to discuss the named character's specific role in contributing to the play's tension within scene four and nowhere else.

The Neutral Question

A neutral question is a popular and effective critical questioning style that allows the respondent to consider creative options and ideas but still directs the response. An example of a neutral question is: "In act one, what is your goal for this specific character?" The responder must focus on the first act, the specific character, and identify a particular goal for that character.

The Open Question

A fourth critical questioning style is the open question, which allows the respondent to consider creative options and ideas and direct the conversation. An example of an open question is: "In act one, does any one character drive the action and, if it's one character or a group, how is this done?" The respondent has the firm boundary of act one but can now choose to identify and/or discover which character or characters propel key moments of tension and conflict. With the open question, the questioner doesn't assume where the respondent will go or how an artistic decision was made. Once the ideas are expressed, the questioner can engage with those comments and a creative dialogue may begin.

Yes, each of the aforementioned questioning styles demand follow-up questions, and most especially the open question. The follow-up questions will be more focused and specific, for they seek to clarify points the respondent raises.

Using Critical Questions

Consider the imagined Jack and Jill play again. Imagine the play's story begins with the pair battling each other and ends with a relationship blossoming between them. Whether the Jack and Jill play was a set text or a new work, conversations with the director or playwright could include a similar series of questions. With a set text, the collaboration involves maneuvering the critical elements to tell the desired story; whereas, with a new work, the writer can choose to insert new themes, passages, images or even characters to affect the story. What might the questions regarding shaping and realizing the relationship on stage or page be?

An example of a vague and assumptive question for the Jack and Jill play is: *Isn't their love beautiful?* According to the above description, a *relationship*, not necessarily a *romance*, has begun. To pose a question as if the emotions have developed is assumptive and reveals what the questioner wishes to see, not what the play's story presents.

An example of a closed question is: *Do Jack and Jill fall in love when they fall down the hill?* Again, the questioner assumes the nature of the relationship (Jack and Jill are in love), and by naming a specific moment there is little invitation to consider other moments that transform their combative relationship to one filled with less strife.

An example of a neutral question is: *How do Jack and Jill strengthen their relationship?* The question directs the respondent to consider how the relationship improves (becomes stronger) and does not readily invite comments concerning how they weaken or damage their relationship.

An example of an open question is: *What moments signal the growing/changing emotional connections between Jack and Jill?* The responses can now include arguments, moments of kindness or collaboration, silent exchanges, and so on. As the conversation generates more concrete ideas, clarifying questions may be posed and may include some of the neutral or closed questions, which help further define the conversation and comments.

The Elements of an Open Question

The active dramaturg's arsenal of questions includes five words and one fixed question. The words are: *who, what, when, where,* and *how.* We tend to avoid *why* because this leads to defensive responses. The fixed question is sometimes known as the Passover Question.

True, the above description is not much different than the writer who describes playwriting as the simple act of listening to what the characters say and then transcribing the conversation, or the director who describes directing as letting the actors say their lines and helping them move about without bumping into one another.

Just as there is more to writing than channeling voices or to directing than organizing traffic patterns, there is more to dramaturgy than placing an interrogative before an observation. The active dramaturg's major challenges are timing the question and locating where the moments to investigate lie.

The Goals of an Open Question

The great oxymoron of dramaturgy is that the more general you are when you begin, the more general you will remain; and, the more specific you are when you begin, the more general you will become. This truism means that when beginning with general, unclear thoughts, the thinking is vague and only becomes more so, generating wide-reaching conversations that are specific and detailed but in the wrong ways. For example, many begin a discussion by generally exploring the characters, which leads to an amorphous conversation regarding character journey, foibles, interesting language—the list goes on, but no truly useful picture specific to the play's world or eventual production emerges. Deciding to narrow the focus from the get-go by looking at, for example, images or metaphors the characters use throughout, provides a specific guide to exploring character, language, and the play. The open question aims to balance a wide-reaching discussion with an overly specific one.

Understanding the concept of how specifics lead to more broad thoughts can be illustrated in another way, through painting. Monet's *Haystacks* series appears as brilliant and beautiful impressions of light dancing along the hay's surface or pulsating within and around objects. No hard outlines contain the objects; everything remains general but oddly specific. When art historians studied Monet's technique, they learned he didn't simply apply a general wash of purple or orange to the canvas with bits of white applied atop to indicate the cool light of evening or pre-dawn light. Instead, Monet sculpts his so-called general wash using very specific layers of color, bits of white, blue, orange, red and yellow, to capture the glow of a sunset in a field in southern France. Only through such precisely placed points of color could Monet capture the general look of a haystack at dawn or high noon.

Like an Impressionist painting, an open question is a delicate creation, and the crafting of it is the active dramaturg's art. With practice, experience and preparation, a dramaturg or artist using dramaturgical approaches will be able to craft open questions spontaneously throughout the collaboration.

The Dawn of the Neutral Question

Liz Lerman, choreographer and MacArthur Fellow, coined the term "neutral question" as part of the Critical Response Process she developed. Lerman originally designed her Critical Response Process for critiquing evolving dance projects. Theatre artists adopted the Critical Response Process to better support writers as their work evolved. The Critical Response Process reminds everyone that the creator is responsible for the work and deciding what to do and how to do it. Lerman's revolutionary process outlines five distinct steps artists and audience can follow when trying to offer constructive feedback. A key element is the neutral question. By definition, neutral questions avoid shrouding comments in bias or hinting how the artist should address the concern. Both the open and neutral questions avoid prescribing solutions and accept that creativity is a process, and both avoid asking the artist to defend specific choices. However, the two types of questions differ in their scope.

The Difference Between Open and Neutral Questions

Many consider neutral questions a dramaturg's friend. Neutral questions do open an artistic discussion and open questions can be neutral, but a neutral question isn't open. Neutral questions suggest where the creative team might begin their development inquiry. Simply put, neutral questions can *direct* the respondent. An open question, however, establishes a context for the conversation and attempts to cultivate understanding without basing observations on assumptions—thoughts regarding how character, story, or other elements should be used—without directing the respondent's answer.

As open questions *make way* for a cascade of neutral questions and a fruitful discussion, neutral questions help the artist sharpen the comments into direct, active storytelling points. The open question seeks to elicit information and connect an observation or theme to a number of comments raised during the discussion. The trick is to include various facts from the play (or conversation) when crafting a question that is simple, clear, and heralded with little or no preamble. The questioner then navigates the responses and forges connections between those comments and the observations, reflections and research done in preparation for the conversation. Open questions foster a conversation that is both focused and broad.

Using an Open Question When Working on Set Texts

The nature of what informs the open question changes somewhat when the active dramaturg works with a director on a set text or a playwright on a new play. For both types of dramatic works, the dramaturg works to identify the play's rules and facts of the text and then grounds the open questions within these ideas. However, because set texts are fixed, the play's rules and facts remain relatively static, changing only when the production's concept or vision shifts. For example, if choosing to stage an uncut version of Shakespeare's *Richard III*, in a Weimer Republic-like era, the artistic team must consider how the line, "A horse! A horse! My kingdom for a horse!" (*Richard III* 5.4) will resonate if automobiles, trains and bicycles are the preferred modes of transportation. Perhaps the team will establish a visual and aural metaphor that equates horses with cars (or trains) and provide Richard with a bicycle when he is desperate to avoid the chaos and destruction that surrounds him. Or, the team may choose as Richard Loncraine did in his 1995 film based on the stage adaptation by Richard Eyre, to indicate that all cars, trains, and bikes have been destroyed, and in desperation Richard III pleads for a horse to aid his escape.

Using an Open Question When Working on New Plays

When working on a new text, the rules and facts of the play may change with each rewrite or adjusted line. As a result, the active dramaturg (or anyone helping the text grow) needs to acknowledge and address the play's current and future rules, causing the open question to morph. Working on new plays also begins with formulating open questions designed to better define the facts or rules of the play. It isn't uncommon to discover through conversation provoked by the open question that what appears most unclear on the page is in fact the clearest idea in the writer's head. In other words, that particular moment often doesn't need to be rewritten, but everything surrounding it does. In this situation, the open question becomes the primary tool used to foster discussion and uncover how to develop the play further.

How to Shape an Open Question

Open questions are not easy to formulate. If they are too formless they may come across as accusatory or negative, or too journalistic and broad, and if they are too specific, they are not open.

To begin forming open questions consider the following:

1. Ground the questions in the observations and reflections made following the various readings of the play and any initial research;

2. Focus the question on or inside the play's world or story;

3. Avoid making assumptions regarding how a story should proceed or a character behave or other elements be used when forming the open question;

4. Focus the question on a specific event, person or character with an eye to using that specific example to open the play's entire world or a large portion of it.

Remember, open questions are structured in such a way that whenever the conversation veers off track, repeating the question—or parts of it—immediately returns the artist to the initial topic.

What Makes an Open Question Open?

Open questions avoid placing artists in the position of defending choices or work and show possibilities for exploration while establishing a parameter for the discussion. Although it's impossible to imagine every way to pose an open question, it is possible to explore why some questions appear to be open but aren't, and what to do to make a closed question open. Taking the time to dissect the following common questions helps clarify what makes a question open, neutral or closed.

Why This Play at This Time? Open or Closed?

This question appears neutral, but from a dramaturgical perspective it's closed. It's broadly phrased and invites a number of long ambling responses ranging from today's political situation to the story of the writer or director's lost cat and the subsequent constant longing for companionship all inspire this play. Similarly, the phrasing can lead the writer to consciously or unconsciously defend the play, its characters or topic. A director might launch into a long exegesis on the importance of theatre in the world today. Worse still, the writer or director could choose to respond with the retort that stops the conversation entirely: Because I need to.

How to transform the closed question *Why this play at this time?* into an open one?

Tweaking a few words to focus the thought and create an open question may salvage the conversation and the artistic relationship. But which words? Certainly *why* is a great word, and one that opens the mind to consider possibility at every juncture, but alone it's also quite broad, because it suggests no boundaries. *Why* also invites a series of defensive answers that attempt to justify a choice rather than discuss the substance of the choice. The phrase *this play* remains quite narrow and helps restrict *why* a bit. The phrase *this play* also encourages a discussion of the writer's *oeuvre* and influences, which is good. The responses will help direct the listener to specific aspects of the play that will resonate with the director or writer's initial impulse.

What about the phrase *at this time*? Again, the phrase is neutral, for it avoids an overt agenda or bias, but the listener may hear one. *At this time* could be interpreted as someone asking an artist to defend the choice to present this play at this time in history. Also, the question *Why this play at this time?* implies the word *you*, a word that can sometimes be considered accusatory and alienating. The writer might hear the question as *Why did* you write *this play at this time?* and begin to feel unsupported. Some might even hear an attack on talent. The director might hear the question as *Why did 'you' choose to* stage *this play at this time?* and also feel unsupported. What the active dramaturg or inquiring theatre artists wants is discover what specifically compels the creating artist to engage with the story.

So what can the question: *Why this play at this time?* become?

A neutral option might be: *What current event connects to this play?* Certainly the question encourages the writer (or director or other artist) to respond in a personal and creative way. But the question directs the respondent to connect current events to the play and limit the discussion. If current events didn't inspire the writer, director or other artist, a wrong assumption has been made and a lot of good will governing collaboration may have been lost.

A possible open question is: *What draws you to this story?*

The question is purposefully broad, for many ideas and events may have led the writer to this story at this time, but it allows for a more focused inquiry, because it uses the word you to focus the response. Yes, usually you should be avoided or used judiciously. Here, however, no one can misinterpret the meaning of *you*—there is no question of credibility or ability, merely a desire to know what personal connection the writer (or director or other artist) has with the material. Because the question explicitly invites the artist to voice a connection with the story, the question is both broad and limited; it is open.

The writer or director's focused response can be used to improve the rehearsal process, the rewriting process, and the active dramaturg's ability to write notes or establish a collaborative vocabulary with which to discuss the play. The answers help the active dramaturg frame observations and comments around a core of specific thematic ideas and critical elements.

The answer to this open question may be long, but when beginning a creative conversation, the goal isn't to seek short answers or whittle responses down to one sentence. All members of the artistic team—but especially the dramaturg—need to first acquaint themselves with the many thoughts that led to the project and listen for particular ideas, themes, images, or other critical elements that repeat.

Only after responding to the question asking how the story began and the many ensuing follow-up questions can artists begin to craft the *why* of the play's journey or main idea in a single sentence. Just as an actor needs to articulate her character's journey in a sentence that takes her through the entire play, obstacles and all, directors, writers, designers and dramaturgs need to do the same for the play's journey. That sentence is often difficult to fashion for everyone—writer, director, designer or dramaturg.

Overusing the phrase *what inspired* as well as *you* will reveal a limited dramaturgical vocabulary and poorly mask a possible lack of interest in the project. So varying the word choice is as key as keeping the question focused on the most basic and simple critical elements.

What Story Do You Wish to Tell? Open or Closed?

I still remember the first time I posed this question to the artistic director of the theatre I worked for—my first job out of graduate school. We were producing a world premiere, and I was eager to put the lessons I'd learned at Yale into action. I went into his office and asked the question: *What story are we going to tell with this production?* The artistic director, with whom I had a strong professional relationship, simply stared back and said, "The play's story."

Thus ended our creative conversation.

I went back to my desk to contemplate what went wrong. Of course we were telling the story of the play, I thought, but which theme would get us there? Which character would underscore that theme? Who did we want the audience to connect to? What did we want them to go away thinking? These questions may be natural offshoots of my initial question, but something was lost when I posed the initial question. It did not lead to discussion; we had a 10-word exchange.

What story do you wish to tell? is an example of a closed question.

My relationship with this director was strong, and I managed to re-phrase the question in a conversation a day or two later. (Read on to find out what I said.) Although it's a funny story now, few dramaturgs have an opportunity to start over and, sad to say, since that day, I've heard others ask this question and noticed how it starts the process badly.

Although this question appears neutral, it risks placing artists on the defensive. Certainly tone mitigates some of this, but when dissecting the words themselves it's possible for artists, especially directors and play-wrights, to hear this question as a threat to or an attack on their artistic ability. Basically, the question asks, *Do you have an idea or vision or focus for this play?* Sometimes the director doesn't have a clear vision but plans to go into rehearsal or the design meetings to uncover it. Regardless, the active dramaturg's job is to facilitate creativity, not supervise it, and not to evaluate an artist's ideas and process.

When I returned to my desk after the 10-word conversation with the artistic director, I realized three things. First, although one might approach a reading of a new play differently, it's sometimes important to approach the *production* of a new play as if it were a set text; it's the direc-tor's and dramaturg's job to help realize the writer's intentions as fully as possible. Sometimes applying a concept may not be the appropriate ap-proach with a new play.

The second was that the story and all concepts and themes related to the production are rooted in real and tangible aspects of the play that the active dramaturg must suss out and bring to the team's attention. Rather than waiting to discuss the play with the director and using this conver-sation to understand the themes, and subsequently which theme to push forward, the dramaturg should use the reflection process to identify a number of themes and prepare ways to discuss these ideas and observa-tions. Many emerging dramaturgs erroneously believe that bringing in ideas diminishes the collaborative process. Active dramaturgs prepare to drive or at the very least help steer the conversation with the director or playwright; we aren't passengers on the road to creativity.

The third realization was that I needed a question that acknowledged this thought process but wasn't as long as *War and Peace*.

How to rephrase: *What story do you wish to tell?*

The first step is to never ask it. By beginning with a more open question that asks how the artist connects to the story, it may become clear which story will be told or aspect emphasized. The second is to ground questions of story in observations regarding theme and other elements of the play's style. Take, for example, Parks' *The America Play*. The dramaturg or other collaborating artist working on the play might offer the theme of abandonment to the director and note how the various characters respond. The conversation could expand to consider disenfranchised populations in the United States or those in other countries adversely affected by short-sighted American foreign policies. The question would then become: *How might this production address the issues of abandonment in the play?* With this question, the focus sits squarely in a specific theme and the play's world, and allows for the conversation to roam into a more global context as long as it remains focused on issues that resemble those raised in the play. By using *might* or another conditional term or phrase, the dramaturg avoids telling the artists what the play is about, limiting the play's scope or directing the director.

What did I choose as my follow-up to my decidedly inappropriate question? The play, Cheryl L. West's *Holiday Heart*, had two subplots, one dealing with a mother's drug addiction and the other the drug dealer's strong paternal relationship with the child who is not related to him. Given these emotionally wrenching and possibly distracting subplots I asked: *Are there any aspects of the story we plan to underscore more than others?* The conversation that followed helped us clarify which of the play's elements and plot points strengthen the story and which dramatic turns we wished to emphasize.

How to Connect Character X to the Story We Wish to Tell? Open or Closed?

This question shapes many an artistic conversation and rehearsal process. I remember when I thought it was a simple, unbiased, and beneficial question; after all, the question refers to specific character journeys and bringing certain stories to the fore. In this sense it's a wonderful beginning to an open question—for later in the process. Focusing the question on a single character closes it, and as a question to initiate and foster a creative conversation and the production's parameters, it falls short.

A more specific example of this closed question might be: *How do we connect Amanda from* The Glass Menagerie *to this world, especially if we're exploring the idea of Tom as narrator?* The opening phrase *How does Amanda connect to the world* funnels all answers through Amanda, forcing a specific connection that begins and ends with her character and events that carry significance for *her*. Amanda drives every answer, closing off discoveries regarding the action of the play and new insights this production might enjoy. Amanda may not drive every scene, and even if she does, this neutral but too narrow question does not allow the director and dramaturg to readily explore moments that emanate from another character or source.

By changing the question to: *How do the characters (major and minor) support this play's major themes or the production's ideas?* the subsequent discussion has definite parameters. The artists will look at Amanda, the play's entire world, and all other characters who directly serve the production's vision. Such a question supports creative thinking, for the director and active dramaturg must now respond to the play in a new way. The bias suggesting that this is Amanda's play no longer colors the question.

The Passover Question: Open or Closed?

The Passover Question is: *Why is this day or night or moment different than all others?* or *What makes that day or night or moment unique enough to warrant this story at this time?*

In part it's one of the strongest open questions, and it's also one of the most purposefully closed questions there is. It's an open question because any answer will require the artist, in particular the director and playwright, to discuss the entire play and focus on relevant events, and this sets strong yet flexible limits, the hallmark of an open question. It's a closed question because ultimately only one answer exists for why this play begins—and that will be specific to the artist answering the question. This particular closed question facilitates clarity for the creative team and a specific reference point for everyone to refer to when fashioning their response to the play. This is why it is rarely the first question a dramaturg asks, even though it is a standard dramaturgical question.

The confusion surrounding the Passover Question isn't whether to ask it—every theatre artist must ask the question—it's when. Because the question functions as both an open and closed query, it's possible to alienate collaborators, if it's posed too early, as the question may suggest the impetus for the story is unclear or not present. The Passover Question may also stall the writer's creativity with the many options the question offers. Similarly, collaborators may balk if the question appears too early in the process, because it may appear that the dramaturg's thought process is ahead of the artist's and she prefers telling her collaborators the answers, rather than brainstorming alone and then bringing ideas to the group for discussion.

However, the question must be asked and asked relatively early, as it informs so many creative decisions. When working on a developing text, it's best to ask the Passover Question after the writer clearly articulates what drives or inspires him to write this story. When working on a set text, be sure to learn what inspires the director and connects him or her to the play before introducing the Passover Question.

How Does the Play's Action Begin? Open or Closed?

This question has greater importance when working on new plays; it's closely related to the Passover Question, for it establishes the difference between the play's current state and what the play's world was like before the play's action began. When considering set texts, the above question refers to context and setting rather than an exploration of a single line or event. Clarifying the question will help it become a strong opening for discussion. Consider rephrasing it so the response can be grounded in context: *What is this world like before the play begins?* or *What or how do the events of this play change for this world?*

Other Ways to Craft an Open Question:

Prepare a Social, Historical or Political Context for the Question.

Using the outside world to frame the discussion helps the artist create an open question. For example, consider what anniversaries surround the play or if the writer has reached a creative landmark (e.g., a major literary award). This approach may appear more journalistic than dramaturgical, but it's a beginning. Here are two examples: *For a classic play celebrating its 450ᵗʰ anniversary, what similarities exist between our time and the writer's world?* or, *For a playwright who has just received a Nobel Prize and spoken out against the atrocities at prison camps, which of her plays reverberates strongly within today's political and social context?*.

Turn Observations that Could Appear Judgmental into Useful Inspirations.

Midway through the rehearsal process for the world premiere of Karen Zacarìas' *Mariela and the Desert*, the artistic team acknowledged that the play mentions a painting with two figures, an orange bird and a green figure. As the dramaturg, I noticed that keeping the identity of these figures unclear as long as possible was integral to fostering the story's mystery and play's dramatic tension. As a result, no one knew whether to proceed with presenting a series of videos that visually identify the characters with their respective colors, for doing so could give the audience too much information too early. And yet, for the designers to fully realize Mariela's vision of her world, we needed to know which character relates to which color. Because the video element wasn't going to be cut, the concerns were which color corresponds to which character, and could we get away with realizing it visually? We decided yes to the second part, because the video was part of the opening sequence; but the question of which color related to which character remained.

Closed questions to the collaborative team would have been: *Why isn't the daughter represented by orange? Doesn't she have a fiery temper and didn't she escape from her parents?* or, *If the young boy dies in the fire, shouldn't he be connected with the orange bird?*

A neutral question that inspires both the writer and the designers would have been: *What is the significance of each color in Mariela's painting?*

An open question would have been: *What or which colors represent the characters?* Immediately listeners, including the writer, begin to consider color choice, the thought process that accompanied it and, more than that, begin to think about the play and what the play says (or doesn't say) about color. This open question also allowed a broader discussion of all characters, not just the characters who inspired the question. Suddenly, specific color choices emerge for all characters within the text, which helped the actors and designers.

When to Pose an Open Question

Open questions initiate conversation and re-ignite the creative process. However, some questions serve the process early on and others should be held in reserve. When to ask a question depends entirely on the collaborative relationship, the production or workshop's timeframe, and purpose for the production (is it a reading, thesis production, a showcase for the director, a world premiere or a Broadway-bound revival). Certainly an open question to ask early on is what attracts each artist to the project. The Passover Question also works well earlier in the process. The other questions should be asked when it seems most appropriate; when the conversation demands.

How to Listen to a Response and What to Listen For

The second part of asking an open question is listening to the response. To develop a strong dramaturgical ear means to listen not for the answer one wants or assumes it should be, but for what is said at length or mentioned briefly—and sometimes what isn't said.

Listening to the answer and noting comments regarding an artist's process, biases, joys, and the connections the artist overlooks, separates the experienced from the emerging artist employing an active dramaturgical approach. Pricking the ears for certain types of repeated or unique language accelerates a dramaturg's ability to grow a single response to an open question into a focused conversation that reveals solutions to the individual artist and the artistic team as seen in the previously mentioned *Mariela* example.

Listen for Assumptive Language

When an artist begins describing actions or scenarios, pay attention to the details mentioned. Or, listen for general descriptions. What's missing? What needs clarification? What does the artist assume the audience or character brings to the table? Is this an acceptable level of assumption? If not, create questions that point to the assumption and begin to build a road to clarify the assumption. Consider Ibsen's *A Doll's House*. An assumption would be that because Dr. Rank has very few lines when sharing the stage with Nora and Torvald, he simply and politely fades into the background. Such an assumption comes at the expense of exploring how Rank responds or how Nora and Torvald depend on his presence to make certain conversations possible and inhibit others. Another assumption involves the children, for few productions include them even though their presence increases the story's tension.

Another assumption may arise during a creative conversation regarding Laertes in *Hamlet*. A creative choice may be to have Laertes seek single-handedly to avenge his father's death. However, this assumption ignores the observation that when Laertes returns to Elsinore, the Messenger announces that the people support Laertes and his desire to revolt against the current rule ("They cry 'Choose we: Laertes shall be king:'" *Hamlet* 4.5.109). Such an observation can transform the assumption that the Polonius/Laertes/Ophelia subplot is a distraction from the other plots of political intrigue.

While working with José Rivera on a reading of *Boleros for the Disenchanted* at South Coast Repertory, very little needed to be clarified;

most of the development process focused on trimming the text and balancing the emotional tension between the first and second acts. However, some assumptions were made regarding the character Eusebio. During a rehearsal break, Rivera described an entire imagined encounter and other bits of character background. When I asked him about this event and whether it might be added to the play (in an abbreviated form), he classified it as actor background. I agreed that most was, but the information that Eusebio saw the woman of his dreams waiting for him was crucial to their love story. After some consideration, Rivera inserted this touching revelation in the play's second act, thereby providing the actor with another essential bit of ammunition to use in a play about love and testing its limits. Assuming this conversation was simply character or actor background could have led the team to ignore a possible solution to balancing the emotional tug-of-war in acts one and two.

For another example of navigating assumptive language, consider the imagined Jack and Jill play. If while discussing the play the writer quickly states, "There isn't a lot of water in this world and the teens take on a lot of responsibility," and then begins to fully describe Jack and Jill, the active dramaturg notes the writer's assumptions regarding the desert environment and social structure. The active dramaturg should ask, "Is it important to know why there is little water here? Why or what led to the young people assuming responsibility for the world?" At the very least, exploring these points by clarifying these assumptions will help to better define the world; at the most, the responses may provide fodder for conflict and dramatic tension.

Listen for Language That Judges a Character or Event

Just as an actor must find ways to like or love his character even when playing a reprobate, a director, writer, dramaturg, or designer must articulate a compassion and passion for each character. Because some artists are less sensitive to language than others, active dramaturgs can help raise everyone's awareness of how characters or plays are discussed, so that nuances may be heightened to provide balance or deeper insight. A play should direct but not restrict an audience's response by telling an audience exactly how it should feel. Stacking the deck unnecessarily limits the play's scope.

Listen for Ideas or Word Choices That Repeat

Repetitions shed light on what ideas attract or confuse the artist. Well-placed and considered repetitions provide insight and meaning; however, repetitions that cause the repeated words to lose their meaning and impact suggest confusion.

Listen for Imagistic or Vague Words

In the context of the artistic collaboration, ambiguous words may come to have meaning to the artistic team. For example, creators of a play about space exploration may use words like "spaciness" and "floaty" to describe the nature of the world; however, outside the rehearsal hall these words may be used as derisive descriptors. A dramaturg's ability to use this project-specific vocabulary will make rewrites and rehearsal notes pertinent to the artistic team. If the terms "spaciness" and "floaty" are used to describe a character, posing questions to probe deeper and better define the character's demeanor or personality will help. Artists who choose to be sensitive to this project-specific language will likely notice that communication speeds up without losing of clarity.

Listen for Words the Artists Use but the Characters Do Not

At times the play's voice encourages artists to imagine the world in ways that conflict with or a character's specific behavior pattern, or the impressions of the rest of the team. For example, a writer may describe a self-important character by adopting a different vocal pattern and inserting the word "fabulous" every fourth word. An active dramaturg will note this and point out that although in the play the character does not overuse a single word ("fabulous"), in conversation the writer did; perhaps adding this linguistic quirk will enliven the character and the play.

Listen for Places to Push the Artist to Be More Specific

While I was working on the premiere of *Mariela and the Desert*, the artistic team noted that the play's major themes included women who give up their art to save and nurture their families. As Zacarìas envisioned rewrites for this production, identifying which theme ignited her passion for the play became a primary concern. Conversations covered many topics but whenever the discussion veered toward the idea of women losing connection with their creativity, and focusing the play through a feminist lens, Zacarìas always stopped the discussion. Given the play's title and its focus on a female character, the question in everyone's mind had been: *How does the play illustrate the challenges female artists face, especially when their spouses are also artists?* It's easy to see how closed this question is. At some point in every rehearsal process a question this closed must be asked, in particular to the actress or actor playing a role. But when looking at form/pattern issues that inform rewrites, I, as the dramaturg, needed to listen to the writer's response to this closed question and its assumptions to craft an appropriate open question.

The playwright clearly articulated that she didn't want her play infused with feminist or post-feminist thought, because her drama dealt with *all* artists trying to remain creative as their responsibilities to people other than themselves grew. Listening to this important distinction made it easier to moderate the subsequent dramaturgical conversations. Instead of *How does the play illustrate creative female artists and their challenges?* I shifted the question to: *How does the play illustrate how artists from different eras meet threats to their talent and creativity?*. This open question includes men, women and, if applicable, the children of artistic parents. By listening and changing one aspect of the question—by making it more pointedly general—the question allowed the writer to articulate more specific answers and invites an on-point creative discussion.

Listen for the Passion

Sometimes what the artist identifies as the point of inspiration isn't actually where the passion for the project lies. A careful listener will hear this and orchestrate the discussion toward this idea. Identifying what fuels the actual passion is crucial to establishing a successful project. It's passion, nothing else, that keeps the journey going when times get rough.

Listen for the Fears

Identifying an artist's fears is as important as identifying passions. Dramaturgs aren't psychologists, but to create a safe environment within which artists can create, it's often useful to note what triggers creative blocks.

Listen to That Initial Impetus for Creating

When an artist becomes overwhelmed, especially the playwright, remind them that what they said fueled that initial impetus; it was brilliant the first time, and it will be brilliant the sixth time, too.

Listen for Exhaustion

When a writer, director, designer, actor, or dramaturg has hit a limit, end the conversation. It doesn't take long to get to this point. Ideas are options feeding the creative process. The process of considering which path to travel and how to incorporate those new insights can overwhelm any artist. Exhaustion can come after a fabulous 15-minute chat or a two-hour *tête-a-tête*. Good artists see this and continue with other points; great artists stop entirely or ask the other artist what else, if anything, she might want to explore. And then draw the conversation to a close.

Final Thoughts

The questions artists ask rarely demand finite, objective answers. An open question provokes a discussion that leads to specific and unique responses. Artists who begin with specific and narrow thematic ideas participate in conversations that lead to more traditional, expected discoveries that often produce lackluster ideas and vague impressions.

Because active dramaturgs play a key role in forming open questions and navigating these discussions, it's important to notice and listen for ideas that repeat or float away, and decide when old points should be raised again. Remember, all artists benefit from and use open questions. The difficulty isn't remembering ideas or taking good notes, rather it's the art of knowing how to incorporate the ideas into the questions that inspire new paths.

The better the preparation, the better the open question. Preparation isn't a multitude of notes and dog-eared essays describing how to apply Aristotelian theory. Preparation is time spent looking for ways to create the more general and therefore thought-provoking question. This type of thinking enables the dramaturgy-minded artist to actively participate in the conversation and quell the misconception that theatre artists wait for the director to tell them what to do. Similarly, when working with a playwright, the prepared dramaturg asks open questions that in no way run the risk of writing the play or dictating to the writer how to solve the play's questions. When active dramaturgs and the artists who think like them use their observations and listen to their artistic partners' responses and language, they are better able to shape the conversation and further the creative process.

Chapter 4

Preparation for and Collaboration with the Director and Design Team

In the early days of American dramaturgy, many theatre artists did not always consider dramaturgs a part of the production team and sometimes viewed these early dramaturgs with contempt. Some dramaturgs were either actual critics hired to protect productions from bad reviews or theatre scholars sent in to doctor the plays and thereby guarantee success, an impossible burden to place on anyone. Today most artists welcome dramaturgs into the pre-production and rehearsal process, for they consider the dramaturg's insights vital for these contributions help shape a thematically rich dramatic production.

An unfortunate legacy of these early days is that some artists believe dramaturgs tell directors how to improve the production or direct the director. Because of this incorrect belief, many have difficulty differentiating between the director and dramaturg's duties, and yet distinct differences between these two artists exists as does how they use dramaturgical information.

First, there is only one leader per production—the director. The director captains the ship, sets the boundaries and the limits with specific impressions and ideas for all to explore. Dramaturgs focus on the play's voice and look to retain its clarity throughout the process.

Like directors, dramaturgs read and consider plays with an eye to how the drama will play on stage. Directors and dramaturgs also use themes and metaphors to root their vision. However, the director uses the critical elements to lead the creation of the artistic vision that captures the play's visual and aural environment; the dramaturg uses the critical elements to enhance the director's vision and any additional contributions by the artistic team. In addition, the director works directly with the actors to identify and shape how the character tells the story. The dramaturg rarely works directly with actors. If a dramaturg discusses the text in rehearsal—and never the actor's performance or acting choices—the dramaturg assists the actor in dissecting the language or textual ideas to foster greater understanding of the story (or line of dialogue). The actor then takes this information and discovers possible choices to perform either alone or with the director. In short, active dramaturgs help root the production in the text, designers make the metaphors tangible, actors bring the characters to life, and the director conducts everyone while rooting the play's emotional life in action.

The first meeting between the director and the dramaturg may be a single private conversation before meeting with the other members of the artistic team (the playwright or designers or both) or take place after this initial group meeting. In addition, the initial collaborative conversation may be a single lengthy conversation or series of brief chats transforming the term "first meeting" into "first meetings". Whatever form the encounters take, the goal remains the same: to establish a framework for the collaboration and a language to facilitate the creative and rehearsal processes.

In addition to meeting with the director, the active dramaturg often joins the design meetings, a series of conversations that establish a strong working vocabulary for the artistic team (designers, director, dramaturg and playwright). Before the group assembles, the director often meets or talks with each designer individually. If the writer isn't a part of the artistic team, the active dramaturg should try to arrange a private conversation with the director before the group design meeting. However, if the playwright is part of the team, the first meeting should involve all three collaborators: playwright, director, and dramaturg.

Some dramaturgs find this initial conversation challenging and, at times, intimidating, especially when the director is more experienced. The greatest mistake dramaturgs and those who work with dramaturgs make is expecting the director to take full responsibility in determining the dramaturg's role. When the student or emerging dramaturg works with a professor or well-established professional director, the power balance often inhibits the process. When grades or written evaluations are involved, the student often begins to serve their GPA or career rather than the play. Even freelance dramaturgs may enter imbalanced collaborations and face some of these same challenges, for the freelance dramaturg or the hiring theatre may see this collaboration as an audition. If all goes well, the theatre will hire him again; if not, the thought is that another job will never arise. The truth is, evaluations accompany any working relationship; accepting this fact can help the dramaturg avoid trying to please the director at the exclusion of all else, and leave her free to focus on devising an active way to serve the production, play, writer and director. Looking for others to lead the process places dramaturgs in a passive position, resulting in an unfulfilling collaboration for everyone. Just as a designer doesn't wait for a director to dictate the shade of a dress or basic needs of the set neither should a dramaturg wait for a director to identify the play's thematic and metaphoric landscape.

Preparing to Meet the Director

To begin formulating active ways to prepare for this initial meeting, dramaturgs should consider themselves a fully valued, integral artistic partner. Similarly, it's important for the artistic team to know that dramaturgs do more than act as researchers and helpmates. Considering how other designers approach a play, suggests ways to pursue active dramaturgy.

In general, designers shape the theatrical space so that the story stands out in greater relief. Select design elements—set, costume, sound, light, video—reinforce particular metaphorical and thematic ideas providing the actor more room to create a character. Before meeting with a director, a designer develops a sense of which design elements can convey aspects of character or story and then propose these possibilities. The director and designer then discuss the images, ideas, and message based on the designer's text-based observations.

Like designers, active dramaturgs bring observations and ideas about the world to the first meeting. The active dramaturg also considers what themes and metaphors hold the world together as well as why characters behave as they do. Just as designers bring concepts and renderings that morph over time so do the dramaturgs. However, without first proposing ideas and actively contributing to the creative process, the relationship between dramaturg and director will remain imbalanced and artistically unfulfilling.

To begin formulating a creative plan, active dramaturgs need look no further than the play itself. In preparing and analyzing the text, the dramaturg begins to craft their job description for the project. The specific observations and impressions that follow reflecting on the critical elements, establishes the parameters governing what to research and how to best to support the rehearsal process.

Enter the Meeting with an Intention

Active dramaturgs begin the meeting with an intention or goal. This may be something you set and keep to yourself. The idea isn't to walk in with a secret and an agenda, merely thoughts pertaining to specific areas or a general game plan. The dramaturg's intention—similar to an intention that activates an actor's performance—exists to shape your contributions to the conversation and provide direction. The game plan also establishes a place to begin or veer from depending upon the director's comments. Without an intention or game plan, the dramaturg enters the conversation without direction and quickly transforms from a collaborative partner to a gopher. Nine times out of ten the dramaturg's intention will correspond with the directors because an active dramaturg grounds all observations in the play and the reflections that follow the initial read. The ultimate aim of a director/dramaturg meeting is to narrow the play's world and discover topics and themes to investigate so that the actors and artistic staff can activate the story more fully.

How does an active dramaturg determine an intention or game plan and use it to prepare for the conversation?

Reading the Play

Prior to meeting the director, active dramaturgs often re-read the play at least twice. After the initial reflection period, an active dramaturg reads to find answers to the questions and observations the first reading provoked. The third read provides an opportunity to notice things missed during a first read, such as ways the writer realizes the critical elements. For example, when first reading *Hamlet* one may miss that when Laertes returns from Paris it is he—not Hamlet—who has the people's support; or, in *The America Play* it may be unclear who is related to whom. Taking time during the first read to search for character clarifying information, may distract the reader from discovering the larger metaphor surrounding the notion of family within the play. For both examples, a directed second reading can help determine the active dramaturg's knowledge of the play's family and political structures.

Subsequent readings often take place over time and lead to artistically rich discoveries. The third pass allows active dramaturgs to examine the play's form and discover what activates the story. What, for example, triggers Sarah's emotional onslaughts in *Funnyhouse of a Negro*? How often does Ibsen have Nora in a scene with more than one adult? When do Nora's children appear, and what does their presence add? Why does every scene in Caryl Churhill's *Far Away* appear separated by many months if not years, and would it work to separate most scenes by only days? Does the play need an intermission and is the intermission at the act break? All of these discoveries provide rich material for the initial conversation with the director and subsequent design meetings.

After those initial readings, it's important to begin assembling information that informs the active dramaturg's basic outline, the information that comprises 80% of what the dramaturg uses to prepare for the rehearsal process and related work.

The 80% Rule—Critical Elements

The rule is simply this: whether the script is new or a set text, active dramaturgs can use the dramatic text as a guide to complete at least 80% of the work before the first meeting with the director. It may sound as if this advocates that dramaturgs become rogue artists; however, nothing could be further from the truth. In short, the 80% is what's fixed; the aspects of the play that will never change. It's the remaining 20% that generates the heart of the artistic team's approach, and the ideas that will shape those underlying, always present ideas into new, fresh sounding story elements; the concept or shape of the production that will affect how these elements tie together to create a unique production. Identifying and pondering these fixed elements of the play can and should be done well before the first meeting.

The temptation to focus solely on the concept, which makes up the flashy 20%, distracts and disempowers many dramaturgs, largely because the concept is often initiated and defined by someone else, leaving the dramaturg to answer questions rather than actively participating in forming and then answering them.

In general the 80% includes a variation on the critical elements: the plot, the basic events that shape and drive the story or the play's action; major characters; factual references or locations; major themes; metaphoric images.

Plot

Often artists confuse story for plot, which is why an active dramaturg should determine and define the plot immediately. The facts that drive the story comprise the plot. Story, however, is *how* the plot unfolds.

Understanding and differentiating between plot and story is crucial because each suggests different creative possibilities. Even in conceptually-inventive productions of set-text plays the basic plot points rarely change but the story can. Of course one can eliminate scenes essentially affecting the plot but the overall plot will remain. For example, some basic facts in Shakespeare's *Hamlet* are: Hamlet's father has been murdered; his ghost appears to his son; Hamlet kills Polonius and Laertes. A production may choose to cut the gravedigger's scene, but the basic plot of a man seeking to avenge his father's death remains.

If a production chooses to change a character's gender or make cuts that alter relationships within the play (such as combining two characters into one), some of the facts will have changed. However, the basic facts pertaining to the overall story have not. Casting an actress to play Hamlet might embolden a production's concept regarding gender-related facts including possible succession issues. These twists can fuel the play's tension and Hamlet's choices, but the play's overall facts remain: the child outwardly mourns the murdered father more than anyone in the court and seeks to avenge his untimely death.

The story, however, is the *how* and *why* of the plot; or, *how* to consider or reveal the plot on stage. Although lines may be cut and concept may change the reading of certain lines or scenes, the play's basic facts shouldn't. For example, consider the story surrounding the ghost and Hamlet in Kenneth Branagh's and Michael Almereyda's respective film versions of the beleaguered Danish prince. In Branagh's epic, The Ghost haunts his son, barks his lines, and assumes a form at least ten times larger than that of his earthly body. In Almereyda's sleek and modern adaptation, The Ghost walks through his son's room, speaks only occasionally in loud tones and looks as he did when alive. One ghost has the quality of a possessed spirit and the other, a loving father who met an untimely end.

Although interpretation fascinates and motivates all artists, an active dramaturg prepares for a meeting with the director of any play by noting the facts, and, for a production of *Hamlet,* that might be the facts surrounding the ghost's appearance. An active dramaturg describes the ghost's appearance to Hamlet by avoiding language that implies how the ghost manifests himself (no use of words like "haunts", "plagues", "terrorizes", etc.). In addition to noting the facts, the active dramaturg prepares the question by addressing how the ghost behaves: What sort of appearance does the Ghost make? How does the relationship between Old Hamlet and Hamlet influence the ghost's appearance? Questions like these lead to creative conversations between the director and dramaturg rather than recycled interpretations of an ages-old scene.

An active dramaturg acknowledges preconceptions and assumptions before the first reading in preparation to be neutral. Reviewing these assumptive thoughts and the reflections following the first read, leads to questions that guide the conversation with the director toward less parochial or expected productions.

Major Characters

The second fixed critical element is the major characters. Even if a production cuts some characters entirely or fuses two or more into one composite figure, active dramaturgs need to identify what informs and shapes each of the original characters' journeys, desires (wants and needs), and the metaphors or linguistic tics woven into the dialogue. Similarly, the facts of the characters remain more constant than the themes. For example, that fact that Shaw's Major Barbara performs missionary work will not change nor will her high ideals. Another solid fact is that Major Barbara eventually questions her mission or herself, but when and how others impact her journey lies in interpretation. The active dramaturg identifies the facts, and then participates in shaping how the production will unveil the conceptual ideas in ways that strengthen the play's language and themes by posing open questions. If the dramaturg has identified specific moments when the characters' views shift, these points may be shared with the director, and the production and performance can remain sharp and nuanced.

Certainly actors and directors look for these moments, but sometimes the emotional nuances overwhelm key storytelling moments, which can lead to confusion. Active dramaturgs help maintain clarity by identifying specific moments and sharing these signposts with the director throughout the production process, grounding the critical comments in the text.

Researching Facts and Reading Critical Essays

The third element active dramaturgs use to guide their preparation are the play's factual references, historical or otherwise.

Most theatre supporters and artists erroneously believe that a dramaturg's sole responsibility is to find relevant articles, perform Google searches and reign as the keeper of the copier machine. Yes, dramaturgs do research facts in plays, the playwright (if the playwright isn't involved in rehearsal), and other related topics no matter how esoteric. But this is only a small portion of a dramaturg's responsibility and work. This misconception persists because many early dramaturgs in the States simply copied critical material and presented it to the cast with little or no context, reinforcing the idea that the answer to a production question lies within a ten-page Harold Bloom, Enoch Brater or Sandra Richards essay. No doubt these critics provide a number of valuable and fascinating insights into Shakespeare, Beckett, and Alice Childress, respectively, but how many of these ideas apply to a particular production or directorial approach? Only a few. Similarly, not all scholars write and think with the precision and acumen of Bloom, Brater, and Richards, demanding that the active dramaturg locate the specific ideas or points that apply to a particular production or question.

If a dramaturg primarily studies the play's facts and secondarily synthesizes the article, much more dramaturgical work will be used by the artistic team. In the initial meetings with the director and the design team, active dramaturgs use critical writings to launch ideas or questions and clarify specific moments. The director may also work with the active dramaturg to select the few articles to include in the Actor Packet, materials the actors use to inform their character and the world of the play.

In addition to clarifying historical fact and providing textual insights, critical and academic essays reveal the changing thoughts surrounding a writer or play, particularly set texts. These writings accelerate an active dramaturg's thinking by reinforcing certain observations or pointing out new areas to explore. These critical articles make the dramaturg's job easier but not easy, largely because many of these articles engage in thinking about the play and its themes and influences rather than determining the theatricality of the work. Production dramaturgy's fascination with literary analysis exists only as long as the literary criticism assists the active dramaturg's ability to clarify questions in ways that the production can realize the story on stage or use to shape character. The key to using essays well is to recognize that often only one useable idea will emerge to impact the production. The active dramaturg also understands that these readings do more to help expand ideas and opinions gleaned during the first two readings.

For new plays, the playwright serves as the point person regarding factual research and dramaturgs as the secondary source, because in the writing process the playwright has conducted enough research to become a *de facto* expert. However, the active dramaturg also devotes time to researching key factual references.

Identifying Major Themes and Metaphors

Themes and metaphoric images provide the greatest fodder for creative discussion for designers. It should be no surprise to discover that these elements also lie at the heart of an active dramaturg's design. The key is to first acknowledge the metaphors and themes that jump out and to then shape them into questions that open the play and lead to discussion, rather than steer the director to consider your singular approach.

Certainly aspects of character related to specific themes and metaphors, as well as researched facts and facts in the play, should be identified. Active dramaturgs go a step further and corral the observations and ideas around one or two major themes before meeting with the director. These groupings will, at times, be loose and sometimes tangential, but openness helps the active dramaturg forge new connections between their observations and the director's. The ensuing conversation is the basis for a dynamic collaboration.

The initial reflection process will also identify one major theme or metaphor, but following some research the active dramaturg's approach will reveal more, because character and context (political, social or historical) are now better understood. For example, researching the character Abraham Lincoln for *The America Play* can lead to varied thematic interpretations. Research may reinforce the famed president's role in the emancipated slave's life and in turn generations of African Americans. A dramaturg may also come across language that describes Lincoln as a father figure whose untimely assassination left his vision for freedom unfulfilled, aligning the sixteenth president with a man who is forced to abandon his family. Now, the play's ideas of fatherhood and family have moved beyond the nuclear definition. A theme initially articulated as the importance of a child knowing both parents becomes, following some historical research and a subsequent understanding of major characters, the theme of a particular ethnic group's search for connection to the United States and the sense of displacement that some African Americans experience as a result.

Dramaturgical Language

Dramaturgically inclusive language implies word choices that avoid assumptions. Inclusive language does not necessarily imply language that is politically correct or reveals a sensitivity to other cultures, ethnicities or religious groups. Inclusive language goes beyond this social requirement to convey an honest appreciation of difference and revel in the new perspectives that difference brings. Dramaturgically inclusive language avoids pandering.

To move beyond the limited scope of ethnically inclusive language, the active dramaturg can simply work to eliminate phrases like "everyone will get this" or "everything relates to this." In most contexts, these phrases reveal the unrealistic hope that every person who encounters the play or production will bring the same experiences and ideas. We know that a group does not and cannot ascribe itself to a single belief; and yet, when discussing a play or expanding dramatical ideas the tendency is to lump audiences together. Good dramaturgs identify assumptive language and ideas; active dramaturgs watch for opportunities to broaden these ideas and encourage all of the collaborators to do the same.

Inclusive language also suggests something more than cultural awareness—it responds to a number of observations and ideas. Open and broad language makes it possible for the active dramaturg to adjust an observation, impression or question to keep the lines of communication open. In turn, inclusive language begets flexible thinking. Flexible thinkers work with others and actively contribute and sculpt the conversation. For example, an active dramaturg embraces a director's vision and thematic or metaphoric interpretation but also questions these ideas and presents additional views. Active dramaturgs use language that keeps the play open and then refines thematic ideas in preparation for the production; this is the heart of active dramaturgy.

In the Meeting

Discuss the Set Text with the Director

The greatest challenge when working on a set text is to balance the expectation to know the text cold as well as all scholarship surrounding the play and its writer. If it sounds like a lot, it is. No artist should feel the burden of having all of these topics well under control by the first meeting; even so, some directors will foster an environment and expectation that suggests otherwise. This drive to negatively challenge what dramaturgs or other collaborators know reveals a need to control. This behavior may also signal an unproductive or artistically frustrating working experience. Yes, some people know certain writers and plays better than others. But rest assured, no one is an expert on the production of a work, because the nature of theatre is that the mysteries the story tells shift with each production and its context.

When discussing the set text with a director, first listen to the director's perceptions and parameters for the production. Do not, however, listen in a passive way, which means to simply absorb and blindly reinforce the director's comments. Active dramaturgs listen in an active manner by noting ideas that reverberate throughout the text, scholarship, and personal observations. Active dramaturgs also use the general groupings of themes and metaphors to identify other places where the play intersects with the director's impressions.

Ignore the Compulsion to Be Right or Know Everything

Many of the questions discussed concern ideas and responses rooted in known facts or specific observations. What about the confusing moments in the play? For example, is Hamlet contemplating suicide in the "To be or not to be" speech (*Hamlet* 3.1.55) It's tempting to put forth an answer or a definitive argument. Succumbing to this temptation makes a dramaturg appear to know what the production should look like and eliminates the desire to explore. At times thinking aloud with the director is the best choice, at other times, to admit more research is needed. Good dramaturgs identify moments that reveal the play's pulse and present them as a *fait accompli*. Active dramaturgs aren't afraid to admit what they do not know.

A director willing and interested in collaborating will invite questions and pursue a conversation that will explore uncovering answers or a path to finding those answers that works well with their production. Directors who function more like authority figures rarely engage in conversations and often fail to hear questions. Even open questions appear as limiting to authoritative directors, because answering them means shaping and connecting ideas and delving into the unknown, which for many authoritative directors remains a frightening and unsettling stage in the creative process. Art ruled by fear remains general and vague to the audience and rich only to the creative team. Active dramaturgs work to make the ideas rich to both the audience and the creative team.

Active dramaturgs use/view the first conversation with a director as an opportunity to raise questions about the play, the things they do not understand as well as how the play challenges their view of the play's world. Commit to searching for the answers with colleagues. Bring the questions that confuse to that initial conversation. By identifying what one still grapples with, it's possible to remind one's self to remain open to surprise and discovery throughout the process.

Because dramaturgs collect the information and images that shape the play and do a lot of this work before the other artists, it's possible to appear to be ahead of the group. Finding ways to balance sharing discoveries and informing the director is part of the dramaturg's artistry. As long as sharing lies at the heart of these conversations, the collaboration should become strong and healthy. Once the conversations become intellectual and artistic face-offs, the relationship has little chance of surviving.

In short, active dramaturgs stay focused on what they can bring to the artistic table and work hard to raise these ideas as questions to explore, to foster a successful and creative relationship with the director.

Prepare for the First Meeting with a Director for a New Play

When working on a new play, the first meeting with the director usually includes the playwright. If the director and dramaturg meet or talk before including the playwright, the conversation usually establishes who will lead the meeting with the playwright to avoid a sense of an unfocused meeting or of ganging up on the writer. Because the play is in process and many of the play's facts and rules may change, the preparation for the meeting largely resembles what's done prior to meeting with the writer, discussed in Chapter 5. If the director has comments or concerns not covered by the dramaturg, the decision may be to have the dramaturg raise them or to have the director voice the ideas. The dramaturg should attempt to connect the director's questions to the general theme governing the first meeting, offering feedback to the writer.

While in the Meeting for a New Play

During the meeting with the playwright, active dramaturgs do everything to honor that initial agreement and avoid pitting the director and playwright against each other. If the director makes comments and observations that go against the conversation's flow or the agreed discussion points, active dramaturgs work to connect those comments to the overall theme of the conversation. This will help reduce the sense of overload for the playwright and keep the comments focused. If anyone behaves or speaks inappropriately, address those concerns with the theatre's artistic or management staff after the meeting; and during the conversation, do as much as possible to refocus the conversation or end it gracefully.

Assemble a List of Things to Do for Set Texts or New Plays

As the meeting draws to a close, it's good to identify what needs to be done before the next meeting. As obvious as this is, many dramaturgs, playwrights, and directors leave meetings without a sense of what to accomplish before the next meeting. Unlike the other designers who must coordinate their work with many departments and staffs, many artists mistakenly believe that few departments depend on a dramaturg's work because failure to find an article or thematic outline rarely impacts the budget. However, a dramaturg's input effects many significant creative decisions. When working on a new play, this to-do list is crucial because every department depends on the script to complete their work in a timely manner. Taking time to build the list with the director helps establish boundaries for thinking and a research process that will avoid becoming diffuse. It also clarifies the active dramaturg's responsibilities so that all involved can appreciate and recognize the dramaturg's contributions.

Complete That To-Do List

This means just that, do what's on the list. Make serious attempts to complete the to-do list and add to it. If impasses develop, find an alternative solution or look ahead and complete those tasks. Communicating whatever conceptual or research hurdles arise gives the director an opportunity to help establish a new to-do list or refocus part of the project.

Final Thoughts

The true key to a successful meeting with a director is to actively contribute to the conversation. Active dramaturgs come to the first meeting with ideas and questions rooted in the play, which will inspire conversation and artistic debate, which results in articulating and defining common terms and a sense of what will work best in a given situation—artistic compromise.

Active dramaturgs do not wait for a director to define the dramaturg's tasks. Dramaturgs actively mine the play for clues that make the play dynamic, which helps the director create a specific job description governing the dramaturg's duties, enhancing active participation throughout. And remember, preparation doesn't mean bringing a number of preconceived ideas or notions and fighting to hold on to them. Preparation means coming to the meeting with strong sense of what the play is doing and where it does this well and less well. Also, dramaturgs do not need to answer the questions right away, but demonstrating a willingness to grapple with challenging matters sets you apart. The more inventive/imaginative the choice, the more exciting the conversation will be, and your dramaturgy will never appear passive.

Chapter 5

Preparation for and Collaboration with the Playwright

The first meeting with a playwright is one of the most exciting and daunting events for a dramaturg. It's exciting because the dramaturg can help form the creative space for the writing and rewriting of a work; daunting because without the proper creative vibe the collaboration can implode and the final project stall. That said, the active dramaturg is not entirely responsible for a project's success or failure, but as the artist charged with cultivating the creative environment it's important to approach the collaboration with care.

The initial meeting between the dramaturg and playwright helps establish a solid foundation for developing the written word. In addition, this inaugural meeting informs the active dramaturg how to best communicate with the writer; help determine the writer's agenda and how to best facilitate it and how to support the writer's creativity while maintaining an objective eye.

If the dramaturg works for a producing organization, the active dramaturg has the challenge of representing and balancing the questions the play asks with the ideas that the artistic director, managing director, and even the marketing director have for the play. Given these varied and sometimes conflicting responsibilities, it's important for the active dramaturg to remember that the playwright drives the relationship. Even when a producing organization assigns a dramaturg to the production, the playwright is the client, and a skilled, gifted dramaturg works to facilitate and encourage this writer's process.

How to Not Help

To train as a dramaturg means to study the history of dramatic literature and then focus specifically on a few periods or writers. This education enables a dramaturg to point out what makes a play unique or derivative and what elements in the play currently in development relate to past works. However, this information rarely helps a playwright. This isn't to suggest playwrights are fragile creatures, or that knowing theatre history detracts from a dramaturg's effectiveness. Playwrights are some of the bravest artists as they regularly enter an unknown world and discover the language needed to place it on paper. But, it's unproductive to categorize the playwright by comparing the writing style or the play to preexisting works. Doing so stifles rather than frees. The active dramaturg knows how the play resembles or connects to theatre history—and uses this information judiciously—to develop the piece.

If a dramaturg thinks a set-text provides an excellent example of a solution or problem, discussing set texts or assigning the writer a reading list does nothing to move the project forward. In fact, it wastes a lot of time. If the writer takes the list and reads what's recommended (especially the writer who is eager to please), the number of possible rewrites dwindles daily. Yes, a solution or key to solving a play's question may exist in that Arthur Miller or Goldoni play or a Sixties charmer like *MacBird!*, but the active dramaturg strives to articulate how that moment works to inspire a revelation. Assigning homework transforms the dramaturg into a teacher, not a collaborator.

My first experience as a dramaturg illustrates this point a little too well. During the first term at Yale, first year actors, directors, playwrights, and dramaturgs were paired for what is known as The Fifty—the first years' new play collaboration. I worked on a wonderful one-act three character play by Dora Litinakes titled *The Fly*. Flashbacks helped tell the story. Eager to do well and put all of my theatre history to work, I remember encouraging Dora to read or at least look at a number of plays that use flashbacks and memory to tell the story. What seemed well intentioned and an excellent way to find examples of how to best use this storytelling device did nothing but mire the entire team in confusion. I couldn't distill why or how these plays used memories to propel the present action. I didn't do what a dramaturg should. I couldn't help the playwright use these examples. The play stalled and confusion reigned. It's an experience I've never forgotten largely because I learned what not to do. But at what expense?

Some may say such failures are fine in an academic setting, indeed encouraged. True. But in a professional setting, such behavior serves no one well.

It would be nice to think I was the only one making these mistakes. However, as a professional and professor of dramaturgy, I see similar well-intentioned missteps occurring at every level. I have seen dramaturgs ignore a playwright and push the writer to pen the play the producer wants. I have heard of interns giving cuts to veteran writers and seen veteran dramaturgs push plays to fit a personal agenda not the play's. I have heard my students encourage a conversation focused on everything but the play at hand and propose first meeting questions such as: What dramatic theory informs your writing and how does this play compare with your other work, the work of your idols? Experience is a wonderful a teacher but it is possible to minimize the number of damaging mistakes through a little preparation.

Step Out of the Way

In order to give the playwright the space to create while simultaneously shepherding the development process (its deadlines, organizing workshops), a dramaturg must learn how to step aside, which means placing the needs and concerns of the text and the writer above those of the dramaturg or the institution. Too often external pressures negatively impact the creative process, and a play that began as a somewhat coherent whole may end up addressing the needs of many cooks and lack a clear voice. Active dramaturgs listen to the writer's wants and responses to the open questions asked and then juxtaposes the rules of the play with these comments to develop a plan that best serves the writer's needs and maintains the play's voice.

Listen to the Voice of the Play

In Chapter 1, the play's voice was defined as the way the critical elements combine to shape the story. In addition, the play's voice is the spirit and tone of the world that houses the story. The voice isn't *genre*, which is the type of play, such as comedy, tragedy, realism or magical realism; it's the play's individual personality. The writer may choose the language and craft the tensions, but it is the play's voice that regulates the parameters for those choices. Plays exist as dynamic stories told through dialogue driven by a character's wants and needs at a particular moment or in a response to a given situation. When dramaturgs and writers say that a proposed solution might work if it were in the play's voice, they are suggesting that the idea is intellectually on the right path, but its spirit and tone aren't yet right for the play.

To hear the play's voice, the active dramaturg explores the ways characters speak, interact, observe silence, and pursue their wants and needs. A play in which characters tell their every thought and deed rather than act suggests a play with a confused or bland voice. A play in which characters pursue wants and needs and actively describe their world in various ways suggests a vivid, lively play.

Balance the Play's Voice and the Wants of Others

Sometimes dramaturgs pursue their own agendas or push the writer (or the play) to explore paths or ideas that do not interest the writer. A dramaturg who fails to listen to the writer might be tempted to craft notes that brings the play away from what the writer discovers is the true goal. The active dramaturg's role is to foster the play and, in turn, the writer, and to not push the play and writer to assume insights and perspectives of the dramaturg or producing institution. Negotiating this political terrain and these experiential differences can sometimes be the active dramaturg's greatest challenge.

Worse still, the dramaturg's zeal may lead to pushing the writer beyond the writer's experience causing both the play and writer to implode. This happens most often with early career playwrights who seek to please their collaborators and demonstrate their ability to play well with others, but in the end they sacrifice their voice and their play. An active dramaturg acknowledges a writer's experience and works to cultivate a process that increases expertise without questioning competence.

If, for example, a writer initially seeks to create a serious political drama that includes a few scenes that lean toward satire. What may become clear through a conversation shaped by open questions is that the writer actually wants to pen a ribald comedy, but has managed to create an insightful political satire, not a drama with satirical moments. The active dramaturg may then need to articulate the difference between comedy and satire and note when and where the play is more comedy than satire, followed by a conversation to create an appropriate artistic plan and goal.

Play development has two equally important components: to serve the play and to serve the writer. When dramaturgs fail to listen to what a writer wants to pursue or where the writer is in terms of process, tensions flare and the process stagnates or erupts.

Acknowledege the Distinction Between Dramaturgy and Writing

Before meeting with the writer, it's important to remember a dramaturgical rule: dramaturgs do not write the play. Yes, some dramaturgs write their own original plays or craft exciting adaptations and translations. But writers who accept a position as dramaturg for someone else's play should remember that their official function is as a dramaturg and they should not craft a single word. The playwright writes everything. If a dramaturg begins to write, the collaboration changes and the dramaturg becomes a co-creator and ceases to maintain the objectivity needed to function well as a dramaturg.

When an active dramaturg brainstorms with the writer to discover a story's path, writing isn't taking place. To avoid writing, an active dramaturg may point to preexisting characters, ideas, or comments from earlier conversations. For example, a conversation might reveal a rough outline—the character needs to arrive, discover something that angers him and then deal with it before his girlfriend re-enters the scene. Here, the dramaturg is clearing a path for creation—not writing. Writing would be stating specific actions, lines of dialogue, and step-by-step ways to achieve those actions. Put simply, active dramaturgs aid in shaping the creative process; writers imagine and realize the result of that process.

When a high level of trust exists between the dramaturg and playwright, some lines blur. A dramaturg may offer more than shape to a scenario, adding character nuance and specific ideas for conversations or motivations. To suggest nuance a dramaturg might ask: *"Does this character's speech ever alter?"* To go beyond nuance, the dramaturg might suggest that this character stutter when in the presence of women, or use a particular greeting. The key is knowing how to shape creative thinking without crossing the line and composing dialogue.

How To Not Help 2

Writer and comedian Steve Martin's 2004 satirical essay exploring the Hollywood rewrite process for Mel Gibson's *The Passion of the Christ* in *The New Yorker* magazine best captures the mindset governing a flawed theatrical development process. Martin takes the screenplay through a gauntlet of Hollywood executives' comments summarized in a letter[1] penned by a

---

1   Martin, Steve. "Studio Script Notes on 'The Passion'." *The New Yorker*, March 8, 2004, p. 94

fictitious producer named Stan. The producer begins as a writer's friend and then launches into with prescribed fixes without understanding, "One thing: I think we need to clearly state 'the rules.' Why doesn't he use his superpowers to save himself?" Stan goes further and asks to omit the crucifixion of Jesus Christ because "It seems the cross image has been done to death," and keep the moment where Jesus changes water into wine because "History compression is a movie tradition.... Great trailer moment, too." The word Aramaic confuses Stan to the point of worry, "I'm assuming 'The dialogue is in Aramaic' is a typo for 'American.' If not, call me on my cell, or I'm at home all weekend."

Martin's satirical essay exemplifies what a dramaturg should *not* do—bark orders based on assumptions. It also reveals why a playwright's creative life differs so much from a screenwriter's. In the theatre, the artistic team should respect the writer and avoid such prescriptive rewrites. As with anything, telling others what to do produces a superficial solution; if, however, an individual crafts an idea alone or with others, the end result proves rich and satisfying.

What to Listen for

Relationships evolve over time. No one disputes this. The first meeting with the playwright establishes how the dramaturg/playwright relationship might grow. However, dramaturgs often work with playwrights at festivals, workshops, or reading series, which last a few days, so there may be only one opportunity to meet with the writer to forge a creative relationship. A short time frame adds to the stress surrounding the need to make a good first impression, certainly not the ideal, but a reality writers and dramaturgs live with.

So, what does a dramaturg actually do with a writer during that initial meeting?

The Importance of Understanding the Writer's Goals

To help shape the creative process a dramaturg seeks to understand how the writer currently sees the development process and what, if any, the goals are. The development process bends to the writer's process and needs, and the active dramaturg serves the writer best by learning these needs or wants. If the writer has no specific goals, asking questions to uncover concerns and areas to explore will help.

Once the basic goals or hopes for the process are clear, the active dramaturg begins posing open questions. A dramaturg's best tool is the question, in particular the Open Question. As described in Chapter 3, these questions inspire creative options and a flexible boundary as well. An effective open question does not lead to a specific or biased answer; nor does it present the asker's opinions or personal thoughts. An open question stimulates discussion and thought. When working with a writer, an active dramaturg's sense of timing or when questions are asked determines a large part of their effectiveness.

Ideally, the dramaturg may choose to begin with a question focused on inspiration but, if time is short, the Passover Question. Whichever question the dramaturg chooses, it should confirm that the dramaturg has read the play and wishes to avoid assuming anything about the story or the writer's intent. More important, it's crucial to hear the writer articulate the play's vision or inspiration to ensure a productive and satisfying development process, for three major reasons discussed below.

The first reason: learning the writer's initial intent and vision for the script will help the active dramaturg connect the responses and observations from the first reading to the writer's passion and help everyone have a better sense of what fuels the play. Not until the actual dramaturgical and development process begins do the writer and dramaturg discover how much—if at all—the initial impulse resembles the writer's true intent.

Many dramaturgs succumb to temptation and begin with personal responses and impressions as a way to demonstrate a keen level of interest to the playwright, an observant eye, and skill. Sadly, this approach has the opposite effect, often alienating the writer because the comments (no matter how right-on or insightful) do not speak to the writer; the comments reflect the dramaturg's language, not the play's or the writer's unique vocabulary. When dramaturgs rush in, the discussion often leans more toward the dramaturg or producer's vision rather than the writer's. And although the producer or producing organization often pays the dramaturg, the active dramaturg's primary goal is to assist in shaping an excellent play. The play is the client; the text drives the process.

The second reason active dramaturgs listen to the writer articulate the play's vision is that engaging the writer in conversation reveals what the writer would like to work on. When a writer reveals a writing challenge or question, the odds that it will be addressed with some success are quite high. If, however, someone tells the writer what to change or how to change it, the possibility for a stalled creative process and confused storytelling (if not total failure) increases exponentially.

The third reason to engage writers in conversation, rather than inundating the writer with responses and observations, is that a guided conversation helps the active dramaturg and writer discover a common vocabulary. It is the dramaturg's job to learn to speak and think in a way that facilitates the writer's process. Listening for how a writer articulates what he or she wants to grapple with during rewrites to solve writing challenges helps the active dramaturg build a linguistic shorthand with the writer. It's more difficult to develop the script if the dramaturg hasn't found a way to talk with, rather than at the writer.

What Goes into Crafting the First Meeting?

First Meeting Questions

In preparing for the first meeting, the active dramaturg considers what issues, themes, and challenges call for attention and composes open questions for each. Grouping these observations around particular themes will usually reveal one or two well-phrased open questions that will encompass all of the areas of concern. This preparation, informed by reflecting on the critical elements, enhances the active dramaturg's ability to listen and helps to generate a potential game plan, with boundaries stable enough to focus thoughts but flexible enough to shift when the collaboration warrants. If the active dramaturg listens openly to the writer, many of the inspirations, challenges, and concerns the playwright raises will connect with the dramaturg's observations made from various readings, and fuel a fruitful creative conversation and productive collaboration.

Preparing questions along thematic lines leads the dramaturg to corral the writer's comments or answers to questions around specific thematic or topic areas. By looking for areas to place each response, the active dramaturg can focus the discussion so it covers one, two or three major topics. Imagine Shakespeare's *A Midsummer Night's Dream* was a new work. After reflecting on images in the play, the active dramaturg notes that Oberon laces his language with references to herbs like wild thyme, and Hermia and Helena refer to flower-bearing fruit trees. (*A Midsummer Night's Dream* 2.1) Imagine for a moment that no other character made mention of flora and fauna. A dramaturg could engage the writer in a conversation that focuses exclusively on the poetic impact horticultural terms have on Oberon and then repeat the conversation for the young female lovers. An *active* dramaturg would simultaneously consider the metaphoric import of language fecund with flora in Oberon's lines *and* the young women's, to engage the writer in a conversation that explores whether references to flora and fauna within more characters' dialogue would enrich the text and characterizations. Making global comments allows the observations to appear similar as well as the solutions, increasing the sense that the changes require the same thinking process. Comments that indicate small, periodic and separate references make the adjustments seem tedious and numerous. One approach inspires and the other overwhelms. An active dramaturg's goal during this first conversation is to inspire and outline how the various questions connect and generate solutions globally.

Framing the Conversation

For many writers a desire to probe a social question or explore a fascinating figure, rather than dramatic form or metaphor, drives the first level of writing. The second, third, and fourth level of writing, however, is always rewriting. Rewriting or deepening the current script remains difficult, if not impossible, if the writer cannot fully reconnect with those moments originally shaped by inspiration and/or the creative need to tell the story. To facilitate this renewed relationship, the active dramaturg encourages writers to articulate questions or key moments within the play that they wish to pursue.

Ideas that aren't true to the play or writer's vision stall the writing and often lead artists to make changes that destroy what made the play exciting. To foster an environment where the writer is working hard and not in danger of hitting a creative wall depends on a dramaturg's ability to notice how a writer responds to criticism and the pressure of rewriting, and the writer's actual experience level.

Have a Game Plan or Intention in Mind

Active dramaturgs begin the meeting with a specific intention in mind: to facilitate the writer's process. Dramaturgs also enter the meeting with a game plan that will help identify ways to nurture the project. The idea isn't to walk in with a secret and an agenda, but a game plan: that is, organized thoughts pertaining to specific areas of interest and questions that will help shape a focused conversation. The game plan is based on the play's voice and designed to help the writer explore the play's questions and needs with focus and relative speed. The game plan's general outline can help shape the conversation, even when it becomes clear the writer needs and wants to discuss something else, for the game plan is flexible. More important, if the questions are open and relate specifically to the critical elements and moments in the play, nine times out of ten your goal and the writer's questions will relate. The active dramaturg identifies specific topics, areas, or open questions based on the reflections that follow the initial reads to forge that game plan. The writer's questions, wants, needs and comments drive the exploration and conversation. If it's difficult to connect the current conversation to the game plan, stop and listen. What is the writer addressing? What is the writer asking to explore? How does your preparation relate to these questions and concerns? Don't push forward with your game plan: adjust, wait for another opportunity to pursue that question (especially if the writer has hit overload), but know that, in time, the ideas unearthed while crafting the game plan will serve the process and the writer well.

Using the Game Plan to Prepare for the Conversation

First, think back to the reflections and notes made following the first and second readings. When noticing events, characters, or themes, did any seem extremely compelling or somewhat inconsistent or provoke questions left unanswered in the script? Were there aspects of the story or the play's voice (its tone and pattern for revealing information, twists and tensions) that excite, remain vague, confusing or disconnected? Whether you are an aural or visual reader, these pattern elements inform your thoughts. An active dramaturg steps back and determines what, if anything, connects these observations. They can often be divided into several groups, which is helpful when assembling a game plan. Addressing the issues in large groups will produce solutions that have somewhat of a cascading effect and can lead the writer automatically to a simple global solution. Addressing three areas or groups per meeting is a lot. Any writer would hit overload and stop listening out of exhaustion, not rudeness. So look for the group of observations that contains issues that impact the majority of the play. When this level of prioritizing isn't possible, look for the strongest examples of where the ideas present in any group work well and where there's room for further exploration. Active dramaturgs shape the transitions between groups so the writer's comments and observations are included, so the examination naturally progresses into a conversation where solutions emerge.

A Conversation of Options, Not Nots

In preparing for the meeting, active dramaturgs have an opportunity to discover a vocabulary that will feed rather than extinguish the flame of creativity. This terminology differs from the language or shorthand vocabulary the artistic team develops. Inspirational language is the language of options. The words focus on what the writer has achieved and where the play can grow as well as ways to accomplish this. The unique lexicon avoids articulating finite solutions, and it isn't ruled by nots (comments that reinforce what the play isn't.) Frankly, who wants to rewrite a play comprised of a series of nots?

How might a dramaturg accidentally enter a language of nots? Perhaps after reading a script with four or five characters the following observation emerges: the script follows a limited structure of two-person scenes where the action develops and concludes at each scene's end. The result gives the audience a fabulous scene for scene-study class, but a weak play. In a play with more than three characters a varied scene pattern heightens the sense of mystery whether the overarching form adheres to chronological, non-chronological, realistic, or episodic patterns. Stating this to a playwright means certain death for the play, for this is the language of analysis. It isn't the language of options, nor is it articulated in a way creative people can readily use. The active dramaturg's task is to take analytical points and language and translate them into an active vocabulary that stimulates creativity.

Finding a Creative Language

To tell a writer the play limits itself to two-person scenes that conclude too easily doesn't encourage rewrites, but injecting the conversation with pointed examples of the necessary dramatic mystery and tension may. Letting the writer know *what* in the play intrigues or heightens a sense of curiosity will begin to direct the conversation toward positive options. Such an approach enables the dramaturg to point out how most or all of the scenes conclude too tidily, deflating any air of mystery or tension. An active dramaturg opens the dialogue by revealing that this regular two-person dialogue form forces the writer to work three times as hard to reestablish the play's mystery. The play's information needs to be repeated and action stalls, leading the writer to force a spark of dramatic action rather than generate one organically. No writer likes to work three times harder than necessary, and no one wants to believe the work looks contrived. By simply alerting the writer to how much dialogue the characters repeat and the emotional delays this creates for an audience, the writer might be eager to work on the scene, and in turn, the play. By avoiding a series of nots, exciting possibilities abound.

If a writer wonders whether to explore those options or how to approach those possibilities, take that wondering as an opportunity to talk. It is not, however, a time to lecture or demonstrate a keen knowledge of dramatic structures. Instead use knowledge to buoy the conversation and provide the writer with inspiration and options. Solutions may be found while discussing the points. Pose questions like: what's confusing or what's interesting about these points or what inspired this scene? The ensuing conversation creates more opportunities for the writer to brainstorm and clarify thoughts, and for the dramaturg to identify which comments clarify the various questions under discussion. Remember the ultimate goal of a dramaturg/playwright conversation is to empower the playwright to rewrite, not to overwhelm or confuse.

When a Playwright Responds with "I Don't Know"

Throughout the conversation, the writer may state that the options are clear but the actual path to affect the needed changes isn't. That's fine. Dramaturgs aren't looking for instant fixes. Similarly, active dramaturgs acknowledge this internally, and regularly remind writers that the path to creation is more important that the final result. Pretending otherwise places the writer on the defensive. A basic rule to remember: defensive writers do not write, rewrite, talk, or participate. The same is true for any artist. Simply put: Defensive attitudes kill creativity.

All writers (and artists) have the right to not know the answer to a question, and the right to say, "I don't know." When a writer repeats the phrase without actively pursuing a conversation to either clarify or find a path to knowing, something's amiss. Typically this indicates the writer's unwillingness to engage fully in the rewriting process. It's possible the writer fears the process, convinced it will be impossible to recapture the creative spirit that fueled the initial draft. It's possible the writer has no rapport with the dramaturg or the other collaborators. When this phrase becomes a stalling tactic, the best countermeasure is to simply stop the meeting. Take the time to discover the root of the problem. If necessary, shift the conversation to investigating the root of the fear. True, a dramaturg isn't a psychiatrist. But helping the writer articulate why the phrase "I don't know" is repeated can help the writer understand the creative process and in turn the reason for the block. If it seems appropriate, let the writer know that to avoid discussing the play will simply leave more work once rehearsals begin, when turnaround time is less generous.

Hopefully the questions and creative conversation will lead to a number of possible solutions and not stall tactics. Then again, some writers cannot rewrite. Few dramaturgs want to admit that, as our role is to help everyone remain in touch with their creative inspiration. But some writers start from scratch every time—the new pages do not take a pre-existing scene or idea and flesh it out or clarify confusion, rather they reveal an entirely new take on the same question with the same problems or challenges; worse still, the new material may present more confusions without moving the writer closer to the stated goal. This often produces interesting and varied drafts, but it's merely the illusion of progressing forward.

All writers are not equally proficient at rewriting. Even the most dedicated and focused writer sometimes simply ceases to move forward.

Learning how to rewrite means navigating between a conscious, creative place and the inspired, muse-driven place where many first drafts come from. The dramaturg encourages the writer throughout the process, perhaps even identifies small changes just to keep the writer writing. An active dramaturg works to consider what fuels the impasse.

Open Questions That Fuel a Creative Conversation

The goal and vision for the conversation will help shape the meeting, but open questions will drive the encounter. The three most important questions to ask a writer are the most difficult to answer. They are also difficult to ask, because how they're framed will determine the level of rapport between dramaturg and writer. There is no set order regarding which question to ask when. What follows is the rationale and key concepts for the questions that regularly inform the new-play development process. These questions lead to other, more focused questions or direct comments that help the dramatic work progress.

A Key Question: Uncovering Inspiration

A basic key question encourages an exploration of what inspired this particular dramatic story.

This basic question establishes a framework for the discussion. As the writer articulates the ideas that drive the need to write, it will become clear that some of these ideas will not be present in the play, and shouldn't be, but knowing the context will generate a vocabulary that fits the play and the writer's world view. The writer's response may also reveal a connection between challenges to explore and the creative impulse; an active dramaturg uses the information discovered to encourage the rewrite process. The challenge to this question is phrasing it to reveal interest rather than an inability to understand why the writer chose this topic. Asking the questions is just like writing the story, the nuances and twists make all the difference.

A Misleading Approach

Knowing what inspired the play is important, but it's all about how the question is raised. If phrased: *What inspired your play?* with an emphasis on "your," be prepared for a windy response laden with self-discovery. If the play or inspiration does come from the writer's past, fine. The trick is to keep the writer in the creative world rather than a personal past.

An Approach to Consider

Frankly, it is sometimes best to simply avoid the inspiration question and look for a way to ask for the same information in a more focused manner. For example, acknowledging that a play is set during the Weimer Republic or New York post-9/11 and then asking how these events inform the action or character journeys, or which elements of this event propel the characters, may prove more successful.

A Key Question: Revealing the Story and Plot

Because the active dramaturg asks to understand story and plot, another key question asks the writer to reveal the story of the play in no more than three sentences. Plot should be distilled to one sentence. Remember, story and plot are not the same.

Early-career writers balk at this question. For some it suggests the reader's inability to understand, an imbedded sense of failure on the writer's part, and that the writer has to divulge the story because it isn't clearly written. Many a writer wonders, if the story has to be summed up briefly, why write 80-plus pages? Hence, the need to make clear why this question is important for active dramaturgs' to ask, and to pose it carefully.

A Misleading Approach

The question: *Can you tell me about your play?* may appear to be similar to the question that asks a writer to describe the action of the play in one or two sentences, but it isn't. The difference is that the earlier open question promotes a focused, succinct answer, while this question encourages a diffuse, wide-reaching answer that could encompass what the writer likes to read or eat for breakfast. To talk about something means to describe it, to expand on ideas, to explore the philosophical aspects. A lengthy, unwieldy discussion that introduces ideas about the play inhibits the active dramaturg's ability to create a framework for the discussion. Talking about a play will distract everyone from discovering its active components, and dramaturgs help writers cultivate a rich, more active play. The discussion won't consider active ways to address or consider issues. The end result will be a fascinating conversation that stimulates everyone's mind but moves no one closer to making sure an audience will have a similar conversation once the curtain falls.

An Approach to Consider

The short answer is to simply ask for a straightforward, brief, and simple description—one sentence, two at the most—of the play's story. Such a question enables a writer to activate the play and provide a framework for the discussion. The long answer follows.

Obtaining a focused description of the story or plot will help the dramaturg articulate how events connect and if any unclear moments exist. The writer will have determined the language and scope. Often, the distilled story guides the writer to recognize the play's less effective moments, accelerating the conversation and the development process.

In addition, when talking about the play, the writer can innocently or deliberately defend the play and prevent questions designed to open up new solutions or creative avenues. A defensive playwright does not rewrite; a defensive playwright rationalizes why the play works despite obvious unclear moments. A dramaturg discourages a defensive environment.

A Key Question: Identifying the Playwright's Questions

Another key question asks whether the writer has questions. This can and should come throughout the conversation but certainly be used to conclude the conversation.

An Approach to Consider

The earlier two questions generate context for the play. This third question, however, comes from the writer and overtly places the control in the writer's hands. Anything is fair game: thematic or pointed queries based on specific characters, moments, or events.

When to ask this question depends largely on the conversation. It may come up naturally during the playwright's reasons for writing the play, or during the discussion of the dramaturg's observations of the play. In the end, when doesn't matter, but it is important to ask. Even more, it's essential that the dramaturg facilitate connecting the answers to the questions and observations raised during the conversation.

If a question begs for a simple response such as "yes, this works," or "no, this isn't clear," give it. Don't forget, however, that active dramaturgy means going a bit further and articulating concisely why a moment is successful or unclear. Addressing the why also allows the dramaturg to move the conversation toward a particular focused end or game plan.

The art of the active dramaturg's conversation is keeping the game plan in mind while incorporating the writer's questions, needs and revelations regarding the play's genesis.

Creative Obstacles

Once the conversation begins, glitches in the dialogue are bound to occur. Sometimes dramaturgs pose questions or discussion topics that inspire great artistic conversations but do little to set a path that clarifies the text. Below are a few of the most common creative obstacles.

Obstacle #1: A Discussion of the Philosophy or Structures

It seems obvious to avoid posing a philosophical question such as: "Tell me about your play's structure," or "What is the overall meaning (intention) of your play?" in an effort to develop the play. There is such little time to work on the play. Such questions are as distracting as "Which writers influence your writing?" Pose such questions over coffee after the work session ends. Why? It allows both writer and dramaturg to discuss their knowledge of theatre and writing, which helps them appear qualified in the other's eye (perhaps their own) but does little to move the play to the next level.

Instead, consider questions that explore how characters actively pursue ideas. For example, if the Jack and Jill play were in development and the writer began expounding upon the issues surrounding water conservation in today's society rather than the play's issues, an active dramaturg might ask: *In the play, what is the community's view toward water usage; what are Jack and Jill's individual views?*

Obstacle #2: A Discussion of Influential Figures

The Influential Figure question is just another version of the philosophical question. The topic may appear to engage the playwright's inspiration, but it actually invites the writer to discuss outside influences and other plays, not the work at hand. Let's say *Funnyhouse of a Negro* influenced the play's genesis and the writer cites Adrienne Kennedy as an influence. The result is a discussion about Adrienne Kennedy and *Funnyhouse,* not the writer in the room or the play in question.

If a previously produced play illuminates a challenge or potential solution, discuss and describe that feature or specific moment and how it applies to the play—and nothing else. If, for example, Kennedy's ability to indicate an anxious emotional state through stage directions describing floating heads applies, discuss that.

Obstacle #3: Journalistic Questions

Consider the question: *How does this play relate to your other works?* Doesn't this read like a classic interview question? It's a great example of a basic journalistic question. Does any artist want to collaborate with someone who begins with this question? And yet it is sometimes asked during the play development process. The question is so objective it makes the dramaturg appear uninterested in the current script.

Instead, discuss an element of the play—how it works and where it excels or becomes a bit fuzzy.

Obstacle #4: Challenging the Writer

Sometimes artists working with writers will ask: *Why did you write (fill in the blank) this way?* The subsequent glare of the insulted playwright usually ensures this question is never uttered again. But the damage is already done. Such a question leads the writer to defend the play (or character or scene) and potentially shut down. End of conversation. Active dramaturgs work to build a relationship of trust and appreciation of the play and the writer.

To pose an effective question, consider changing and focusing the question to produce more exciting conversation. For example, a play that includes a number of flashbacks or remembered scenes but it isn't clear why the action moves through time. Asking what the writer sees as the trigger for the flashbacks, begins a conversation that looks at specific moments in the play's action and the writer's specific thoughts governing the flashbacks and memory.

More important, if the question is posed in a more open way, the active dramaturg has an opportunity to build rapport and gain insight into the writer's thought process. And remember, sometimes dramaturgs ask questions to simply gain a better understanding and make certain they are on the right track. Don't be afraid to tell the writer if the flashbacks appear to shape a character in a particular way. Remember, everyone loves to hear when the ideas make sense and come through clearly. Active dramaturgs provide honest praise and happily identify when moments soar.

Obstacle #5: Demanding Work from the Writer

Asking or actually telling a writer when and what they should complete by the next meeting can destroy all of the good will generated during the meeting. Yes, all meetings should conclude with some sort of to-do list, but active dramaturgs do not assign tasks the way a teacher doles out homework. It works well when the dramaturg takes the lead in summing up the meeting and the questions or topics raised, after which the writer can identify what to address and in what order. If that doesn't happen, it's good to get a sense during the summation of how the writer prioritizes the tasks and what he wants to work on. Active dramaturgs can also help generate a realistic schedule for the writer, if asked.

Sometimes, however, the script seems written in a fit of divine inspiration and the writer demonstrates difficulty accessing its point of origin, making rewrites impossible. At this point, it does seem best to engage the writer in a few pointed tasks. The question is how to shape the need to rewrite so it less like homework. Planning together will help. The dramaturg sums up the conversation, perhaps asking the writer what interests her most or what she connects to. Active dramaturgs can also help the writer fashion a framework or outline with specific questions to answer throughout the rewriting.

Sometimes it's as simple as avoiding the word "rewriting". "Tweaking", "smushing", or "molding" may make the list of words that suggest restructuring but seem less onerous than "rewriting".

If the writer returns without having completed or furthered the exploration, one of two things is happening: a desire to stall, or an inability to execute the exploration alone. Both bode poorly if the theatre commits to the project and the project needs clarification before rehearsal. If the writer is young (in terms of career) no one wants to write him off, especially if the promise of a strong playwright manifests itself, but an unwillingness to rewrite establishes a reputation difficult to shake. It is not the dramaturg's job to preserve a writer's reputation. But if you believe in the writer, continue the search to help unlock the creative block.

As a last resort, if the writer hasn't suggested a timeline of projects or questions to explore (based on the conversation), encourage the writer to explore certain areas. Say, for example: *To help the play move forward in terms of the questions we've talked about today, it will help if you address or look further into (and insert a section). I'm happy to look at what you've come up with before we meet next or feel free to bring it in when we see each other next. It will help me prepare, if you can email or call me with what you're looking at and what section of the play you're focusing on.*

A writer's inability to fulfill any of these requests reveals a lot about that specific process, or lack thereof, and whether you and the theatre wish to continue the relationship. Don't write a playwright off entirely; this inability to execute changes or fear to review work may be a mark of inexperience, not necessarily lack of talent.

After the Conversation Ends

Taking the time to summarize the conversation or compose a helpful email for the writer can also serve every member of the artistic and producing team well. In addition to summarizing the conversation around three key themes, the active dramaturg should include the game plan or schedule for the rewrites that the writer and the dramaturg crafted together.

Final Thoughts

By discovering a vocabulary that allows direct, honest, and kind communication with the playwright, the dramaturg will avoid appearing ineffective or unsure. Of course it's natural to be nervous, but finding a way to move forward and make a positive contribution to the process will do more to alleviate nerves than anything a collaborator may say. Remain focused on the dramaturg's main responsibilities.

Active dramaturgs take time to prepare for meetings by reading, considering the areas of concern, and developing what connects these ideas and how to hold onto these ideas throughout the conversation. Careful preparation makes flexibility possible; the more done before the meeting the more likely the dramaturg will be able to follow the playwright's lead and introduce the comments in a manner that makes them most helpful to the writer.

To ensure that questions remain honest, direct, and open keep the following in mind:

- Focus comments on specific issues or points presented in the text. This will help both the dramaturg and writer discuss actual moments rather than remembered moments or events. People often recall information incorrectly and think we've added something when we actually haven't. And when the question inspires a conversation, which is necessary to any

creative process, be certain to return to the specific issue and
point in the text.

- Focus less on defining a text as linear or non-linear and look
  to discuss the play in terms of its rules and how they shape the
  characters' journey.

- Focus on ways to make the possible solutions active. This will
  help the conversation avoid becoming too philosophical and
  keep the writer's next step, rewriting, alive.

- Remember, dramaturgs do not write the play. Solutions or
  ideas that attract the playwright remain the ultimate goal. Be
  honest about an idea that intrigues you and why it intrigues
  you, but don't try to impose your vision for the play's evolution on the writer.

- Ask open questions and be willing to listen to the answers
  they inspire.

- Don't look for ways to tame the play or rid it of its challenging
  moments; instead, look for ways to increase understanding so
  that the challenges appear less difficult.

- Assemble these guiding principles into a game plan designed
  to generate active responses.

Chapter 6

The First Day of Rehearsal and Working with the Actors

The first day of rehearsal is an energy-filled event when everyone comes together to realize the imagined vision. The specific agenda for first rehearsals varies everywhere, but often the designers present more concrete expressions of the play's world and the director shares the production's vision, including initial perspectives on characters and story. What's more, the dramaturg has the rare opportunity to directly address the cast and articulate a personal vision and perspective that supports that of the artistic team.

The first day of rehearsal usually has three components, and their order depends on the production and the director. The three major parts are: the designer, dramaturgy, and concept presentations; the reading of the play; and discussion of the play. If it's a new play, there's an additional part: the writer addresses the group throughout the rehearsal, but usually at length after the first reading. The director often shares the vision or concept throughout as an introduction to each of the three major parts.

The dramaturg's presentation primarily includes presenting the cast with the information and themes the artistic team wishes to emphasize, and active ideas that shape the play, often (but not always) through the Actor Packet. Active dramaturgs also moderate the discussions following the first readings.

The key to a successful first day is to remember that the actors have had less time with the play and the production concept than the other collaborators; this means the dramaturgical presentation will need to review ideas and discoveries the design team made weeks if not months before. One of a dramaturg's worst mistakes can be to tell an actor or writer how these questions were solved by the artistic team or to articulate how the actor should solve a particular character challenge. The information presented should ignite the actor's process by presenting information that can fuel many paths clearly rather than one definitive, creative journey.

Preparing the Actor Packet

The Actor Packet is a document—paper or digital—that includes articles, images, and other relevant materials compiled to help the actor better understand the play's world, characters, images, and themes. The Actor Packet is not an exhaustive publication but a select set of materials designed to fuel the actors' creative process as they bring the play's world to life. Frankly, the term Actor Packet is a bit of a misnomer, for designers, marketing directors, education directors, and anyone else interested in probing beneath the play's surface may also refer to and benefit from the Actor Packet. Even so, the information primarily addresses the actors' needs, which drives the active dramaturg's, director's, and writer's decision of what to include.

Simply put, active dramaturgs gather information guided by a single question: *How will this information enhance what the actors do on stage and how the artistic team shapes the production?* The questions that emerge following the reflection process and initial conversations with the director or writer also often inform the first stage of research for the Actor Packet, as do the play's historic or social references. The Actor Packet may also be informed by the ideas and questions raised during the reflection process. Even if the production or play is in great flux, 80% of the work for the Actor Packet may be and must be completed before the first rehearsal.

A Philosophy for Shaping the Actor Packet

Many consider scholarly research and incessant fact-finding active dramaturgy. It isn't. A dramaturg must learn to resist the urge to include research for every question or fascinating reference because too much information overwhelms and stymies creativity rather than inspires. The Actor Packet supports key moments of the story. Without a game plan, the Actor Packet can become a large unwieldy beast. Using the following seven areas as a standard starting point will help the active dramaturg assemble a dynamic packet. Of course, an active dramaturg can expand the following list to fashion an Actor Packet that exceeds expectation.

In general, the Actor Packet should address the following seven areas:

1. The playwright;

2. Each character;

3. Historical, political, or religious movements or areas of concern (e.g., science, aviation) specific to the play;

4. Information that creates a social context for the play such as art, music, literature or popular magazines;

5. Images (aural and visual) of the period;

6. Images (aural and visual) that evoke the play or individual characters' voice or mood;

7. Themes present in the play and concept that are separate from political/historical topics.

Two areas to include depending on the material:

1. The play's genre or style, especially if the director wishes to shape gestures influenced by a particular performance style, for example, commedia dell'arte;

2. The significance of specific music stylings for musicals or plays with incidental music.

The Playwright[1]

All playwrights deserve an introduction. A brief biography can help the company learn about the writer's interests and accomplishments. If articles by or about the writer exist, include a select few. When appropriate, address where or when the writer wrote the piece, what plays precede and follow the play you're producing, or what inspired the play's genesis. Be sure to include major biographical dates and any quotes or writings that relate most specifically to the play or the writer's vision.

When little published information on the writer exists, if possible interview the writer. An interview can accomplish more than three critical articles, because the conversation can focus on production-specific topics. If this is the writer's first play, focus on the open question: *What draws you to this story?* Any background or insight into the writer's creative process will excite the collaborators and encourage them to delve beyond the play's surface, enriching the rehearsal process and in turn the production. Do not, however, craft this section so that it merely repeats what the writer will say when addressing the cast during the first rehearsal. Obviously some overlap will occur, but strive to generate an original and exciting

---

1   If the production is a musical, remember to include the composer and lyricist in addition to the person(s) responsible for the book.

biography. If done well, the interview may become an important component of the marketing campaign or education director's materials.

The Characters

Take time to isolate each character and present specific information for each. Whether the play has as few as one or as many as 13, including specific character-related research can immediately gratify a curious actor. However, it doesn't take long before a dramaturg becomes overwhelmed by the amount of information to include. Take time to notice references the character made that you may not have understood initially and begin to research those. Places the character mentions, people, events, and the things this character knows also provide ways to organize information. Should the play include numerous characters, look for ways to group like figures and present information that addresses them; for example, assembling Shakespeare's fairies and including a few additional notes for Puck may help organize information for part of the *A Midsummer Night's Dream* Actor Packet. Keep in mind, the packet doesn't replace the actor's homework, it merely provides help locating a research path that fits with the production's vision and the director's concept.

If a historical figure informs the character, locating images, articles and short biographies not only provides background information but may also illuminate the play's form/patterns. For example, a historical figure known to suffer from mental illness may inspire a story realized in complete scenes that give way to fragments when a manic episode occurs. That said, watch the tendency to overwhelm the actor with history. Remember, only some aspects of the historical figure will inform the invented character. The actor will enliven the character the writer imagined, not the actual historical figure. Shakespeare's Richard III is nothing like the historical king, who was neither disabled nor a proven conspirator in the murder of his nephews, the princes.

Too much historical detail may distract the actor from creating the dramatic character. Consider Marilyn Monroe as another example. It may seem tempting to include information regarding Monroe's marriages, career, and now-understood chemical dependency. But in Arthur Miller's final play *Finishing the Picture,* the Monroe character he offers remains partially revealed or completely unseen and utters unintelligible lines throughout. Also, Miller's final play depicts a time when her prescription drug habit was not understood by anyone; Miller shows her friends to be as lost as she in terms of how to deal with the emotional agony and fallout such addiction caused. How much background on Monroe's life, marriage to the writer, and drug addiction does the actress or the company need? What information best relates to the times? Research that reveals that Monroe, considered to have it all, faced inner demons that no one, not even her many husbands, understood, and that her inner struggles remained a mystery might be enough. Of course any character affected by Monroe's behavior needs background information on the doomed star, which will help ground any imaginative creative process, especially the actor's. An active dramaturg shapes the information so that it reflects the basic truths each character would know.

Historical, Political, or Social Movements

Anything from yesterday, last week, last year, last decade, to last century or millennium qualifies as historical. It can be a popular song, the name of a baseball player, or a minor political intrigue. For a play, seemingly insignificant details weave together to craft a believable world. Even if that environment is more fictitious than historical, a greater understanding of the period's reality will accelerate the actor's process.

If historical periods or issues frame much of the play's action, a few pointed articles that discuss the background, impact, and significant events will go a long way. More important, these articles or excerpts should address the emotional tenor or knowledge from the period. All too often, research materials contain articles that reflect a contemporary perspective. If the packet fails to address the chaos of the times—for example, the hysteria surrounding the Bubonic plague or those initial years of the AIDS crisis—how will the production elicit the requisite emotional tension the play demands? In *The Normal Heart*, for example, a climactic moment could occur when the two men kiss after one has revealed he had a purple lesion, a tell-tale sign that a man had developed what we now call AIDS. At the time Larry Kramer wrote his groundbreaking drama, not only was it highly unusual for men to kiss each other onstage but the general population believed a non-infected person kissing an infected person was extremely dangerous. In short: the kiss is explosive. A dramaturg must convey its importance and the circumstances for its import to the cast and director to reinforce the original impact a dramatic work or passage had. If, however, all the research reflects the modern medical miracles and contemporary knowledge surrounding transmission, the tension surrounding this kiss will never appear and this climactic moment will fall flat.

The same holds true for Shakespeare's history plays. Understanding the turmoil surrounding the English throne and the role religion (and family) played in the lives of the Yorks, Tudors, and Lancasters means dialogue and plot will be clearer and the tension palpable.

Images

Does the play include symbols and/or recurring images? Are specific paintings mentioned as in Stephen Sondheim's *Sunday in the Park with George*; or, is a specific city referenced, as in Tony Kushner's *Homebody/ Kabul?*. If so, an active dramaturg may use these facts to shape the question: *What images to include?* At times, images are more metaphorical as with Suzan-Lori Parks' *The America Play* where it's hard to miss the recurring image described in the stage direction as "the Great Hole of History." But what is the "Great Hole"? Is it an actual opening in the ground, or a metaphorical absence? If it's the latter, what is missing? If the hole signifies both, how to help actors and designers realize those metaphors on stage? The possibilities are many. For the active dramaturg, the goal is to first recognize that the "Great Hole" may have significant metaphorical meaning and to begin to shape the dialogue and research question, and the second is to collect images that may trigger thoughts of what holes are used for— for example, burying or hiding objects, or trapping animals. Although the set designer ultimately conjures the physical image, the active dramaturg can influence the team's imagination by providing a few initial visual references. Including a written introduction or specific questions with the images will help the actors and the director focus on crafting an answer to the dramaturgical question throughout the rehearsal process.

Sometimes images appear in the mind's eye but not in the actual script. Take *The America Play* again. During a master class exercise I led, a student revealed she imagined a huge map with items out of place hanging over the stage. As she explored this image, she was able to connect the idea of a map to the dialogue and bring specific lines to life by enhancing their meaning and interpretation. The student also assembled a list of items to explore or images to gather for the Actor Packet and for the designers. Were this student to organize her Actor Packet like a map or use the map to illustrate the play's ideas, her dramaturgy would prove original, useful, and relevant. An active dramaturg assembles a packet using personal and factual connections.

Information That Creates a Context for the Period

Do specific social and etiquette behaviors influence behavior? Usually this question brings thoughts of Emily Post and Miss Manners to mind. However, with a number of contemporary plays focusing on Goths, Geeks,

Preppies and Jocks, it's clear that there's more to social comportment than removing your hat when in the presence of a lady. Researching what a gentleman should do with a hat is much easier than researching contemporary modes of behavior. But active dramaturgs embrace the challenge and locate examples or at least direct the company where to find information that will help shape a believable physical dynamic throughout the production. Photographs and film clips also help convey period-appropriate physicality. Dramaturgs are not movement coaches and shouldn't try to be; however, information or images that help focus or clarify why or how certain behaviors came to be or what clothes are associated with particular groups does help actors (and movement coaches) generate a physical life rooted in authenticity but organic to the play's world.

Identify Themes Past Productions Overlooked

Themes lie at the heart of the dramaturg's work. When assembling an Actor Packet, the temptation is to focus on and research the obvious questions, but an adventurous dramaturg looks beyond the norm. Themes help active dramaturgs do this. Take Caryl Churchill's fabulously inventive *Cloud Nine*, which takes on a number of taboos, cultural and sexual. It begins in the sexually repressive Victorian era and ends with the promiscuous and sexually androgynous world of Margaret Thatcher's England. When the play was first produced in 1979, such frank discussions of sexual preference rarely appeared on the London or American stage. However, producing this play in the late Nineties or during John Major's final years, different themes resonate. There are two reasons for this: 1) any strong play will support a shift in emphasized theme and 2) what's important and daring in one era or decade may not be in another.

Between the premiere of *Cloud Nine* and the second millennium, films such as *The Crying Game* and *Brokeback Mountain* and television programs such as *Will and Grace* or *Queer Eye for the Straight Guy* captured the general (American) population's interest, encouraging heterosexuals to reconsider their attitude toward homosexuality and homosexuals. The changing cultural landscape impacts how the audience responds to Churhill's play, and an active dramaturg keeps this evolving perception in mind whenever looking for support materials. The dramaturg's challenge is to discover how to make once-groundbreaking themes relevant and edgy again. An active dramaturg pushes the envelope further and looks for ideas that live below the surface, awaiting a chance to shape a production. The question for the active dramaturg becomes, what other than homosexuality, colonialism, and transvestitism in *Cloud Nine* shapes the play? Perhaps parenting issues interest current artists and collaborators. Maybe issues of city life versus suburban or country living and the debate about this changing environmental focus could inspire a vigorous new interpretation.

Identifying thematic shifts regularly accompanies productions of Shakespearean plays. The 1995 film version of *Richard III*, directed by Richard Loncraine and starring Sir Ian McKellen, sets the story in an imagined 1930s fascist Britain. This shift heightens the play's themes of violence and tyranny, for Richard III no longer appears as an ancient, Medieval example of evil but as kin to the last century's most evil men, Hitler and Mussolini.

Dramaturgs interested in exploring the full extent of their art apply the same rigorous questions to a contemporary set text as to one ages old. Thinking outside the box allows the active dramaturg to impart a personal stamp on the process, but it only works if the basics are covered. Overlooking the basics listed above will only frustrate the actors and lead the director to think you want to direct the play. Look to strike a balance.

The Dramaturg's Personal Vision

Often dramaturgs think they should divorce their curiosity from the project and research topics, themes, and issues they think others will need or want information on. Nothing could be further from the truth. As an artist and collaborator, the dramaturg's questions are valuable. However, dramaturgs must be careful and avoid overwhelming the Actor Packet with ideas that fascinate only them. Strike a balance between what the company needs, what the play asks for, and what you're curious about. Investigating questions or topics that hold personal appeal will boost your morale when the research lags. In truth, what makes a person a strong dramaturg is a willingness to bring personal questions to the research. Actors bring their life experiences and perspectives, why shouldn't a dramaturg? For example, if a dramaturg working on Tennessee Williams' *A Streetcar Named Desire* considers herself a foodie, she might use this personal interest to inspire a presentation regarding the city's culinary history or how ethnic recipes blend in New Orleans; such an approach to history and culture enlivens the play's world and the actors' connection to it more deeply and immediately than an article about ethnic diversity.

Whittling Down the Information

The packet needs content that helps the actors *do*. Heady, analytical articles may fascinate and illuminate scenes or characters, but often the discussion is just a dissection of ideas. Ideas are not actable. Yes, they can influence choices, but an actor is often best served by the argument that most directly and actively applies to the rehearsal hall and performance. To help determine what should go into an Actor Packet, establish a predetermined page or article limit. If page and article limits prove too daunting or inappropriate, choosing to organize the guide by character can provide focus and immediately reveal when and where an imbalance of support materials exists. Fine details or references to minutia can work their way into notes or discussions around the table later in the process. For example, an article identifying repeated words and phrases: this article, though inappropriate for the Actor Packet, is good for the dramaturg, because it points out how to look at the play's dialogue and language. The active dramaturg can use the information to listen for moments when the production's humor lags or becomes maudlin. The active dramaturg may also choose to use these observations to influence notes to a director willing to explore linguistic humor to relieve the play's tension.

Identify Key Points in Articles

Imagine the director wants to explore the Freudian aspects of *Hamlet*. Locating an article that exclusively explores Hamlet's incestuous love for his mother may satisfy the Freudian question but serves little dramaturgical purpose. In a sense, the article resembles a closed or neutral question, and inappropriately restricts the actor's choices. What if the actor wants to consider an incestuous relationship between King Hamlet and his son? This mother-son article runs the risk of stunting that actor's exploration. Essays that explore the nature of incest, what it looks like to those involved as well as outsiders, may prove more useful. Better still, passages rather than the entire article may benefit the actor more. When including excerpts, be sure to indicate clearly why this section was included, in writing and during the presentation. Once the actor makes a specific choice, articles supporting this decision may be appreciated. Including all of the bibliographical information in the packet allows the actor to read the entire article, if he chooses. Rarely will a single article speak directly to the challenges of creating an active choice.

How to Determine What Else Goes In

When searching for information, dramaturgs have complete artistic license to include material that not only grounds the actor but could direct character exploration. However, the active dramaturg must take care to suggest options, not a single, specific path. For example, if a play takes place during the Great Depression, the first impulse is to find a lot of information on life during the Thirties. Of course this is important, but if the characters are adults, they represent people who came of age during the Roaring Twenties, World War I, and before. It's important to balance the Depression-era research with information from these earlier times. In truth, one of the greatest mistakes dramaturgs make is choosing to focus exclusively on the time period within which the play's action is set rather than the many eras that shape the characters' perspectives and views. In fact, information referring to these past periods helps all designers (set, costume and sound) a great deal, as they look for ways to establish a sense that this world belongs to each character and in turn a number of eras.

Addressing any questions or ideas the director wants to be sure the actors know about will also contribute material. Finding ways to connect these ideas to the dramaturg's vision of the play and the play's voice will keep the research process and the packet active. Sometimes the information the director wants will distract the actors if the dramaturg does not find a way to forge a strong connection to the play, theme, or character. Simply including information because a collaborator wants it guarantees a lackluster Actor Packet.

It's tempting to include all information that relates to the play no matter how esoteric. For the dramaturg connections exist, but remember—all information isn't equally important to the actors or useable in a rehearsal hall. Including too many scholarly articles or neglecting to introduce them in the packet can also dilute a packet's impact. As much as a production dramaturg looks for ways to activate everyone's creative process, most dramaturgs enjoy reading about plays and amassing factoids or esoteric information. All of the research makes sense to dramaturgs but not necessarily to anyone else. Embracing this truth can lead all dramaturgs, but especially the active dramaturg, to find articles that will be useful in the rehearsal hall.

The Actor Packet's Design

Design and layout are as important as the information included, perhaps more so. Actors, like dramaturgs, fall into two basic groups: linguistic learners and visual learners. What's more, actors are doers; they bring ideas to life with their body, mind, and spirit. When dramaturgs present information in a way that embraces that reality, the actors will use the material. Weighing the packet down with grey photocopied pages with large sections crossed out and notes in the margin further diminishes the incentive to read. Take care and present the research in a way that generates excitement and matches the actor's resolve to give 110%.

Many dramaturgs photocopy their information and add color copies or color dividers to enliven the material. Others use modern technology. With CDs, webpages, and blogs, it's possible to assemble the information in a more user-friendly manner than the traditional photocopied packet. Dramaturgs who remain technologically current may find that the theatre or company does not have the ability to use the material as it was designed, but that shouldn't prevent innovative thinking. Simply keep in mind that everyone may not have the same operating system or high-speed Internet connection. In short, provide alternative ways to access the information, namely a hard copy actors can take with them on the train or read on breaks if the rehearsal hall doesn't have a wireless connection.

Assembling the Information

Since actors use the packet outside the rehearsal hall, it should be both easy to use and clearly show what section or article refers to what part of the play. There are many cosmetic suggestions, but stronger choices regarding user-friendly packets involve introducing each section and editing articles in ways that focus attention. Two key ideas are:

1. Include introductions to all material or at least major sections. These brief passages are the active dramaturg's chance to frame the content according to the dramaturgical vision and design, which helps ground the actor and compliments and embellishes the director's, playwright's and other designers' views. The active dramaturg aims to bridge and accelerate the imagination process so that the actors have more time to deepen and finesse their discoveries;

2. Design and format the packet to suggest conventional and unexpected connections, to encourage interesting actor choices For example, the packet may be organized to correspond to the play's chronology, thematically, or by character.

When building a packet chronologically, consider arranging the articles, historical information and images by scene, act, or page number. For one-act plays, consider the play's sense of time rather than organizing in-formation by act or scene.

The Theme-Focused Actor Packet

A thematic Actor Packet follows two lines of thought simultane-ously. Here the active dramaturg identifies and underscores the play's major themes while presenting background information. The packet presents how to activate the idea by example. Within each section, the ac-tive dramaturg collects information that links each character or group of characters to those specific themes.

The Character-Focused Actor Packet

Character-focused Actor Packets require the dramaturg to organize information according to what relates most strongly to each character or groups of characters (e.g. the fairies in *A Midsummer Night's Dream*). This packet allows for more character-specific research, however, it can also encourage a lot of repetition. The active dramaturg must present informa-tion in ways that reduce the tendency to isolate character from the play's structure or thematic issues. A benefit of this organizational design is that actors can hone in on their character immediately and explore the rest of the world later in the process.

No matter which organizational format the dramaturg chooses, the Actor Packet should be fun. The packet can and should include a separate section dedicated to the playwright as well as background information that does not easily connect to other sections, and include photographs, paintings or unusual images that you or the designer found for the play. Include all bibliographical information near the article and in the back of the packet. Remember, the packet is an extension of the play. The play works as a cohesive whole, and so should the packet.

Presenting the Information in Rehearsal

Certainly a lively presentation piques everyone's interest. Some dra-maturgs opt to adopt a character or dress in ways to evoke a period to demonstrate their connection to the production, play, and design. Others choose a more conventional presentation style, but augment the stan-dard oral presentation with props, food related to the play, or other items that the production team can use to forge tangible connections to the play and the Actor Packet. Envisioning the dramaturgy presentation as an informed advertisement or movie trailer will compel the company to explore the active dramaturg's handiwork and use the packet throughout the rehearsal process.

A Final Thought on Actor Packets

Approaching the Actor Packet as a permanent, fixed document will cause every additional request to frustrate rather than excite. The packet's initial goal is to address major issues and questions for as many characters and collaborators as possible without diluting the play's power. During the rehearsal process and the all-important first reading, numerous questions and areas for further exploration will and should arise. Active dramaturgs look out for these questions and the best way to share information that will inspire creativity but also keep the exploration focused.

The Second Part of the First Rehearsal: The First Reading

The true purpose of the first rehearsal is to hear the play. As tempting as it is to sit back and let the words mesmerize, the active dramaturg uses this first reading to determine what additional observations and information might influence her comments during the tablework phase (usually the first two to five days of a three week rehearsal) and what to add to the Actor Packet. Also, listening with the most challenging questions the directors and designers posed during the pre-production process in mind helps focus attention during the first read. As the actors read and enliven these challenging scenes or moments, they may reveal instinctive solutions or stumble. Moments when actors stumble over words or lines indicate places to mark and return to during the group discussion or to review privately with the director. In addition, the active dramaturg might listen for ways the actors confront the troubling transitions, confusing passages and lines, or strong images or metaphors that influenced the artistic team. Active dramaturgs take note of both the insights and confusions.

Ways to Listen Well

At every step the dramaturg listens; listening is the single most essential aspect of the job. Without listening well, it's impossible to craft strong, open questions. This is why many active dramaturgs do not follow along in the script during the first reading, in an attempt to truly hear the play for the first time.

Another way to listen well is to remain aware of the room's changing dynamics. As the reading progresses, the ideas of the play will begin to transform the room's atmosphere and how the actors relate to one another. The vibe in the room may concretely indicate a thematic shift or a reaction to a particular aspect of the world that the rest of the team may not even consciously recognize. The active dramaturg works to identify when this shift begins. How well does the play sustain the shift? Or, are the actors manufacturing the shifts because they know the play should become serious (e.g., *King Lear*) or the theatre's blurb suggests it's a serious drama. The active dramaturg's job is to help ensure that the play's story comes across not as everyone remembers it, but as it is for that group at that particular time. Just as dramaturgs work to read a play openly, they apply that process to the first reading, noting when the company reads less openly by listening for passages that are read through quickly or watching for expected acting choices (especially when the director asks the cast to read without making conscious acting choices).

Set Text vs. New Play

In general the first day of rehearsal for both set texts and new plays is the same. The company meets and reads the play, after which a discussion follows; that said, differences do exist. Set texts rarely receive textual changes throughout the rehearsal process, so actors have little need to prepare themselves psychologically for major character or story changes. Yes, cuts may be given and they can prove disconcerting for an actor and some designers, however, the basic story and character journeys for a set text will remain intact. A new play, however, may undergo a major transformation during the rehearsal process. A new twist may be added or a character cut—it does happen. An active dramaturg works with the director to prepare the company for the possibility of receiving changes throughout the process and what those changes may look like or what questions the writer plans to explore.

What to Listen for During the First Reading of a Set Text

During the first read of a set text, listen for the surprises. What line comes across as unexpectedly funny? What line had you or the artistic team missed entirely? What moment or scene jumps out as particularly and unexpectedly relevant in today's society? The actor's choices change the play and the active dramaturg notes those moments of discovery to find ways to connect to the actor's take on a character or scene, and feed the director's vision.

Reading a Play With Cut or Shortened Scenes

Sometimes set texts, in particular Shakespearean plays, are cut. The reasons for reducing the plays by a few lines or scenes are many, and the possibility for unclear transitions great. This is why the first reading holds such importance for cut or amended texts. Active dramaturgs, who often play an active role cutting texts, listen for clarity and flow of story. It's easy to forget that clarity also includes character journeys, because a well-edited or cut story that builds logically according to the rules of cause and effect can eliminate key moments of a specific character's journey and cause confusion for the actor and character. Moments when actors stumble or seem confused may indicate unclear cuts, as well as areas to research or the need to restore a line or two.

What to Listen for During the First Reading of a New Play

When listening to a new play, it's tempting for dramaturgs to listen for a series of nots. What's not clear; what's not present; what's not working. That is *not* an active dramaturg's job. Active dramaturgs listen for what works, what excites, and what will lead to a stronger, clearer play. For example, everyone may agree that the ending is unclear, but listening for what informs the confusion will only confirm what everyone knows. Instead, the active dramaturg listens for moments or storylines that suggest solutions. Choosing to listen for how the protagonist interacts with others, and what possibilities she ignores and why, may provide more avenues for development.

Listen for Joy

The first read introduces the cast to the work that lies ahead, but what makes the event so much fun is the sense of endless possibility. The temptation to focus solely on the challenges can make the dramaturg appear to be all work and no play. Active dramaturgs have a strong sense of play. So, listen for these moments of joy throughout the reading, and use them throughout the discussion and the rehearsal process, especially when the mood becomes more tense and serious. Gaining a sense of how and when the joy enters the room by observing and articulating what happens when and why, as well as noting the actors' instinctive word choices, will help build the company's vocabulary for the rehearsal.

The Third Part of the First Rehearsal: The Discussion

Every artistic team member eagerly anticipates the post-reading discussion, for it's the first time everyone expresses their excitement for the project, play, team, or concept. It's a conversation that shouldn't be underestimated. Through listening, the active dramaturg learns what language or vocabulary to use when composing notes.

The need to listen to how actors speak about their characters might suggest that dramaturgs should resist participating in the discussion. In truth, this conversation and those that follow during the tablework phase present the best opportunities for active dramaturgs to interact with the actors (by participating in the textual investigation). However, remember that the dramaturg's level of familiarity far exceeds the cast's. In short, active dramaturgs sometimes temper intellectual enthusiasm by timing comments and offers them in a way that encourages exploration and full ownership of the discoveries.

The actors' initial responses will often resemble the reflection phase following a dramaturg's first read. As the actors' quick hits give way to more instinctive yet grounded comments, the active dramaturg also gains deeper insight into a play's truths and strengths. The goal of these conversations at the table is to clarify the questions for the rehearsal process, which means that a number of questions will be deferred with the comment, "We'll know more when we revisit the scene and put it on its feet."

Dramaturgs tend to participate when the discussion veers toward thematic issues and historic or factual questions. Active dramaturgs fuel the discussion with information that exposes thematic or symbolic references that the company can use to develop its own ideas, and continue to offer insights as the rehearsal progresses.

To Pose or Not to Pose a Question

The dramaturg's comments during this discussion period needn't always take the form of questions, however the dramaturg also understands that a lengthy relationship with the text colors comments and runs the risk of making newcomers to the script feel less equipped. This may be why a number opt to pose questions rather than offer comments during this discussion. The flipside of this approach is that the questions come tinged with an air of knowing.

How then might an active dramaturg solve this conundrum?

One option is to use the research in the Actor Packet. If, for example, the Actor Packet for *Funnyhouse of a Negro* includes information on Queen Victoria and Patrice Lumumba, the initial impulse might be to discuss each historical figure as a separate entity, since they never met in life. However, an active dramaturg may point out that Lumumba's revolution involves fighting Belgian colonial rule on the African continent, and may relate that to British rule and Queen Victoria. So an active dramaturg listens for actors asking why and how these characters connect within the play. In this instance, look to biographical information to expand the cast's questions and ask how the uniting of European and African personalities during America's civil rights struggle shapes the lead character. Instead of phrasing these issues and ideas specific to the play, the active dramaturg might choose to bring them up as ideas that were part of the Sixties' zeitgeist. Eventually the conversation moves to the current era so that the company discovers how or what of Adrienne Kennedy's play remains relevant today.

Another option is to point to recurring themes or images within a writer's *oeuvre* that appear in the play to be produced. For example, noting that Lynn Nottage often uses direct address for comic effect in many plays may lead to a discussion of style and form for a production of her satire *Fabulation: The Education of Undine*, the sister play to the award-winning *Intimate Apparel*. This observation creates an opportunity to discuss the fabulous moments in her play *Crumbs from the Table of Joy*, when Ernestine Crump shifts a scene's reality with a simple sentence that begins with a variation of "at least I wish…" Highlighting these similarities allows the active dramaturg to place Nottage's wry sense of humor within a context that extends beyond a single play and potentially informs the interpretation of Undine's asides without directing the scene. Waiting to share this dramaturgical information during the discussion, rather than during the Actor Packet presentation, establishes the dramaturg as a team player aware of the creative process and comfortable presenting information.

A third option may be to simply point out which characters use similar imagery. In Shakespeare's *A Midsummer Night's Dream*, the young female lovers use language laden with fruit and flower imagery. Highlighting this may lead to a discussion of what makes Helena and Hermia similar, or encourage the actors portraying Lysander and Demetrius to explore their language and discover what connects them. Before leaving the discussion, however, the active dramaturg encourages all cast members to investigate their character's language. The question of what is, if anything, the significance of floral imagery in Oberon's speech should arise. Should it not, the active dramaturg could initiate this exploration, even if it's tabled to a later rehearsal.

What to Listen for When Discussing a New Play

Hearing a play aloud for the first time can overwhelm the writer, who often hears only what to change, not necessarily the play's successes. The active dramaturg supports the writer by listening for what works and what concerns or questions the actors have following the initial take on the play. Also, as the actors ask questions and explore the text, their comments may appear to question the play, leading the writer to defend the play or focus on areas that do not need clarification. The active dramaturg and director work together to distinguish between actor questions and those questions which apply and may inform the writer's rewrite process.

Sometimes, however, members of the company appear reluctant to make comments. The writer's presence may account for this tentativeness. The dramaturg's role becomes more important in these situations. Active dramaturgs facilitate the discussion to tease out what excites or distracts the actor and articulate these points using the language the writer and artistic team developed together.

Moments of Opposition

When the cast points out stellar moments, the active dramaturg listens for hints that an opposite image (or opposing comment) may benefit the production. Someone may comment, for example, that they enjoy when the protagonist breaks the fourth wall. The active dramaturg immediately begins to note or silently review the play to see if the character always breaks the fourth wall in the same manner or pattern. If not, ask the writer, and perhaps the cast, what advantages occur when the character violates this expectation. It's important to note that variations are *not* inconsistencies, necessarily; they do have benefit. Not unless the writer begins to tell the company that the variations are signs of writer fatigue can the group call them inconsistencies. Active dramaturgs listen and remind the writer what rules she's established, and work to recreate and incorporate these successful moments throughout the play's action. Certainly, whenever the dramaturg clearly articulates how the play functions, a writer may choose either to maintain or to change these moments.

Active dramaturgs embrace the play's rules and use them to help finesse a change and clarify a form that works with the writer's initial intentions. However, an attentive dramaturg will remind the writer that these moments of writer fatigue can result in opportunities to change the play's rules.

Active dramaturgs listen for questions regarding storytelling as it pertains to performance or acting. For example, comments revealing uncertainty regarding where a character is or why an event take place at a given time are comments that indicate the actors aren't sure how to bridge the actions; something in the transition doesn't reveal itself immediately. Yes, sometimes events will become clear as the rehearsal process progresses, but dramaturgs listen for these questions and then revisit the text to determine with the director and playwright whether this a problem in writing, an actor block, or an unactable moment.

Dealing With Time

All writing reflects its current era, either in topic or the way ideas or language are arranged or assembled. These observations affect how characters evolve and what some audience members will or won't need in order to follow the story. The temptation during these early conversations is to dwell on how to fix time and use it to establish a rhythm for the world. Frankly, some contemporary plays do not wish to adhere to chronological, easily managed depictions of time on stage, and to force a change would mean a plodding drama. Active dramaturgs listen to determine whether the actors see time as a way to organize events or create events that control character. Later, the active dramaturg, writer, and director will revisit the conversation and determine whether the use of time in the play is still unclear.

Final Thoughts

The conversations following the first and second reading present the dramaturg with the most options for speaking directly with the cast. It's the time before any actor has committed to a choice and, usually, the director has only briefly presented the parameters for the production. As such, this is an excellent opportunity for active dramaturgs to connect comments, questions, and observations to the materials collected in the Actor Packet and the ideas discussed during the production meetings. The trick is to introduce information in a way that inspires conversation and exploration, yet doesn't make the actors feel as if they have come to the process late. One of the best ways active dramaturgs achieve this is to present any discovery by grounding it in the questions it raised, and infusing the response with the emotional excitement or temporary frustration that directed the search for answers.

Chapter 7

Active Production Dramaturgy:
From Rehearsal to Previews to Opening Night

Transitioning from the excitement of the first rehearsal to the regimen of daily rehearsals is, for all artists, difficult. The shift can be even more challenging for the dramaturg who wrestles with how to remain active and present as the actors and director begin to explore the text that you've been dissecting for weeks if not months. The dramaturg can speak freely with the actors during the discussions that occur during the tablework phase, which can be as few as one or as many as five days in a three-week process. However once tablework ends, the dramaturg often communicates directly with the director and writer, through notes, and so can appear inactive in the rehearsal hall. To remain connected and involved, the active dramaturg watches the rehearsal with simple and specific goals in mind: to gain insight into the evolving creative vocabulary; to observe how the cast retains the story's clarity as they move from the page to the stage; and to observe the visual storytelling and how it relates to the written story. The active dramaturg transforms these key observations into questions that shape the dramaturgical game plan and process until opening night.

Even with a game plan it's possible for the dramaturg to be unsure how the role evolves during the five phases of rehearsal: tablework, scene work, runs of scenes and stumble-throughs, complete run-throughs, and previews. Although each rehearsal process will follow its own path, understanding how the dramaturg's role evolves during these five phases, and the three key challenges to look out for, can increase the active dramaturg's effectiveness and ability to collaborate with the director.

What to Look for During Rehearsals

Watching initial rehearsals and listening to actor discussions allows the active dramaturg to obtain a sense of the cast's concerns, their take on particular scenes, the evolving vocabulary, and provides the active dramaturg with the insights and tools needed to shape comments. Even if the active dramaturg opts to visit the rehearsal hall only sporadically, the questions from earlier artistic and cast discussions will guide what to look for and think about, and will focus the dramaturg's eye. The active dramaturg connects those observations to the play's themes in ways that inspire or reinforce active performance choices/discussions between the director and actors. Referencing other critical elements will also help reveal how the text supports a director's ideas or an actor's choice.

Unlike assistant directors who watch for movement patterns and the individual choices actors make, active dramaturgs observe how the story and visual clues—set pieces, props, body movement—connect, and consider how the general story the actors conveys relates to the play's major themes. Dramaturgs may also notice the hand gesture or upstage cross that detracts from or adds depth to the storytelling. To prevent the sense that the dramaturg's comments are veiled directing notes, the active dramaturg grounds comments or observations to the director in the play's thematic reality, and connects the physical life of the play to the narrative.

Throughout rehearsal, active dramaturgs listen and watch for those moments when the actors loosen their connection with the text's language or appear unsure of what they're saying. When the director and actor work to sculpt a character in the rehearsal hall, they often explore sections of dialogue and on occasion will work word-by-word or line-by-line. Yes, the expectation is that the actor engages in such detailed work at home, outside the rehearsal hall. However, even with such diligent preparation, it's possible for actors to miss certain references or innuendos. The active dramaturg discerns whether the actor is uncertain about why the line exists, what the line means, or its significance to the story.

Active Dramaturgy During the Tablework Phase of a Set-Text Production

During tablework, often three or four days, the company assembles around the table and slowly reads each scene. At regular intervals the director stops the reading and gathers impressions. Scenes or sections may be read numerous times before moving on. During this time, actors may stop the reading to make comments, share observations, and pose questions. Dramaturgs rarely interrupt the reading, although the active dramaturg regularly adds information and insights to the discussion. These early days are important for the entire company, and the active dramaturg attends each rehearsal devoted to tablework.

What to Look or Listen for During Tablework

The conversations during the tablework phase will reveal how the active dramaturg should shape the next steps. The actors may ask questions that suggest new topics to research or indicate where additional research is needed. The discussion will also suggest additional thematic concerns to explore. Sometimes an actor will offer a direct question, and at other times the active dramaturg must listen between the lines. For example, an actor may ask a direct question regarding what a certain word or set of words means in Hamlet's "To be or not to be" speech (*Hamlet* 3.1.55). If the same actor begins to ask what the speech's import is for the character or play, the director will respond. But the active dramaturg can supply what's implied or left unsaid, because the actor may need assistance identifying themes within the production that correspond to the speech.

When, for example, questions are followed by phrases like, "We'll find the answers when we move to our feet," an active dramaturg takes note. The scene or moment in question may prove challenging throughout the rehearsal process, and an active dramaturg will review it—many times before attending the rehearsal—to identify ways to help the company crack the scene. Active dramaturgs may also notice line readings that lead the play's themes in new and exciting directions, taking the time to consider how and why these nuanced readings work and how this discovery might apply to other scenes, moments or actor performances.

Communicating During the Tablework Phase

Because the active dramaturg regularly contributes ideas to the discussion, written notes to the director are not needed. If and when additional information is found, the active dramaturg might write this in a note to the director. It's more likely, however, that the information will be shared in an upcoming rehearsal as a global note from the dramaturg to the cast or additional information for the Actor Packet. Otherwise, directors rarely receive notes during this phase, because dramaturgs will be constantly contributing to the dialogue. For ideas that pertain directly to the director's vision, concept or interpretation, active dramaurgs often compose a note to the director or discuss the thought in person. These comments should be shared as soon as possible. If, however, the artistic director or representatives from the theatre would like rehearsal hall updates, the active dramaturg pens brief summaries of the day's conversation for them.

The Active Dramaturg's Role During Scene Work

As the company moves to its feet, the active dramaturg's role changes. The dramaturg may visit the rehearsal periodically throughout the day or every few days to gain a sense of the production's creative vocabulary. Although some directors invite unfiltered dramaturgical input, rarely during this phase does the active dramaturg communicate directly with the actors. As actors work on scenes, dramaturgs often sit in the back of the hall, jot down the occasional word, and watch and make notes for themselves alone. The active dramaturg uses this time to become better acquainted with the production and its evolving creative vocabulary.

What to Look for During the Scene Work Phase

As the company shapes the scenes, the active dramaturg attends the rehearsals looking for what moments work, what remains unclear, and why these situations exist. The active dramaturg will watch how the actors use gesture, movement, and language to connect to and communicate the play's larger themes. More important, the dramaturg identifies how the staging charts time, during transitions between scenes, and how this impacts the storytelling and the play's larger themes. If, for example, transitions between scenes haven't yet been considered or they've been overlooked entirely, the active dramaturg prepares possible ways to articulate how enacting these shifts will strengthen the production. Again, rather than considering blocking choices, the active dramaturg looks for ways to use thematic ideas or other critical elements to build tension either by connecting scenes or placing them in opposition. The active dramaturg and director may discuss transitions before rehearsal begins or throughout rehearsals.

Early during the scene work phase, it's best if the active dramaturg acknowledges these ideas as moments to watch. So much changes during these early days that notes to the director may ruffle feathers or appear as if the dramaturg neither trusts nor respects the director. However, taking the time to chat about the rehearsal process and listen to the director's

general or specific interests/concerns will help the active dramaturg prepare for the next rehearsals.

Helping an Actor to Prepare

Consider Oberon's monologue "I know a bank..." from *A Midsummer's Night Dream* (2.1.249-267). The language is dense and full of references to nature. A well-prepared actor may research every herb and flower men-tioned and create a mental image for each. Such detailed delivery can distract everyone from noticing that the purpose of the speech or what connects each line is less clear. The speech's through-line may become the dramaturg's responsibility. Without directing the director or the actor, the dramaturg might begin to dissect the speech (through written notes to the director or a private meeting with the actor if the director agrees) using questions that help the actor understand the monologue's build.

For example, when I was the dramaturg for a production of *A Midsummer Night's Dream* at Syracuse Stage, the director Ron van Lieu asked me to assist a few actors with text work. While working with the actor playing Oberon, I helped him discover the aforementioned speech's organizational build. The first set of lines (249-252) describes a distinct place and the next four lines confirm that this is where Titania sleeps. The next six (253-258) clearly describe what Oberon will do with the flower's juice and its effects. Then Oberon begins to direct Puck, and the next set of lines (259-263) establish what Puck should do. In the next lines (264-266), Oberon clarifies his directions. The final line establishes when he and Puck shall rendez-vous (267). In this case, it was important to simply help the actor divide the speech so that he could discover distinct choices for each section. The challenge when working with the actor or pointing out the distinct breaks in the speech, is to steer clear of language that di-rects or tells the actor what the choice should be. It's tempting to note that Oberon warns Puck in line 265, but to do so gives the actor a choice and tells the director what to have the actor do—this is not an active drama-turg's job. Asking the actor what happens in line 265 avoids this just as writing a note stating: *"the next five lines establish what Puck should do"* allows the director to decide what to do with the shift; this is an active dramaturg's job. The active dramaturg also knows that the actor and di-rector do observe these very shifts; however, the work of breaking down large ideas with questions that provoke solutions a performer can perform assists these creative colleagues as they contend with many other responsibilities and obligations.

Many incorrectly assume that productions of Shakespeare, Restoration dramas, and highly poetic contemporary plays alone call on a dramaturg's linguistic deciphering skills. If a play purports to tell a story, a clear understanding of events and language is always needed.

Communication During the Scene Work and Blocking Phase

Throughout the blocking phase, the active dramaturg may discuss ideas with the director, write notes, or do both. What makes or breaks the director-dramaturg relationship during this phase is how the dramaturg communicates an idea. The *how* extends beyond word-choice to include the overall presentation of the observation or argument. Many dramaturgs overstep their role and skip right to the opinion-laced question, or compose a note that appears to direct the director. An active dramaturg avoids directing the director by penning notes that identify the areas of concern in as specific but objective way; articulate the facts of the situation; present a question; and finally, if appropriate, articulate an informed opinion. The active dramaturg grounds each of the comments in the text by using the critical elements whenever possible. The active dramaturg avoids directing the director by offering insights into the text and its meanings, not by pointing out choices the actor could or should make. The goal is to provide possibilities for the actor and director, not just a single creative path.

Crafting Effective Dramaturgical Notes

Composing helpful notes that avoid directing the director is an art. At the heart of this skill lies the essence of dramaturgy: understanding how a play's form and the other elements work to create a world. The dramaturg's temptation is to assume a certain intimacy with the text, and write notes in a way that assumes others lack similar familiarity and must be told how to fix the problem. An active dramaturg knows that every artist has a unique relationship with the play and appreciates that these connections reveal different insights. An active dramaturg looks to magnify these differences or points out when they distract from the collective vision, while always considering when to use research to for support; where and how unique actor choices bring the production closer to the desired end; and which images and thematic ideas may finesse transitions.

The notes generated during this phase of the rehearsal process should be delivered to the director—sent through e-mail, hand delivered, or placed in the in-house mailbox—at least two hours before the next rehearsal.

When completed poorly, dramaturgical notes can rapidly destroy any positive collaboration the team established before entering the rehearsal hall. A similar roadblock can occur with the writer. If a dramaturg crafts notes that ignore the play's needs, the writer's concerns, or re-write the playwright's play, the relationship can combust, and rather spectacularly.

But how to write these notes?

How to use language to help, not hinder the relationship with the director or playwright?

Dramaturgical Notes: Proactive and Responsive

There are two types of dramaturgical notes: proactive and responsive. The **proactive** note addresses concerns as the artists develop an approach, and anticipates artists' needs by providing information or analytical assistance before rehearsal. The **responsive** note comments directly on work in the rehearsal hall, or presentations such as a stumble-through, a run-through, or a preview performance. The responsive note articulates what comes across and how that compares with the director's intended vision. Both types of notes provide information that can be used the next time the cast runs that particular scene or the next time the actor is called to work on any scene. Active dramaturgs offer responsive notes with the understanding that the director also notices the hiccup or fabulous moment; the dramaturg's notes consider why the scene goes awry or excels, and roots comments in textual and visual facts so that adjustments may be made quickly. Dramaturgy notes prove most helpful when worded in language that is actor-friendly. Active dramaturgs should offer written responsive notes to the director at least four hours prior to the next rehearsal and, if possible, share initial impressions verbally (a sense of what worked and what the notes might address) at the rehearsal's end.

Another question dramaturgs ask is at what phase in the process to offer certain notes. Should comments about unclear performances be given at the end of the first week, second week, or the first moment it appears an actor is unsure of the text's meaning? The *when* depends entirely upon the specific rehearsal and the director's process. If an active dramaturg remains vigilant, preparing dramaturgical options as soon as she notices a moment when her input can enhance the performance and has notes at the ready, she has done her job well.

Crafting a Proactive Note

To better understand the proactive note, let's explore a fictitious production of Ibsen's *A Doll's House*. Imagine that the scenes with Dr. Rank, Nora, and Torvald are on the day's agenda. A proactive note might include the observations regarding Dr. Rank's silent but palpable presence. The director will certainly have planned to tease that tension to a distinct level. The active dramaturg, however, explores the scene for particular moments when Dr. Rank's presence might alter the perception of marital intimacy and impact the couple's conversation. The supposition in these notes is that the active dramaturg can help the team identify explosive artistic moments and additional ways to dissect them, *not* that the director or actors haven't done their homework. By creating artistic openings, the active dramaturg assists the artistic team to quickly delve deep into the text, so they can spend more time exploring creative choices. In short, the active dramaturg looks at the larger dramatic picture differently than the director. Directors look toward creating and shaping emotional tension and journeys; whereas, active dramaturgs pursue ways to connect those emotional journeys to thematic ideas and add thematic tension. Ultimately, a director addresses thematic issues as well, but the dramaturg focuses on this idea exclusively from beginning to end.

It may also help to consider the notes a different way. When actors begin working on their feet, they often request rehearsal clothes and shoes. These items help approximate their costume so that the actor can better sculpt the character's physical life. A woman who wears skirts moves one way; a woman who wears sweat pants, another. A man walks one way in loafers, another in boots. The rehearsal costumes do not tell the actor what to do but they do open the creative process. Like rehearsal clothing, the dramaturg's notes (should the director choose to use them) help open the actor's creative process and focus the connection to the scene's life and personality.

Of course, to make a proactive note successful and inviting, the active dramaturg writes diplomatically.

A poorly written proactive note tells the director what to do, assumes the dramaturg knows more than the rest of the creative team, and liberally uses the word 'you' in an off-putting manner. An example of a dramaturg's poorly written proactive note for the scene when Dr. Rank tells Nora he's dying might look like this:

> I see that you will be working on the Dr. Rank and Nora scenes
> tomorrow. I know we discussed those scenes a lot, spending

considerable time debating whether Nora gets Dr. Rank's hints at death or she's totally obtuse. Remember, we said she's smart and plays the men, Torvald and Krogstad that is, for fools; Dr. Rank is a bit trickier for her to play and pin down. But she likes a challenge. This scene presents that challenge to her. It's an opportunity for her to explore her charms and what it's like to function like a man. Look out for Dr. Rank appearing like too much of a wimp. He loves her but where's his strength? Even though he's dying, something's got to fire him up. Have a great rehearsal. I'll be in on Thursday to see what you all came up with.

An infuriating note, isn't it? Imagine if you were on the receiving end. The dramaturg who writes something like this shouldn't be surprised to find they're unwelcome in the rehearsal hall; worse still, accused of directing the director.

This note goes awry in the very first line: *I see that you will be working on the Dr. Rank and Nora scenes tomorrow.* This dramaturg chose to use language that separates her from the company, *I see that you...* Everyone on the team works on the production whether they attend each rehearsal or not. A more appropriate and welcoming introduction would be: *I saw the rundown for tomorrow, and noticed the Dr. Rank/Nora scenes are already on the schedule.*

The second sentence manages to avoid insulting anyone: *I know we discussed those scenes a lot, spending considerable time debating whether Nora gets Dr. Rank's hints at death or she's totally obtuse.* But it serves as a set-up to a thoroughly inappropriate comment: *Remember, we said...* The director doesn't need to be schooled as a colleague reminds him of a conversation that took place perhaps two months prior. If it's important to reference a prior conversation or ideas, do so honestly without an air of superiority. A better lead into the third sentence might be one rooted in facts, truths regarding the creative process or the play. For example: *After the first reading, the actors had a lot of the same questions we did regarding what Nora knows. It seems like they'll be open to a lot of the discoveries we made.*

Now, the observations the team made regarding Nora's relationship to the men is important. The director probably remembers these ideas quite clearly (he probably offered them to the group initially, too), so using the notes as a memo isn't a good use of time or space. What's better? Take the observations and ratchet them up a notch or two. With this in mind, the passage: *We said she's smart and plays the men, Torvald and Krogstad that is, for fools; Dr. Rank is a bit trickier for her to play and pin down. But she likes a challenge*...might be rewritten as: *By the time Nora sits with Dr. Rank, she's managed to ask Torvald a few key questions and set Krogstad up with Kristina Linde. With these mounting pressures, is she as energized as we originally thought? Is Dr. Rank less of a challenge because he's more of a friend? If that takes the scene totally off the tack we've charted, we might consider looking at the conversation as her way of searching for ways to make him happy. She found a way to take Torvald on a trip to Italy to renew his health (all those years ago) and Krogstad reunited with the love of his life, what could she do for Dr. Rank?*

As we near the end of this note, the dramaturg loses steam and chooses, rather unwisely, to lecture the director. The original reads: *Look out for Dr. Rank appearing like too much of a wimp. He loves her but where's his strength? Even though he's dying, something's got to fire him up.* With this sentence, the dramaturg functions like a back seat driver rather than a navigator, a true collaborator. An active dramaturg may choose to alert a director to the scene's or relationships pitfalls—that Dr. Rank could appear to be totally useless around Nora and in turn unattractive, and drain the scenes of their palpable sexual tension—and points out lines or moments that the cast could explore. In addition, the active dramaturg could include thoughts on how to shape the scenes. So, a concluding comment might be: *Dr. Rank could appear like a lost puppy around Nora. The moments when this happens might help with this idea (the dramaturg could choose to include a specific physical action the actor makes or line of text). I know we discussed a different type of relationship between them, but the actors seemed to glom onto this idea. Who knows, this puppy-dog approach to indicating an emotionally lost Dr. Rank may play like fingernails on a chalkboard, shifting a bit and looking for ways to emphasize the thematic ideas regarding the legacy of debt, sins of the father, and responsibility versus loneliness during this moment may help.*

Although it's great to sign off with *Have a great rehearsal* and reminding the director when you plan to return, *I'll be in on Thursday,* closing with the phrase *to see what you all came up with* places the dramaturg in the position of control and leadership, and there's only one leader on a production: the director. A better close is: *Have a great rehearsal, tomorrow. I'll be in on Thursday as we had scheduled. Let me know if you need anything for Thursday and if these notes were helpful. I'm looking forward to seeing everyone.*

The complete final version of an active dramaturg's less inflammatory proactive note is:

> I saw the rundown for tomorrow and noticed the Dr. Rank/ Nora scenes are already on the schedule. I know we discussed those scenes a lot, spending a lot of time debating whether Nora gets Dr. Rank's hints at death or she's totally obtuse. After the first reading, the actors had a lot of the same questions we did regarding what Nora knows. It seems like they'll be open to a lot of the discoveries we made. For example, by the time Nora sits with Dr. Rank, she's managed to ask Torvald a few key questions and set Krogstad up with Kristina Linde. With these mounting pressures, is she as energized as we originally thought? Is Dr. Rank less of a challenge because he's more of a friend? If that takes the scene totally off the tack we've charted, we might consider looking at the conversation as her way of searching for ways to make him happy. She found a way to take Torvald on a trip to Italy to renew his health (all those years ago) and Krogstad reunited with the love of his life, what could she do for Dr. Rank? Dr. Rank could appear like a lost puppy around Nora. The moments when this happens might help with this idea [the dramaturg could choose to include a specific physical action the actor makes or line of text] I know we discussed a different type of relationship between them, but the actors seemed to glom onto this idea. Who knows, this puppy-dog approach to indicating an emotionally lost Dr. Rank may play like fingernails on a chalkboard, shifting a bit and looking for ways to emphasize the thematic ideas regarding the legacy of debt, sins of the father, and responsibility versus loneliness during this moment may help. Have a great rehearsal, tomorrow. I'll be in on Thursday as we had scheduled. Let me know if you need anything for Thursday and if these notes were helpful. I'm looking forward to seeing everyone.

Crafting a Reponsive Note

The challenge with responsive notes is that the active dramaturg must begin by describing what happens on stage, much like a theatre critic, but must also search for possible ways to compliment, expand or amend choices. To get a sense of a responsive note, let's explore the final scene from Kennedy's *Funnyhouse of a Negro*, and why this note infuriates rather than inspires:

> Thanks for letting me know the noose will remain as a visual through to the end of the play. That's an interesting choice and a bit off-putting. A hangman's noose has quite a negative history in the black community. Remember those articles on lynching? I don't think seeing Negro Sarah's body swaying limp throughout the scene helps her cause. It says something like, "Look at me I'm dead," and frankly stops the play. It's a tough ending, having Robert tell us everything she says is a lie, and I know you want to call his words into question, but right now it looks like he's free to say anything because she's dead. There isn't a lot of power there. She shouldn't be swinging (I know it's a prop, but still...) because it's distracting and advocating suicide.

If you were a director, would you want to read this? Nothing in the note actually helps the director consider new possibilities for the scene. In fact, the not so subtle demand on the director to change the ending almost ensures nothing will change. But there are a few strong points and ideas to keep. The question is, what doesn't work and why?

To begin the note with: ***Thanks for letting me know the noose will remain as a visual through to the end of the play***, isn't a bad choice. The idea of thanking a collaborator can never be wrong, but this sentence needs to be reworded with more grace and less attitude. However, if this note followed a run-through later in the process, this sentence also reminds the director the dramaturg hasn't been attending rehearsals and doesn't know which moments are left purposefully un-staged until the production moves to the actual performance space. In the end, an active dramaturg may find it unnecessary to include this introduction.

The second sentence offers judgment and opinion rather than dramaturgical evidence and artistic support: ***That's an interesting choice and a bit off-putting***. Adding the word "interesting", the euphemistic critical response for unsuccessful artistic choices, is an obvious slight that the word "off-putting" compounds. A more tactful opening might be a factual comment such as: ***To have an image of Negro Sarah hanging and swinging from a rope (albeit a shadow of her body) is a strong choice***.

If the visual has the potential to distract an audience because it offends or competes with other images or ideas, a dramaturg should point it out. Also, if the choice is strong, insightful or surprising, the active dramaturg should not shy away from using such descriptive and helpful adjectives. Sometimes, however, choices are weak and depending upon the collaborative relationship this word can be used with no damaging effect. Often the active dramaturg simply acknowledges the choice and articulates other possible choices that will help the moment progress differently. No matter what, a clear discussion may help the director and, by extension, the company hone an idea. To facilitate the re-visioning process for this imagined production of *Funnyhouse*, the active dramaturg works to articulate why the visuals have a particular impact.

The example shows a dramaturg walking away from her artistic responsibility with the sentences: *A hangman's noose has quite a negative history in the black community. Remember those articles on lynching?* Active dramaturgy never shies away from thinking of ways to grow a production. Similarly, the active dramaturg doesn't hide the thought process. As long as the notes are clear and articulate, there's no reason to sanitize them; keep your personality and share how the ideas developed. The adjusted language regarding the visual choice and its historical significance might be: *The visual connection to lynching can't be missed, and it makes her suicide take on a larger significance. The problem is lynching is done to you, and suicide is a self-inflicted act. The suggestion that modern society's expectations and exclusions metaphorically lynches Negro Sarah presents an appropriate intellectual argument, but does the discomfort of seeing a woman hanging from a rope support this?* The director has a better sense of how the image reads and why, because the note dissects the image rather than dismisses it. The question at the end gives the director ideas to mull, but the active dramaturg provides evidence and information to aid that process.

Whenever artists collaborate, the temptation to have things look a certain way always rises. This is only a problem when that vision competes with the leader's ideas, in this case the director's. Although the note avoids an outright statement of, "I don't like this; change it," the following sentences aren't too different: *I don't think seeing Negro Sarah's body swaying limp throughout the scene helps her cause. It says something like "Look at me I'm dead" and frankly stops the play.* The relationship between the director and dramaturg may be strong, making it possible to reel off quips like, *"Look at me I'm dead…frankly stops the play."* However, reading this phrase is considerably different from hearing someone say it. Vocal inflection changes everything. Adjusting the language helps the active dramaturg remain a valuable contributor to the production: *Will the audience remain connected to the play and listen to Robert's speech as the hanged body of Negro Sarah sways in the wind? Right now Robert's speech calls Sarah's ability to tell the truth into question and subsequently undermines her, but the proposed visuals are changing Kennedy's argument, albeit unintentionally. If Negro Sarah is shown as having been lynched by society and then Robert calls her arguments a lie while she hangs in the wind, what are we saying about all of the men (and few women) who were lynched in the United States? If we can find a way to have the image trump his argument, force the reality of lynching by mob or society's exclusion, then we may be able to keep the audience on Negro Sarah's side and look at the Caucasian's words and recording of history with the grains of salt the writer intends.*

Here's a look at the entire revised note:

> To have an image of Negro Sarah hanging and swinging from a rope (albeit a shadow of her body) is a strong choice. The visual connection to lynching can't be missed, and it makes her suicide take on a larger significance. The problem is lynching is done to you, and suicide is a self-inflicted act. The suggestion that modern society's expectations and exclusions metaphorically lynches Negro Sarah presents an appropriate intellectual argument, but does the discomfort of seeing a woman hanging from a rope support this? Will the audience remain connected to the play and listen to Robert's speech as the hanged body of Negro Sarah sways in the wind? Right now Robert's speech calls Sarah's ability to tell the truth into question and subsequently undermines her, but the proposed visuals are changing Kennedy's argument, albeit unintentionally. If Negro Sarah is shown as having been lynched by society and then Robert calls her arguments a lie while she hangs in the wind, what are we saying about all of the men (and few women) who were lynched in the United States? If we can find a way to have the image trump his argument, force the reality of lynching by mob or society's exclusion, then we may be able to keep the audience on Negro Sarah's side and look at the Caucasian's words and recording of history with the grains of salt the writer intends.

When to Deliver the Responsive Note

Responsive notes refer to a specific directorial choice. It's possible the director and dramaturg and design team discussed this choice at length before rehearsals began. If so, the active dramaturg should have attempted to share these observations in conversation and then as a proactive note. If the director decided to include a noose during the rehearsal process, the active dramaturg should offer the note after seeing the scene as staged and discussing the idea with the director. Understanding the context will provide the active dramaturg with information and credibility. Ideally, however, this note arrives before tech rehearsals.

Who Sees the Dramaturg's Notes?

For the most part, only the director sees the dramaturg's notes. On occasion the artistic director may consult them to remain in touch with the artistic process. The stage manager's notes track the nuts and bolts of the rehearsal process but avoid any commentary or documentation regarding actor or director choice or designer work. Only the dramaturg chronicles the creative content within the rehearsal process.

As opening night approaches, the dramaturg needs to slightly adjust the way notes are written. Early on, the ideas can and should be broad with an eye to performance and use language that is less immediately connected to an actor's vocabulary. In other words, the notes connect to the story, how it's told; what's clear and what's not or how to use the text to clarify the storytelling. When run-throughs and previews begin, the turnaround time for adjustments significantly diminishes. To acknowledge this, the active dramaturg's notes become more precise and incorporate more actor-ready language—that is, terms actors use to build and execute their characters. Although the actors never see the dramturg's notes, the active dramaturg composes them in a way that facilitates more immediate use by the director.

How Notes Change Over Time

To consider an approach to rehearsal notes, discussing a specific play may help. When, for example, working on any Suzan-Lori Parks play, the company must grapple with the silences, spells and the unwritten lines of dialogue. Parks' essay titled "The Elements of Style" articulates her intentions and goals for these unique dramaturgical elements, but only somewhat clarifies how to execute her dramatic use of unspoken language. An active dramaturg provides assistance in realizing these passages on stage, but only if the comments directly relate to the actor's process. That said, just as the dramaturg doesn't direct a play, it's also important to avoid translating a playwright's ideas regarding performing the text. The active dramaturg simply uses the writer's thoughts to impact and shape the notes rather than definitively explain.

When responding to a director's question about performances that seem stunted rather than freed by a writer's device (a pause, overlapping dialogue or a spell) a dramaturg might proceed without caution and craft a response like this:

> I've spent some time looking into the spells and silences. Parks says they aren't pauses but, as you said, they're playing like pauses. The actors are engaging fully with each other and the story moves on through the silent subtext. The subtext of the scene grabs us, the tension between the mother and son and their concerns regarding their legacy deepens an already rich narrative. I suppose a silence is just that—a time to take a break and be silent, luxuriate in each other. From an actor's perspective it's one of the few times mother and son connect in a loving way. Their individual journeys rarely coincide in such an obvious manner. Maybe a longing to return to that moment could color the spells so that they're silent, reflective moments.

This comment avoids the cardinal sin of directing the director but never manages to help the director explain how the spells and silences function. The note suggests that the director acknowledged a challenge and asked for assistance, *I've spent some time looking into the spells and silences. Parks says they aren't pauses but, as you said, they're playing like pauses*, but the dramaturg has done little to answer this question. True, the dramaturg shouldn't be held responsible for answering any question definitively. Nevertheless, as a collaborator the director expects the active dramaturg to address the issue and provide researched thoughts or educated guesses; dancing around the issue merely prolongs the confusion.

Beginning with an analysis of what the actors are doing, or objectively stating what comes across, can help the conversation and the collaborative search for a solution: *The actors are engaging fully with each other and the story moves on through the silent subtext.* However, to better serve the process, the active dramaturg could do more to compare how a Parks "spell" and Harold Pinter "pause" functions. This concise, production-oriented analysis could help the director identify and articulate what the actors are doing. If, when writing about Pinter, the dramaturg succumbs to literary analysis nothing will be used in the rehearsal hall. Take this for example:

> The ability to tell a scene through silence or parallel, subtextual narrative lies at the heart of Pinter's pauses. Pinter brilliantly illuminates the path even though he doesn't sculpt the journey with plot-specific words. The successful manipulation of weaker characters, in say, *The Homecoming*, depends on the actor's willingness to focus on the spoken words while subtly hinting at a physical attraction or some other distraction. Parks does something else with her pauses.

What can a director readily take from the above analytical comment and use? *Parallel, subtextual narratives* aren't playable and neither is *sculpt the journey with plot-specific words*. A director can invite an actor to focus on language and use the body to suggest the opposite, but how does the rest of the note impact the rehearsal?

What might better serve the rehearsal process and the collaborative relationship is the active dramaturg's attempt to actually define how spells and silences function. The active dramaturg demonstrates a willingness to engage in the thinking process and reinforce a connection to the rehearsal process and the artist team. The active dramaturg might choose to compose something like this:

> We know the spells and silences aren't pauses (Parks tells us this). You're right, when the cast plays these moments as pauses, the action slows and the story becomes overly sentimental and self-important. It seems, then, that the pauses allow the actors to continue to tell the story through silence. They are lulls in speech and action; unlike a Pinter pause, a new power dynamic hasn't been established when the pause ends and the action resumes. Parks' characters can manipulate a relationship by playing an action with focused intention, so that even if their dialogue tells the audience they've lost, it's possible to reverse the outcome with a focused action. Maybe the key to performing a spell and silence is stopping the actor's actions. A bit like a commercial break from the action. Or, to keep with Parks' music analogies, a silence might be the rest, the space in which the last note of music reverberates as at the end of a lengthy orchestral piece. No one applauds right away no mat-

ter how triumphant the final phrases. The conductor holds the applause at bay, allowing the sound to hang in the air and simply be. The silences might be asking the actors to hold on to an action without intensifying it or refocusing it. A true acting challenge if that's the case, but our cast is up to it.

Even with the analogies, this note includes more ideas that a director can explore and an actor can play. The notes may also provide an outline for an in-person discussion. Yes, the active dramaturg's ideas may be rejected, but by focusing on the issue and avoiding sounding like a know-it-all invites the director to consider the insights. Ending with positive reinforcement reassures the director that although the solution may not be easy to find or to execute, the director's talent will lead the cast through this minor muddle, and that as the production dramaturg you will be there to help.

Notes After Runs of Scenes or Sections of the Play

As the company makes its way through scenes, directors periodically schedule time for the actors to run a few scenes back to back. This allows everyone to get a sense of the play's organic flow and discover new truths about the characters and play's build. These runs are a lot like reading and responding to an early draft of an unfinished paper, book, or play. No one expects perfection, but the general direction and framework should be evident as well as the moments that, if not explained or clarified, will lead to audience confusion. During these runs, certain moments flow with ease and others proceed in fits and starts. Confusion regarding blocking and stage movement can occur, but usually a lack of clarity within the storytelling lies at the heart of these hiccups.

While watching these early runs, the active dramaturg focuses on the arc and build of the story and moments where the thematic ideas and linguistic metaphors aren't clear or used to their full extent; whereas, the director may look for clarity of specific choice and how each actor tells the story. Although there is overlap, everyone is working on the same play. Understanding the major differences can help avoid tensions and the sense that the active dramaturg is directing the director.

It's also possible that the active dramaturg watches these runs and notes the broad strokes to gain a sense of how the ideas raised during pre-production change when a company adds their interpretations to the mix. The active dramaturg considers how these adjustments play with the storytelling, character development, and the play's form.

Following a brief run, the active dramaturg's notes acknowledge the actor's journey and highlight additional moments in the text that may fuel their progression or suggest interesting twists by noting where to accentuate or challenged the production's thematic through-line. The active dramaturg may also offer notes that connect movement to text and story, as blocking challenges sometimes stem from an actor's flagging connection to language or story. During this phase, the active dramaturg also responds to internal transitions and the moments between scenes and notes images or thematic ideas that might reinforce choices or increase dramatic tension. These notes should be delivered to the director—sent through e-mail, hand delivered, or placed in the in-house mailbox—at least two hours before the next rehearsal.

Active Dramaturgy and Run-Throughs for Set Texts

These are some of the most exciting and tension-filled days. Actors have high expectations during runs, as they are looking to have their character in place and navigate their emotional journey, and each run introduces new discoveries that somewhat alter performances (as they should) or the dramatic arc. Directors and active dramaturgs watch to discover what works and what doesn't and what needs to be attended to before moving from the rehearsal hall to the stage. A lot of the theatre's staff or friends of the company attend particular runs, ramping up the tension.

Again, it's worth noting how the active dramaturg's focus differs from the director's during these run-throughs. Dramaturgs do note where the energy flags and the story lacks clarity, but instead of trying to articulate what new choice an actor should make as well as how to do it and when, the active dramaturg focuses on what the current choice tells us (what's happening) and where the scene resists that choice—due to text or concept—or where the choice pushes against expectation in an exciting manner. In illuminating these sometimes unwelcome conflicts, the active dramaturg supports the director as he discusses the actor's options. The active dramaturg also looks at the larger story and how the choices either challenge or oppose the play's dramatic through-line, to reveal new insights or establish a new path for the production. Noticing where the drive and energy flags is how the active dramaturg attends to pacing.

As these runs occur later in the rehearsal process, the active dramaturg focuses more directly on storytelling and transitions. For story, the active dramaturg observes how clear the key points are and how well they land. For transitions, the active dramaturg notes whether the scenes end the same way, with a sense of closure, or with an energy that looks forward. Be sure to leave room for design elements to assist with transitions. Writing notes that acknowledge when this might occur may help with the technical rehearsals. Keep in mind that active analysis connects key story points with the action on stage. Remark on what works well and use those discoveries to shape the notes for the sections that still need to meet the strongest moments of the production.

The Bad Rehearsal

During the initial run-throughs, there will be a day when cues are missed, the pacing is off, lines dropped, the story unclear. Look forward to this day. First, all productions must have a bad rehearsal to ensure a successful production—it's one of the profession's oldest myths. Second, it's better to make mistakes in private than in front of the audience. Third, there's little reason to write notes following this rehearsal. Everyone knows it's gone poorly. This is the time for the active dramaturg to remind the director—in person and as soon as the run ends—what's working and the benefits of having a bad rehearsal that day. These rehearsals bring everyone's doubts to the fore and the active dramaturg should remind everyone of their strengths. This is the time to be a grand cheerleader. It's the moment the active dramaturg remembers: sometimes your job is to bring cupcakes.

Active Dramatury and Previews for Set Texts

For these runs—and it's important to consider them runs rather than performances—technical elements are in place and tweaked throughout the day and sometimes during the run. The greatest difference with these rehearsals is that the run takes place before an invited or paying audience.

The first preview most resembles that first stumble-through in the rehearsal hall, because every unexpected laugh may throw off the timing and every unanticipated shift (or ringing cell phone) can call attention to moments the company has yet to entirely own. As the preview process continues, the story tightens, the actors assume a sense of comfort and the active dramaturg has less to focus on. But during those early previews, there's a lot to watch, synthesize, and write about quickly. It is during previews when the active dramaturg proves most useful. The director must manage the design staff, run crew, actors and possibly the playwright; however, the active dramaturg focuses solely on the story and its themes, and how the audience receives it.

A major idea to keep in mind during the preview process is that the play and the production are two different things. The play is the story, the base upon which artists build a production. The production is the collection of elements (few or many) used to interpret the play in a particular way.

To best help the play, the active dramaturg focuses on the story and how it unfolds during the previews. To best help the production, the active dramaturg watches the audience more often than the action on stage. The notes then discuss the story in relation to the audience reaction, making an effort to relate the audience's response to the performed story.

These notes must be delivered to the director—sent through e-mail, hand delivered, or placed in the in-house mailbox—at least two hours before the next rehearsal.

Good Shifts

When watching a preview, a dramaturg learns to watch the play through the audience's eyes; however, an active dramaturg watches the audience experience the play.

The active dramaturg learns to notice which moments elicit rapt attention and which do not. Good shifts precede and follow the dramatic events; they mark moments that draw the audience in. As the emotional truths—these may be serious or humorous—escalate in intensity, the audience will, as if on cue, lean forward in their seats, stop fidgeting and concentrate on the action on stage. The universal silence or, for a comedy, laughter will tell a director, active dramaturg and designers whether their preparation has paid off. The actors might be terrified by the silence or thrown by the laughter, but only until their colleagues who watched with the audience confirm that the stillness or laughter comes from rapt attention.

I worked as the dramaturg for a somewhat expressionistic interpretation of *The Glass Menagerie*. The audience remained fixed and still from the strike of Tom's first match to the snuffing out of Laura's candle. The director's concept was that the memories housed in the play's scenes pursued Tom and were as unrelenting as a nightmare. For this reason, Tom (and the other actors) rarely left the stage, forcing them to live in a heightened emotional state for a little under two hours. The audience responded in kind, refusing to avert their focus for even one second. Such an emotionally unrelenting production grabbed the audience and gave them a new appreciation for the play, but when the play ended there was only silence.

In striving for a production that ends as abruptly as a dream, the artistic team hadn't given the audience time to adjust to the fact that the play had ended. They were rarely ready to applaud. When they did respond, however, they clapped intensely, for a long while.

Bad Shifts

Inevitably an audience will feel the urge to move. Even when a play demands an incredible amount of stillness and attention, the audience will find places to rest. These moments of relaxation aren't bad shifts, just breaks. The difference between a break and a bad shift is that one is silent and almost imperceptible and the other, quite loud and obvious. Bad shifts include rifling through programs, trying (and failing) to find a comfortable position in the seat, visibly surveying the audience, talking, sighs of boredom, exasperation, and a general sense that everyone wants to be somewhere else. Bad shifts come after moments that confuse, irritate or infuriate an audience. Usually the actors will begin to struggle to regain the audience's attention, and the more they do, the more bad shifts result.

Active dramaturgs watch for the bad shifts.

When watching the shifts, the active dramaturg works to remember what took place before the shifting began. It's also important to note when the fidgeting stops.

The equivalent of bad shifts is unwanted laughter. Rare though it may be to have a drama appear like a comedy (it's a lot more common to have a comedy play like a tragedy), it does happen. Whatever the response, the active dramaturg addresses these shifts through notes. If your notes continually point out the same unclear beats, moments or scenes, stop writing the note. Either the director has chosen to ignore the note, or you haven't yet found a successful way to inspire and facilitate an adjustment.

If the director refuses to consider your notes, wait for the audience to speak. One of my first productions after graduate school, a world premiere, was about a woman in mourning. Throughout the rehearsal process, the play dragged. In the rehearsal hall, the performers played the pathos, and in doing so the action seemed maudlin. I felt the choices stalled the play's action and felt too much like movie-of-the-week acting; I tried to write that in more polite terms. The director disagreed, so much so he sat me down to tell me why each of my notes was ineffective. That meeting proved a decidedly unpleasant experience. Then first preview the arrived. The audience responded to the movie-of-the-week acting style in an unusual way. Instead of sobbing uncontrollably, they roared with laughter for two solid hours. The actors were distraught and the director duly stunned. By the play's end, the only tears flowing were those from laughing too hard. The artistic director and I joined everyone in the rehearsal hall the next day and watched a number of my (and his) notes facilitate the necessary changes. That night, the audience began laughing (clearly their friends had described the play as a comedy) but soon settled into the grief-stricken world the playwright envisioned.

When watching previews, active dramaturgs celebrate the moments that work on stage but hadn't worked in the rehearsal hall; the design and how it compliments and enhances the performances; while identifying the moments that lead to the bad shifts and ways to clarify them.

Notes and the Active Dramaturg During a New-Play Rehearsal Process

The greatest difference between a new-play rehearsal process and the set-text rehearsal should come as no surprise: the script changes often. Despite everyone's efforts during workshops and dramaturgical sessions with the playwright before the first day of rehearsal, the script will evolve throughout the rehearsal process. Sometimes the adjustments will include minor line deletions or additions; at other times, the changes involve re-structuring entire scenes, maybe even composing a new ending. Because the rehearsal process helps refine (and sometimes find) the play's story and characters, everyone has two goals in the rehearsal hall: to find the play's story and to find the story for production. In contrast, the rehearsal process for a set text focuses exclusively on the *production's* story.

When the rehearsal begins, the director, dramaturg, and playwright work together closely although they focus on different elements. For example, the director engages in conversation to assist in developing the story, but focuses more intently on what the actors and production need. The active dramaturg, however, focuses on what the story and characters need and identifies with the writer which of the production's needs translate into story needs. A simple example is when and how a scene must change to accommodate a difficult technical effect rather than a storytelling question.

The dramaturg and director's differing areas of concern do not place them in opposition. The somewhat divergent visions complement one another and, when the dramaturg remains active, this split can help the playwright address the arising concerns quickly and effectively.

But how does one know which moments need attention and which simply need to be rehearsed? Practice and experience working on new plays as well as a strong sense of what stories need to effectively communicate an idea will answer the question.

It also helps to know how to identify where the problem is.

The Quincy Long Rule

Mame Hunt, a well-respected and accomplished dramaturg I met while working at a Sundance Theatre Lab, revealed a true dramaturgical secret as we discussed our various projects. She learned this theatrical truth while working as the dramaturg on Berkeley Repertory Theatre's world premiere production of *The Virgin Molly* written by the well-respected and prolific playwright Quincy Long. She even named the secret the Quincy Long Rule.

Simply put, the rule is this: When a problem in the story arises, look to a moment or two before the problem to identify the cause; address that concern, and a number of unclear moments including the one in question will disappear.

It's incredibly simple and applies to new plays and productions of set texts alike.

The Quincy Long Rule acknowledges the temptation all artists succumb to; they see or sense that something isn't working and begin to hone in and dissect the moment or scene when the confusion manifests itself. The adjusted language or performance provides a temporary sense of satisfaction, but as time passes either a new hurdle emerges or the patch for the scene in question begins to fray at the edges. In other words, something still feels a bit wonky. The Quincy Long Rule tells the artistic team to look elsewhere, usually earlier, for the problem area.

When active dramaturgs apply the Quincy Long Rule, one adjustment can set a number of concerns right. The challenge is to locate where the confusion begins. To find the source of the hiccup, active dramaturgs work backward. When actors begin to reveal they're having difficulty with a particular moment, first determine (silently) if it's a question of needing more familiarity with the text and character or if too little evidence exists to support the actor's process. If it's clearly a question the writer needs to address, work backwards, much like David Ball suggests in his book *Backwards & Forwards,* to identify when the necessary information should appear or when it appears but is confused. Understanding the Quincy Long Rule saves incredible amounts of time. Using it can help active dramaturgs, directors, and writers isolate and differentiate challenging areas from gaps in storytelling.

Essentially, plays are mysteries waiting to be solved and every line provides a clue; the active dramaturg works to make sure the necessary clues exist in an order that serves the play and the actor.

Notes During the Tablework Phase for a New-Play Production

The dramaturgical process during a new play's rehearsal parallels the set-text rehearsal process, except that the active dramaturg must work to clarify unclear moments by differentiating between an individual artist's concerns, and the play's true needs, its unanswered questions and unwritten moments. These concerns demand considerable focus and as such drive the dramaturg's duties and the types of notes written. The active dramaturg's notes address the writer and director separately, as each artist must realize the adjustment differently.

When working on a new play, the time spent around the table can last as long as a week. Some theatres might call this a mini-workshop. A more typical time is four to five consecutive days with frequent returns to the table when new pages arrive.

Conversations around the table for a new play also differ. As actors read and then respond to scenes, the playwright often chooses to engage with the actors. Rather than providing answers, writers often use the time to ask actors questions about the character and scene. These relaxed and sometimes wide-reaching dialogues rarely include lengthy contributions from the director or active dramaturg. Unlike the set-text discussion, these first reads provide writers the chance to learn how the play functions and feels inside an actor's body; and since writers write for actors, hearing an actor's response is crucial and important.

Tablework Conversations

During this phase of rehearsal, active dramaturgs and directors listen to the actor's points and questions about character and story, stepping in only when the questions veer toward observations and solutions that satisfy a single performer's need or ego. One listens for comments that impact the entire scene or story or character journey, taking note of when character comments result in revisions that allow the character to win more stage time or scenes by achieving his or her wants/needs. During tablework dramaturgs, playwrights, and directors should expect to hold numerous sidebars. Even if these days at the table aren't considered a mini-workshop, active dramaturgs should plan on a lot of conversations with the writer to follow up points the actors raise and explore options inspired by the cast's comments. Three general thoughts that govern the active dramaturg's process are: note any areas that cause actors to stumble during the reading; track questions and comments that promote additions or cuts to augment a particular character's role without supporting or strengthening the story; identify if and when the writer becomes entranced by the performances and stops listening to the play.

Most of the notes during this phase are for the writer and should be proactive in nature. They may include the following: observations that follow up on ideas raised during the day's conversations and sidebars; questions for the writer to consider as the actors read particular scenes; a possible schedule or outline for the rewrites. These notes should be the result of work completed with the writer and director before rehearsal ends. The active dramaturg should discuss these ideas with the writer and the director and follow up the conversation with written notes by the next day.

Notes During the Scene Work Phase for a New Play

As much as the company focuses on character work and general story flow, once blocking begins new questions regarding the play's form/pattern may emerge. Writers may tend to overwrite to fix non-problems as they watch actors contend with the normal struggles surrounding learning a role; an active dramaturg watches for this and points out when to ignore these non-problems. Unless major rewrites arrive during this phase, this is a good time for both the writer and active dramaturg to simply observe the rehearsal or address other script questions outside the rehearsal hall. The temptation for the writer is to watch the actors, and become entranced. An active dramaturg works with the writer to focus on the pre-established questions and articulate how select moments impact those questions and help the writer remain engaged in the writing process. Throughout the new-play process major discoveries are made and as such at least two members of the three-person artistic team (director, dramaturg, and writer) should always be present during this phase. All three members should attend rehearsal exploring the confusing scenes identified during pre-rehearsal conversations or discussions following the initial readings.

As new pages and possible solutions will be explored throughout this phase, the active dramaturg considers: suggestions that address the moments and remaining awkward sections; how the rewrites play and impact continuity; how to not eliminate purposefully challenging acting and storytelling moments. The active dramaturg's notes address areas where

the Quincy Long Rule applies and celebrate the writer's efforts and successes. These notes must be delivered to the director and playwright—sent
through e-mail, hand delivered, or placed in the in-house mailbox—at
least two hours before the next rehearsal.

Notes After Brief Runs of Scenes or Sections of the New Play

Stumble-throughs provide everyone an opportunity to see what's
been accomplished and obtain a clearer sense of the play's flow. Unlike a
set-text production, however, the active dramaturg watches for moments
when the written story remains unclear and acknowledges when the solution may lie with the director. The challenge is to identify whether the lack
of clarity comes from actor choices, the text, or directorial storytelling.
The active dramaturg may need to address all three as areas to investigate. By presenting scenarios for all three (four if one considers technical
or design elements later in the process) the dramaturg can guide the exploration by presenting options. Over time, experience helps the active
dramaturg identify when an acting choice works well in the rehearsal hall
and less well on stage, or when a storytelling moment requires more clarification. Remember, the dramaturg is neither perfect nor expected to have
the answer.

The act of presenting options develops these prized production dramaturgy skills. These runs often produce tension in the rehearsal hall,
as little time remains for the writer to compose effective changes. If the
company hasn't already established a time to freeze the script—to stop all
rewrites except minor cuts—somewhere during this process the director
may set this date. This is also the time when the active dramaturg and the
director may appear to be in conflict. Active dramaturgs will often advocate giving the writer more time and encourage the writer to forge ahead
with textual changes that clarify the story. Directors must look out for the
actors, their process, and the pressure of learning a world and presenting it
with grace. Both artists have the same goal, a strong production, but their
allegiances can make them appear at odds. The active dramaturg remembers everyone's on the same team.

During run-throughs, the active dramaturg looks for: unclear moments and new ways to articulate questions to generate rewrites that will
clarify the play in production; exhausted or overwhelmed artists (rewrites
take a toll on everyone from actors to crew to designers); transitions that
detract from the story's flow. The active dramaturg's notes tend to include
suggested cuts that will clarify and intensify transitions; ways to restruc-
ture scenes with existing lines (Although a new word order can frustrate

actors, since these lines aren't entirely new the resistance is often less.); moments and choices informed by information no longer in the play. These notes, from this phase of the rehearsal process up to opening night, must be delivered to the director and playwright—sent through e-mail, hand delivered, or placed in the in-house mailbox—at least two hours before the next rehearsal.

Notes After Run-Throughs for a New Play

By this point, the script should be in solid shape. If any changes are bandied about, they usually involve cuts (for length) or story solutions for the next draft. The active dramaturg's goal is to help the writer and director strengthen the story for this production and iteration of the text. To facilitate this process, the active dramaturg continues looking for actor behavior that refers to moments and character traits from earlier drafts; and looks for ways to reinvigorate artists who may be frustrated with the process—it may be a good time to bring cupcakes. The notes an active dramaturg writes often include suggestions that help the director boost the morale of frustrated actors; comments to boost the writer's morale as previews and opening night approach; questions that point to parts of the play to watch when the audience arrives.

Active Dramaturg and During Previews for a New Play

These performances are by far the most nerve-wracking experiences for everyone—except the audience. Preview audiences for world premieres are daring, smart theatre-goers who love adventure and strongly support the future of American theatre. They also enjoy knowing they play an active role in shaping the production before Opening Night.

Because many previews for a new play include post-play discussions (or surveys), those who attend the first or second previews relish the chance to meet the playwright and share their impressions. Their verbal responses during the talkback and physical shifts during the performance tell the playwright where the play, excites, succeeds, provokes, and confuses. Sometimes these physical responses may be all the writer needs, but the audience looks forward to the talkback. Aside from moderating the talkback (discussed in Chapter 8), the active dramaturg watches the audience during the performance, noting good and bad shifts, often while sitting next to the writer. It's best to simply watch and reserve any comments regarding moments when the story or production lags, unless the writer begins sharing observations first. The active dramaturg's notes during this phase will include suggestions to clarify confusing moments;

comments that place the audience's observation within the context of the rehearsal process and team's language; and lessons gleaned from the audience's physical and verbal responses. However, many notes will probably be taken during the meeting following the performance, so the notes might recap as well as introduce ideas, making them a combination of both proactive and responsive notes.

The early previews usually generate considerable notes and comments: remember no artistic team has attempted to solve the play's questions ever before; there's a lot to discover. Unfortunately, most theatres retain the same number of previews for a new play as for a set text. This is almost always an unwise decision. Active dramaturgs should lobby for an additional preview or rehearsal during season planning to accommodate the many added responsibilities of mounting a world premiere. The extra performances allow more time to hone the play and find the production's rhythm.

Opening Night for a Set Text or World Premiere

Enjoy it. Watch the production as it was meant to be seen and be proud of your contributions. If it's a new play, you might continue to learn from the audience and share these observations with the writer during the run or when the play closes, for writers often continue to make changes after the first production. But what every active dramaturg should do on Opening Night is enjoy it and all of its pageantry.

Final Thoughts

The importance of a dramaturg remaining visible during the five phases of rehearsal cannot be overstated. Certainly face-to-face conversations are the cornerstone of strong working relationships, but taking the time to write notes greatly benefits the artistic relationship. For one, it's easier for the reader to digest the content. True, active dramaturgs aren't present to gauge how the comments are landing, which is a bit dangerous, but with some thought, attention and tact the notes can provide a wonderful record of the company's progress and everyone's contribution.

Written notes also help the active dramaturg obtain a better sense of the production. Every time a dramaturg sits down to contemplate how a scene works on the page and then in action, that dramaturg learns more about balancing theory and practice (production).

When writing notes, active dramaturgs pay attention to the team's language, goals and how to avoid overwhelming the director or playwright. A way to do that is identify two major themes or ideas that every observation or note can connect to. The second recommendation is to remember that notes needn't be focused exclusively on what isn't working. Notes are responses to the work—its promise, surprise, beauty, and challenges.

Chapter 8

Festivals, Workshops, and Post-Play Discussions

The Fast Paced World of New-Play Development

The title for this section misleads somewhat. New-play development remains, hands down, one of the theatre's slowest processes. The rehearsal process takes, on average, three weeks at regional theatres and up to three months (if not the better part of a year for a Broadway musical). The build for a set and costumes may take from five weeks to five months, but new-play development can literally become a never-ending process.

The fortunate playwright manages to place a play in a workshop at a festival or with a particular institution only months after conceiving the idea or hammering out a draft of an act or two. For the majority of writers, however, the process takes considerably longer. Scripts that make the rounds from new-play festival to new-play festival to developmental workshop and back to new-play festival are known to reside in what writers, dramaturgs, and directors call "workshop hell," a never-ending cycle of rewriting and consideration for production. No one intends to keep the writer trapped in an endless cycle of writing without production, but sometimes this happens. Attending too many workshops designed to help the playwright develop a deeper connection with the story and a stronger play often backfires, leading the playwright to write the play into oblivion, or fosters a situation where the reasons for writing become less clear and the work becomes a burden shrouded in faint recognition.

That said, writers who attend a select number of festivals and workshops often claim that more writing and creative thinking happens during this period than in an entire month of writing at home. During play development residencies, writers can overcome years of writer's block, as did Doug Wright who cracked the storytelling question of *I Am My Own*

Wife during a residency at The Sundance Theatre Lab. Or, a writer may discover the ending of a play, rewrite entire acts or explore specific characters and dramatic questions. Some claim that the writing gods visit these workshops, but most agree that relief from life's obligations and the joy of having actors, a director and dramaturg to respond to ideas immediately or simply to read the latest version, stimulates an amazing level of creative thought.

Whether a development workshop or festival includes sixteen hours of rehearsal or fourteen-plus days in residence, these events involve a variety of theatre artists committed to and adept at helping a writer move a play to the next level. The invited actors possess an uncanny ability to offer comments that serve the character and the play, and watch a character's significance change without complaint. Directors for development processes display considerable patience as they encounter daily drafts and articulate the difference between an actor or character's needs and the eventual production's demands.

Dramaturgs invited to serve on the artistic teams articulate the play's structural and story needs, identify and voice the emotional or thematic logic within various lines or scenes, and zero in on specific unclear areas that impact the entire work, all in order to help a writer establish and articulate goals for the process. Once the writer declares a desire to fix the ending or look at a specific character, the active dramaturg can use themes and other critical elements to shape questions to help shape the writer's process. The active dramaturg also crafts questions designed to keep a writer motivated and working toward those goals. When the dramaturg has two or more projects within one festival—a normal occurrence—it's important to develop ways to connect with each writer to establish a rapport and a common artistic vocabulary quickly.

Workshop readings or presentations rarely involve movement, props or sets; and if they do, the company uses the most basic blocking (stand, sit, cross, hug) and props. Actors read the script during the presentation, as they are not required to memorize their lines. Many festivals actually require actors to hold the script or a page if they do move about the stage. Everyone involved knows that these workshops provide the writer a precious and rare opportunity—to hear a play that's in process read by actors before an audience—and works to make the residency as successful as possible.

The Basic Difference Between Festivals and Workshops

Because new-play development takes place at both festivals and workshops, the terms are used interchangeably throughout this chapter. But know that differences do exist. Festivals always include a number of plays and a public presentation or reading to complete the residency. Workshops, however, may focus on one play or a number of them, and occasionally include a public reading opting instead to read for the company or artistic staff before the residency ends.

Another major difference between the festival and workshop is the talkback. A talkback follows the reading, and provides the audience with an opportunity to respond to the play through written responses or a 20-30 minute conversation between the writer and the audience moderated by the dramaturg. Workshops where the audience is the in-house artistic staff, usually conclude with a private conversation between the artistic director, the artistic staff, and the managing director. If a workshop includes an invited audience (be it professionals or theatre enthusiasts), a dramaturg often moderates this discussion as well.

A Few Basic Truths About Development Processes and Presentations

Although a director and dramaturg actively participate in the workshop, writers actually drive and shape the process. Writers establish the parameters for discussions, the overall goals for the residency, and what they need to see or hear in the reading. The director actively works with the writer and dramaturg during the artistic conversations, but spends little time developing a unique directorial vision—the purpose of a workshop is to serve the writer's vision and process and the play's development. The active dramaturg explores ways to fulfill these needs and facilitate the writer's vision and process with questions and observations designed to articulate which aspects of the play's voice emerge, how the elements support or distract and, most important, why.

But before there is work to discuss or progress to evaluate, the artistic team must sit down with the writer and establish how to best use the limited time to serve the writer and play.

Helping the Fifth Workshop Work as Well or Better than the First

Every writer differs on how many workshops for a single play is too many. But no one disagrees that too many workshops for a single play negatively impacts the play and the writer's ego. If this is the play's fifth workshop or the first following a longer rehearsal and subsequent rewrite, the playwright's desire to use these few hours to the fullest may be quite strong. Determining the play's development history and the writer's ideas surrounding the play will help the dramaturg and writer avoid working at cross purposes. If, however, a playwright has attended too many workshops and hit the limit, there may be little interest from the playwright to actively engage in the process. Whatever the scenario, when a dramaturg enters the hall eager and full of insights and ideas that a writer might not have time to address, the enthusiasm and diligent preparation can overwhelm everyone in the rehearsal hall and destroy the collaborative relationship even before it has begun. Hence the active dramaturg's need to ask what fuels the writer's creative agenda.

What can an active dramaturg do to prevent artistic overload and help move the development process forward at any stage?

Quite simply, remember the dramaturg's second goal: to help the playwright hear the play.

Helping Artists Avoid a Sense of Overload

For active dramaturgs to impact how anyone, especially the writer, hears the play, they must quickly and clearly articulate why key elements work, even if it seems as if these elements do not relate to the writer's (or director's) concerns. By voicing these observations, the active dramaturg develops a vocabulary for the team and an opportunity for the writer to hear concrete descriptions of why and where the play excels. Active dramaturgs articulate observations and then phrase questions that illuminate ways to bring the entire play to a new level of clarity.

By locating points of excellence and, if appropriate, briefly offering a thought as to why the moments transcend other moments or scenes in the play, the active dramaturg helps the writer see what the play communicates. Such comments also encourage a dialogue where the writer may respond with self-identified areas of concern and thoughts on what works well. This approach also provides a more immediate sense of how everyone can begin listening to strong sections compared to less vibrant moments and, once the workshop ends, a model section may guide the writer's rewrites. Even when scenes work in opposition to one another, hearing the adjustments in the context of specific points can lead to a quicker solution. This approach may even lead to the group performing a few improvisations or discussing scenes through a focused lens. But this isn't to suggest that the dramaturg dictates how the brief development period goes. As with all development processes the writer determines the process. An active dramaturg facilitates the writer's agenda by presenting ideas and questions that feed the writer's plan.

Focusing on what works well also makes it easier to put the Quincy Long Rule into action. The Quincy Long Rule, covered in Chapter 7, simply states that a problem with dramatic action isn't when someone notices it, but actually begins some time before.

The Different Workshop Processes

Most workshop or development processes follow one of three basic structures: a short process that includes as little as 16 to 36 hours of rehearsal; a mid-range festival which encompasses three to seven days; and a long process that ranges from as little as eight days to as long as four weeks. The wildly different residencies demand a different artistic focus from every participating artist. Responsibilities change too, especially for the dramaturgs. Whether the dramaturg works full-time for the host institution or as a freelance artist, the dramaturg's main responsibility lies in helping the writer shape script development time at the festival and helping everyone else navigate the play's needs, *especially* when actors pine for specific changes and producers push for certain adjustments. The active dramaturg exists as the writer's greatest ally during these creatively charged events.

The Quick Turnaround: 16-36 Hour Rehearsed Readings

The most common workshop and festival scenarios are the 16-36 hour rehearsed readings. An incredibly low ratio of accepted to submitted scripts are selected for these short workshops, affording the plays and the workshops a level of prestige. But what can a writer or artistic team hope to accomplish in such a short period of time? How can the dramaturg help writers mine the most out of the experience?

The Typical Agenda for the Quick Turnaround

During a 16-36 hour rehearsal process, the cast might read the play two or three times, and follow each read with lengthy discussion about the play or a few significant scenes or moments.

Because the first presentations occur after 8-12 hours of rehearsal, rewrites rarely appear. Instead, writers tend to arrive ready to tweak scenes by adding or cutting a few lines, or exploring a new order. A writer may even ask that new passages be read in the rehearsal hall but not during the presentation. For these short processes, active dramaturgs focus on identifying ways to help the writer hear the play in the rehearsal hall and during the presentation. Two key questions can guide active dramaturgs. First, find out whether this is the play's first workshop and if it isn't, ask what the writer discovered and worked on at the other workshops. Second, ask what the writer wants to concentrate on during this workshop.

Framing the Discussion Following the Quick Turnaround

To help the post-play discussion for these briefly rehearsed readings, an active dramaturg fashions questions that encourage an audience to explore the entire piece rather than specific moments or characters. As little has been reworked during this limited process, steering a conversation toward the hiccups often does little for the writer. But more open questions that encompass the entire world and the play's major themes, engaging moments and success can help the writer further identify what comes across and how that happens. Of course, any dramaturg will ask any specific questions the writer poses.

What might some of those questions be?

One option is to ground questions in themes. For example, a discussion following a play that explores religion or spirituality through a variety of characters might be worded like this: *How or when do characters in this play use various forms of religion and spirituality? How do these choices impact our (an audience's) sense of a specific character or set of characters? What is the role of religion or spirituality for this or these character (s)? If religion does not play a role, does this absence make sense or seem out of place?*

Another option is to ground the question in a specific moment. An active dramaturg might compose a discussion question following a play involving a grave secret like this: *A number of people gasped when the truth was revealed. Were those sounds of surprise? Contentment? Confusion? If this moment worked and satisfied, what moments fell a bit flat but felt as if they should have produced a similar response?*

Playwrights who want to know what worked or what confused an audience are brave, and should be awarded a medal. To facilitate this request, the active dramaturg works to create a context for the question so that the responses will be worded honestly but with care. Following *Liz Lerman's Critical Response Process* can help. But some well-chosen language will go a long way, too. Take care to not defend the play, which may provoke aggressive comments or craft questions that censor the feedback. An active dramaturg's question addressing what works and what did not might be worded like this: *Throughout this brief process, we began to explore a few areas of concern to clarify points of confusion or unclear aspects of the character's journeys. First, what do you consider the play's story and second, were there any moments that confused you or stopped you from following that story?* The active dramaturg takes care when planning this question to avoid telling the audience what the story was. Making such assumptions denies the writer an opportunity to learn what ideas land and how.

Soliciting Audience Responses

Frankly there is no single way to introduce a work-in-progress, except to openly and proudly declare the reading as just that, a presentation of a work that's still in development. Audiences tend to assume perfection; after all, they're watching professional artists at work. Taking time to invite the audience into the creative process reminds them how important their role is, especially with a new work. A few people may choose to snub an invitation to nurture a work by ignoring the ground rules and assailing the writer with derisive comments. When negative comments occur, the moderator or dramaturg needs to step up and defend the process—not necessarily the play—by politely silencing the dissident and encouraging others to address a new question or a previous point without returning to the controversial statements. One reason it's best to consider these discussions opportunities for responses rather than feedback is that a response implies a personal or even factual observation, whereas, feedback suggests an opinionated comment.

What is Success for the Quick Turnaround?

During such a brief collaborative process, everyone's goal is to help the writer hear the play well. Doing so helps the writer identify where the play works and what to explore further.

After the Quick Turnaround

Following such a short process, the artistic relationship may not warrant or support post-workshop communication. Much work should have been done during the rehearsals to establish the questions that may help the writer move forward with the work. However, should the writer request written comments, the active dramaturg should provide them. If a post-reading discussion was held, it is helpful for the dramaturg or director to record the comments (by writing them down or using a digital voice recorder). Ideally, the dramaturg would then transcribe the comments or summarize the comments and provide context by using either the questions from the rehearsal process, creative conversations, or the post-reading discussion. These comments should be emailed to the writer and the director within a week of completing the reading.

Somewhere In Between: The Four to Seven Day Workshop or Festival

During a workshop process that is somewhat short and long, a dramaturg assumes an even more important role. This in-between process begins with the false sense that plenty of time to explore the play and to welcome the writer's many rewrites exists. If no one manages the time, a sudden and rude awakening occurs when everyone realizes how few hours a week actually holds and how little forward progress has been made. Remember, progress doesn't mean pages written, lines cut, or story completed; rather, that the writer has a substantially clearer sense of the play or a strong sense of what the next steps entail and how to go about moving forward. A dramaturg can, as in a 16-36 hour workshop, help the writer listen to the play, but an active dramaturg identifies key areas to explore and establishes goals, and aids in relieving the pressure when a writer realizes certain goals may not be met and maintains the writer's spirits and interest in the play.

From day one of these semi-brief development processes, the entire artistic team should establish a set of writing goals. The limited time supports focused rewrites. A writer may manage a new draft of an entire act if the workshop lasts seven days, but subsequent rewrites during the workshop rarely follow. Why? A seven-day festival residency actually means four days of rehearsal and rewrite time, a day and a half to prepare specifically for the presentation, and two days of readings or presentations, especially if a number of writers have been invited to the workshop.

Again, active dramaturgs ask playwrights what questions or concerns they wish to address and then work to shape those ideas into single-focused observations that the workshop can support. It's always best to create a short list; adding specific goals that can be accomplished, will make the group—and the writer—feel the time has been quite productive.

The Typical Agenda for the Four to Seven Day Workshop

The agendas for these short-but-longer workshops tend to encompass only a few areas: the concentrated rewrite of a scene or act; exploring a specific character's journey; generating an entire act (rare); exploring a possible production question like music and its impact on story; clarifying a specific theme or storytelling motif. A list of goals may touch on a number of these areas and prioritize them, from which can be best supported at this time to the least.

The Concentrated Rewrite

A concentrated rewrite means a writer focuses on a particular scene (or set of scenes), act, or character. Rarely does the artistic team and staff expect the writer to fashion changes throughout the entire work, although minor adjustments throughout may accompany the major change. The writer may also insert new plot points and depend on the director and actors to reveal a sense of whether these ideas work and what new questions these additions raise for individual characters or production needs. In addition, active dramaturgs distill comments and identify the domino effect particular changes may have on the play's entire story and major themes.

Character-Specific Rewrites

These are exactly what they sound like: explorations and adjustments for specific characters in the play. Of course, any changes in a character alter the play's balance, which is why a number of change usually accompany these rewrites. Active dramaturgs play a significant role helping the writer stay on task by formulating specific questions for one or two characters. The active dramaturg can help note other adjustments needed to balance the information included in future rewrites.

Generating an Entire Act

Sometimes a writer comes to a workshop without a second act or an ending to a long one-act. Often then, a writer sets a goal to write that act or find the ending. Sometimes the solutions come about easily. Sometimes, less so. No one but the playwright, neither a director, actor nor dramaturg, can come up with a play's ending. Yes, these artists collaborate with the writer—if the writer supplies them with the ideas or desired effect—to generate scenarios or ideas through improvisation or extended, focused discussions. Often, however, when an ending or act eludes a writer, too little exists to support an appropriate and fruitful conversation. An active dramaturg can engage the writer in conversations to explore certain metaphors, themes, and characters in hopes of discovering what cries out for further exploration and leads to a dramatic and fulfilling end.

For example, consider the imagined Jack and Jill play, which could conclude with either an engagement, marriage, heartfelt goodbye, Jack's untimely death, or the joyous celebration following a rite of passage. Discussing these ideas and how or whether to explore them through improvisations, or developing questions to initiate conversations with the cast, may help the writer eliminate options and select paths to explore after the development process. Everyone benefits from these focused discussions that clarify the play's world and provide the writer with a different way to interact with or relate to the characters and their world.

Exploring a Possible Production Question

Only two types of plays enter a workshop to explore production questions. The first is a very complete, well-developed, clearly written play that is, for all intents and purposes, done. If the play includes interesting effects, either sound or visual, the collaborators may request a week-long workshop to explore how to add these elements and what, if anything, is needed in the script to accommodate these changes. Here, an active dramaturg watches for the ways the production elements elevate, add or distract from the story and consider what's needed to maintain the balance the writer seeks. The second type is a musical at any stage of development. Because of the many writers—lyricist, book writer, and composer—it's important for them to come together frequently, especially if they do not live near one another. They may simply need time to focus on the piece together. An active dramaturg helps the team focus on specific areas to address, perhaps after the workshop concludes. Yes, that's right—sometimes the active dramaturg watches and learns the piece and wants to offer questions and comments only near the end of a workshop.

Clarifying a Specific Theme or Aspect of Storytelling

This is a lot like focusing on a specific character's entire journey, except revising a theme involves a multitude of characters and dramatic scenarios. The active dramaturg offers questions and observations designed to isolate why certain ideas are clear and others, less so.

Occasionally, a writer will surprise everyone and manage to rewrite an entire play and rework specific scenes numerous times; this is rare and not something to shoot for. Why? Burnout is one reason. If the new pages are particularly weak the realization will negatively impact everyone's perception of the writer. And so, the active dramaturg works to create goals designed to avoid exhausting the writer and establishes, in collaboration with the writer, an outline the writer can return to repeatedly during the process and after the festival concludes.

Fashioning Discussion Questions for the Four to Seven Day Workshop

Unlike the longer residencies, the four to seven day workshops often conclude with a dramaturg-moderated talkback or discussion between the writer and audience. Even if a festival moderator exists, each dramaturg works with the artistic team to prepare appropriate questions for the audience to consider. Inevitably the questions refer to the areas the writer concentrated on during the workshop. On the one hand, this makes focusing the discussion easier. On the other hand, without careful consideration such specific and targeted adjustments can lead to questions that solicit biased rather than honest responses. This happens most often when the questions appear in surveys or program inserts that the audience reads before the presentation begins.

If, for example, the writer wants to know whether the audience knew to follow a particular character in Act Two, and this question appears in the program, the audience immediately begins to follow the character in Act Two. The questionnaire's rather pointed phrasing makes an impartial assessment impossible. The same is true for a question that asks an audience to voice (or write) their impressions of a specific character. Again, the wording directs the audience to focus on one character to the exclusion of all others. An active dramaturg looks to pose a fairer, more open question, and asks the audience to note whose story (or stories) they followed throughout the play or during each act. It's possible to go further by encouraging the audience to consider whether their allegiance or interest changes after intermission or at another specific moment. Asking patrons to identify the specific moment and how their perceptions changed might also aid the writer.

When the rewrites are too fresh to warrant commentary, the writer and dramaturg should look for other ways to focus the questions, especially if the institution actively encourages a talkback. One option is to ask obvious, general questions like: *What ideas did you take away from this story?* or *Which character did you connect with most and why?* These questions seek a patron's response, that is, insight into where or how the play impacts a viewer on a personal level that cannot be argued against; they do not seek analytical comments. Of course, knowing that a patron likes aspects of the play can and does encourage any artist during the darkest times. A discussion proves most successful or helpful when audiences can identify when they connected with the story and then when, if ever, they dropped out and why. This leads to the second possible softball question: *Did your attention ever waiver and if so, when?*

Even with these open and easy questions, the talkback can veer into dangerous territory, with audiences commenting on new scenes or the play's untouched, troubled sections. The active dramaturg circumvents these comments without defending the play or skewing people's perceptions by kindly reminding the audience that some sections are so new the writer and artistic team would like to wait before discussing them.

What is Success for the Four to Seven Day Workshop?

Numerous pages with new scenes or lines do not necessarily signify a successful process. Sometimes generating zero pages indicates success, especially if the writer leaves with a better sense of what the play wants and how to tell that story. In the end, success means serving the writer's process and strengthening his or her vision of the play.

After the Four to Seven Day Workshop

To ensure that the play's voice will continue to strengthen, the active dramaturg works with the writer to craft the major questions or ideas and commit them to paper so that the writer can resume work where the workshop ended. This outline or list of questions takes some time to generate, as it addresses major and minor areas of concern. The major areas are: how the acts flow or build or character journeys evolve, and how these two structural elements impact and shape one another. Minor areas to address often involve the general use of language, imagery and metaphor. The active dramaturg infuses these notes with personality and the energy of the rehearsal or reading, and avoids crafting dry, academic musings. The notes needn't be long. The writer has plenty to process. Whether through email or written notes following the wrap-up conversation active dramaturgs take the step to facilitate the writer's process beyond the residency.

Artistic Feedback for the Four to Seven Day Workshop

Short-but-long workshops often include feedback sessions with the institution's artistic and management staff. At times, the artistic staff solicits comments regarding the writer's work process and goals (and perhaps even audience responses) from the dramaturg a short time after the festival. A writer may be called for a conversation and asked to provide similar feedback on the dramaturg and director as well. The active dramaturg makes every effort to communicate with the writer after the festival and may even volunteer to read subsequent drafts. Because theatre depends upon close relationships, it's important for active dramaturgs to solidify their connection to the play and writer during these festivals by exercising good manners and common courtesies. Even if the relationship was a rocky one, a letter that extols the progress and, if necessary, includes an apology can go a long way.

The Long-Term Residency: Eight Days or More

Although these are the lengthiest, and in many cases, the most prized new-play development retreats (Sundance's Theatre Lab and The Eugene O'Neill Playwright Center's workshops are two of the best-known long residency workshops), don't let a 14 to 28-day writing schedule suggest complacency. The time passes quickly and the writer's creative demands require the entire artistic staff to remain focused and diligent. More important, without a plan the retreat's length can work against the artists who choose to avoid setting daily or weekly goals.

The Typical Agenda for the Long-Term Residency

The producers of longer residencies often provide some structure, such as guaranteed rehearsal time and space either every day or every other day. Whether the writer is on a roll or experiencing writer's block, every effort should be made to hold rehearsal, if only for a few hours. The actors need the time to work on the characters, the director an opportunity to experience the play's world, and the dramaturg a sense of the play's evolving voice and structure. Also, the guaranteed meeting may inspire the writer. The writer might choose not to attend rehearsal during moments of feverish creation, but the artistic team may use some, if not all, of the allotted time.

An Active Dramaturg's Focus During the Long-Term Residency

Whether a dramaturg has one or many projects during a workshop, a number of basic responsibilities exist, namely, to meet and discuss the writer's goals and questions, and to identify the play's strongest moments. Sometimes the goals change each week. Because the writer has many days for exploration, most choose to rewrite or rework the entire play throughout the residency. Of course, some use it as an opportunity to begin a collaborative project or integrate music with text or explore a number of production questions.

When using a residency to prepare for a production, the active dramaturg meets or communicates with the writer for a considerable time before the rehearsal process begins. A similar first meeting should occur days or weeks before the festival or workshop, although it rarely does. However, it's truly important to hold an introductory conversation before a long-term residency. A conference call or a few emails can suffice, but if schedules prevent such conversations, the team should meet in person before rehearsal begins.

Even if the pre-workshop conversation with the director does not happen, an active dramaturg *always* learns what the writer wants to work on and what inspired the play before the workshop begins. After listening to the writer and the reading, the active dramaturg gains a sense of when to ask the other important dramaturgical questions. Learning what concerns the writer has will, as always, determine how the dramaturg can best support the playwright during the development process.

When beginning a long-term residency, the writer may voice general goals like completing an act or exploring scenes that involve certain characters. The active dramaturg works to support these broad goals by identifying key questions to focus the conversations and rewrites throughout the weeks-long workshop. Sometimes a writer may wait to hear the actors read the play before determining a plan of action. The director and dramaturg should respect the wait-and-see attitude. The active dramaturg listens to the post-reading discussion with even more vigilance and makes certain the artistic team meets to discuss the major ideas and questions raised and establish a game plan for the next few days if not the entire workshop.

But how does an active dramaturg focus conversations and ideas quickly?

The short answer: organize responses and observations around a single theme or event. Just as this approach focuses rehearsal notes, it also shapes the new-play development conversation. When the dramaturg can locate the common hiccup in the play's story or logic in a way that makes everything seem related, the problem's perceived magnitude diminishes greatly. This approach also frames the active dramaturg's post-reading discussions with the entire company so that comments facilitate solutions through a single concern. Without such focus—especially within a long-term residency—a writer may attack each hiccup in the play's story individually, spending too much time establishing ground rules for each unclear moment that may lead to opposing solutions. A broad, yet focused approach keeps related issues together and allows the writer (and company) to mine brilliance out of every minute of a workshop. Remember, active dramaturgs seek ways to simplify the path to possible solutions, not by revealing shallow shortcuts, but by offering simpler ways to define, discuss and eventually address the concern.

Setting Goals for the Long-Term Residency

Long-term residencies often demand that the artistic team set specific goals. Although no one knows which idea inspiration will support each day, establishing goals or areas to explore helps the director and the dramaturg organize their respective schedules. A dramaturg assigned to numerous projects rehearsing simultaneously can plan appropriate time to visit the various rehearsals. Similarly, the director can identify areas to work on with the actors so that they will be able to better respond to the changes or adjustments.

These goals, however, avoid prescribing time-oriented tasks like: *Finish act one rewrite by Tuesday.* Active dramaturgs set goals that articulate a prioritized order of concerns that will often impact a large number of problem areas. For example, when I was working on Sarah L. Myers' play *The Realm* at the Bonderman, a two-week residency at the Indiana Repertory Theatre that focuses solely on Theatre for Young Audiences, Myers and I spoke prior to arriving in Indianapolis. During our phone conversation, we established that the play's major theme concerns the idea of choice—what the characters are choosing between and how the story expresses that struggle—and that most of the play's development should revolve around questions this theme provokes. Having identified this overarching idea, any question the actors posed or comments the high school students who studied the play offered was connected to this question. As difficult as the rewriting was, the notes were easier to give and process smoother because of this single filter: *What are the choices in The Realm?* and *What are the rules that govern these choices?*.

So clear was the question and Myers' goal, that identifying which scenes needed to include information regarding choice and its effect was simple. Every rehearsal saw regular changes to a crucial scene and the subsequent moments directly impacted by this single question.

As the workshop for *The Realm* progressed, other challenges emerged, namely how to articulate the male protagonist's (James) diminished capacity for language and his emerging reliance on sound as a language. Again, because of clear goals and using creative, open questions, it was easier for the creative team to find a way to relate the character's situation to the initial goals, the creative 'in' to the logistical problem emerged quite quickly. A character-defining question became: *When does James lose language in relation to losing or recognizing choice?* Yes, the writing took as long as writing takes, but Myers realized what was needed to accomplish rewrites more quickly.

What Is Success During a Long-Term Residency?

Lengthy residencies provide the artistic team many opportunities to hear the play or particular sections read aloud before the director begins to shape the presentation. During these many readings and discussions, the active dramaturg works with the playwright to determine where the story lags or seems unnecessarily long. Often the director encourages the conversations to take place as the company reads, and the active dramaturg joins the company conversation by articulating concerns through the framing questions. Ironically, during long residencies, the temptation for the artistic team and cast to tell a writer how to solve the problem increases. Perhaps it's because the entire artistic team has time to become fully invested in the project.

Again, no one but the playwright writes the play; no one but the writer can cut the text. As obvious as this rule is, many artists break it—especially when the process involves cutting the text for time or story.

There are directors and dramaturgs who play an active role in cutting a script *with* the writer. But neither should propose what a character says or does. In general, however, no one purposefully cuts a writer's work other than the writer. Active dramaturgs try to help the writer see where a scene is too long or when certain points distract or unnecessarily repeat. Even when a producer, managing director, or director demands that the dramaturg reduce a play's running time or cut a particular scene, the active dramaturg reminds everyone that the playwright holds the power. That said, the active dramaturg works to make everyone's concerns known, especially if they improve the play and are in line with the writer and play's wants. But timing is everything. Tact helps, too.

Cutting and certain rewrites cannot happen until the writer has a clear sense of the play and the scene in question. In writing, as in life, clarity happens with distance, and sometimes a residency or workshop situation fosters such renewed connection with a play for the writer creative distance isn't possible. This is also why outside comments and critiques aid in the development process, and why the active dramaturg records these comments and shares them with the writer at various stages during the process. The producer or artistic director's distance allows for insight that may help inform the writer's perception of the play.

Discussion and the Long-Term Residency

Although long-term workshops rarely end with a public discussion, there are usually feedback sessions with invited guests, the institution's artistic staff, or the other resident casts. These discussions provide the writer an opportunity to share thoughts on the process and discoveries made, as well as hear how others responded to the work. The dramaturg rarely moderates these sessions, and it can appear as if the dramaturg plays no significant role in these talks.

Nothing could be further from the truth.

Often a skilled and experienced artistic panel will offer questions and comments that may be tough to hear but are not designed to elicit a defensive response. The goal of these meetings is to grow the play; this may mean identifying venues to submit the script or areas for the team to explore further. An active dramaturg supports the writer and the project by helping everyone prepare for the session, because an active dramaturg helps the team discover ways to avoid defending the play. When this preparatory conversation happens doesn't matter, as long as it's *before* the critique.

In general, try to avoid comments that defend the play by simply and clearly identifying why choices were made. Knowing what informed certain decisions helps the artistic evaluators expand their comments so they too can help the project grow.

After the Long-Term Residency

The dramaturg can also help place the criticism in context following the session, either right away or months later through email. The active dramaturg plays a critical role in keeping the writer motivated and connected to the play, especially by following comments that may question a number of the decisions and choices made during a residency.

What About the Plays That Are Perfect?

It happens.

There are plays that work extremely well and appear as perfect as a drama will be. Perfection may also refer to a play too far along to benefit from a reading. In other words, only a production and its rehearsal and tech process will reveal the solution's to the play's questions. A case in point is Lynn Nottage's *Las Meninas*. When workshopping the story of historical fiction about Queen Marie Thérèse's half-African child, Louise, known throughout France as the Black Nun of Moret, at Crossroads Theatre Company, the artistic team focused on the story's many transitions and how to clarify Louise's movement. In the reading, the narration seemed natural and seamless, but everyone knew that in production these narrative moments could confuse the audience and perhaps stop the action; or worse, make a production feel like a reading. Actors sitting at music stands with some staging could not provide the playwright with the answers to her questions surrounding the structure. Only a production could provide the necessary solutions.

What About the Plays That Are Perfect for a Reading but not for Production?

Without question, this is the number one fear of all artists working in new-play development. Sometimes rewrites answer the narrative questions a reading demands but destroy the story's theatrical lift and mystery. A play's quirks and wrinkles can be excised or smoothed out so well that the play's magic no longer exists. Literary tension exists, but no dramatic tension. The need to verbalize all physical actions in a reading leads to this literary linearity. But, one could argue, once the actors begin to physically embody the language the dramatic energy should return.

Yes and no. Yes, because physical action separates drama from literature. No, because drama thrives on more than movement alone. When plays succumb to the demands of readings, the writing—the dialogue and the stage directions—looks to tell what's happening, to guide the audience to every emotion and action. Dramatic writing, however, remains open to choices by giving the necessary specifics without connecting every dot. It's possible to overwrite a play because during a reading, when actors often stand at music stands looking at the audience rather than at their scene partners, ideas, gestures, and emotions can pass too quickly. And so, to ensure or preempt an audience's confusion, a writer might include unnecessary information. An active dramaturg works with the writer to locate and distinguish between those moments or storytelling facts that need written reinforcement for a reading but not for the production.

A Closer Look at the Talkback or Discussion

Today most dramaturgs who moderate talkbacks or post-play discussions follow Liz Lerman's Critical Response Process exactly or a format loosely based on it. It wasn't always this way.

Before Liz Lerman, a choreographer, founder of the Dance Exchange and MacArthur Fellow, introduced her Critical Response Process, dramaturgs worked like Sisyphus as they recreated ways to fashion a post-play dialogue for each writer or production at each theatre. The results varied. Sometimes, the discussions were successful; other times, opinions replaced questions and patrons began to rewrite the play or flay the production. The result: writers left the conversations damaged and zapped of any desire to continue work on the play.

Also during this time, despite the dramaturg's best efforts, the post-play discussions for set-text productions or new-play readings often centered on the audience's fascination with the actor process or less scintillating questions like, how does one walk on a raked stage, or memorize lines? Every once and a while the discussions soared above mediocrity and allowed audiences to talk with each other or a famous performer about the production, the play and its larger ideas. In most instances, however, an actual conversation involving the thinking surrounding the play or the production occurred in a decidedly haphazard fashion. This is not to say that dramaturgs failed to moderate successful or fascinating discussions. Many succeeded. But the mechanism for recreating a positive and fruitful talkback wasn't considered and the successful techniques did not reach a larger audience.

Everyone created a format from scratch.

The Talkback Pioneers

To help raise the level of post-play discussions for new and classic works, various theatre magazines and industry newsletters printed articles designed to help dramaturgs, actors, and writers craft a successful conversation. David Rush's essay, *Talking Back*, focuses on the discussion for new plays and how to keep the talkback in the writer's control. The essay is based on workshops and conversations Rush held at the American Theatre Educators conferences in 1998 and 1999. Rush lays out key areas for anyone involved in a new-play process talkback to consider from the primary artist's—the playwright's—point of view. Some of Rush's key pointers are: "never ask opinion questions"; "never ask if anyone 'understood' something"; and "make questions open ended and content related." (Rush 57-58) Chief among his recommendations is the importance of including the writer in determining the questions and the guidelines for the discussion. Hard to believe, but there was a time when talkbacks for new plays didn't involve finding out what the writer or artists wanted to discuss. Rush even advocates that the writer craft the questions, moderate the discussion, and establish signals to indicate when the limit's been reached.

A number of essays from *Production Dramaturgy: A Sourcebook* chronicle approaches for running the post-play discussions for set-text productions. Essays by Richard Pettingill, Oscar Brockett, Alan Kennedy, and Michael Bigelow Dixon argue for the dramaturg to shape the discussion with a number of questions that spark conversation among the audience and have the production team point out themes in the play to provoke and propel the debate. The hope is to elevate the conversation and encourage the audience to contemplate the play's ideas, voice, and rules rather than ponder how difficult it is to memorize lines.

The Critical Response Process

What makes the Critical Response Process so amazing is that, with a few adjustments, it works well for both new and, with modifications, set-text productions. Lerman's process, originally created to help shape discussions around her company's dance projects, allows artists and audience to discuss the creative process framed by a six-step process.

The two concerns Lerman addresses with her process are: one, how to allow the artist to control the process; and two, how to help audience members offer helpful responses rather than opinions, judgments, or pronouncements on how to change the piece. Her process allows for specific forms of feedback from viewers and encourages artists to craft and then pose questions to which the audience responds. Best of all, artists remain in control of most of the process. When followed through to the end, the artists have a chance to hear what grabs an audience and, after the questions, process the comments into a few action steps at the end. The Critical Response Process revolutionized the artists' relationship to those who support the development process.

Theatre artists gravitated toward her process even before her 2003 book. Lerman's ideas first appeared in a 1993 essay in *High Performance* titled "Toward a Process for Critical Response."[1] The original process included six steps, and its fifth and sixth do not appear on the Dance Exchange website or the book. The original six steps with brief summaries are:

1. Affirmation: Affirmative responses to the work (words, images, phrases, or moments that impacted an audience member;

2. Artist as Questioner: Questions from the artist to the audience. These questions allow the artist to shape the discussion around specific ideas and solicit pointed responses;

3. Responders Ask the Questions: Questions from the audience to the artist. The audience can now pose a neutral question to the artist. The challenge is that these questions cannot include embedded opinions. In other words, the question cannot reveal the patron's solution or perspective on the questioned topic. Also, the artist may choose to not respond;

4. Opinion Time: At this point, the audience can share opinions regarding certain moments in the work. However, the opinion must be announced and the artist has the right to not respond or to ask that the opinion not be shared;

5. Subject Matter Discussion: An opportunity for the audience and artist to discuss content issues that may not relate to the specific evolution of the piece;

6. Working on the Work. Here the artist can summarize where or how the comments from the discussion may inform the process. Or, the artist can simply state where the project may go without referencing the comments from the discussion;

A number of dramaturgs follow Liz Lerman's process closely, while others use the principles she outlines and adapt them to the playwright's process. The greatest adjustment for theatre is skipping steps five and six. Interestingly, the Dance Exchange website currently lists the Critical Response Process as having four steps, also omitting the original fifth and sixth steps. This change may have been made because many believe that the production is the artistic team's statement and the talkback is

---

1   Lerman, Liz. "Toward a Process for Critical Reponse" *High Performance*, 64.4 (1993) 17-19.

an opportunity to learn how an audience receives those ideas. When the artists pose questions or talk at length about specific choices, they risk defending the production and silencing the audience.

Playwright José Cruz Gonzàlez introduced an additional step to the Critical Response process during the post-play discussions of the 2004 Bonderman new-play festival. His new final step gives audiences a *second* opportunity to share affirmative statements as a way to end the discussion. Returning to the affirmative comments also enables those who were either too shy or simply not yet ready to share their thoughts when given the opportunity to speak up. More important, since writing is so solitary and constructive comments are sometimes difficult to hear (they often indicate more work), why not end on a positive ebullient note that reminds the writer what worked well?

Strict adherence to the Critical Response Process requires considerable training for the moderator and the audience. The basic steps seem simple enough, but comfort in asking neutral questions or sharing an opinion without directing the writer takes time and patience. At times the conversation feels stilted, and when combined with the writer's nervousness, the Critical Response Process can make the talkback a truly unpleasant experience even if the comments are positive. Lerman offers workshops designed to train people in the process to reduce this awkwardness, and has written a book to further describe the process.

A Few More Comments About The Critical Response Process

Oddly enough, asking an audience to share positive responses can often throw them for a loop. When beginning by soliciting affirmative statements, a lengthy pause often ensues. The moderator or dramaturg should not rush to fill the silence. Most erroneously believe that a talkback following a new work means pinpointing what's wrong and how to fix the problem. If it seems important to model what constitutes an affirmative comment or observation, the dramaturg could start the ball rolling with an example of an affirmative comment—but only as a last resort.

For a set-text production, questions often challenge the director's vision rather than explore them, and make the first moments when using the Critical Response Process difficult. And unlike a developing work, the set-text production is often the final step, so the ideas will not evolve further.This will drastically change how the Critical Response steps are framed, for they are geared toward furthering works in progress.

Even so, once the positive comments begin, an audience will want to ask questions.

The dramaturg's challenge for a discussion of a set-text production is to steer artists away from defending artistic/conceptual choices made. To do this the dramaturg can rephrase the patron's question in a way that respects the question but encourages a less defensive response. All questions should be restated by the dramaturg unless microphones are used, and even then it's a good habit to keep, for repeating/rephrasing helps the dramaturg shape the discussion. The dramaturg can also remind the artists participating in the talkback (prior to the talkback) that lengthy speeches designed to explain away confusion or reveal how radical production ideas or design elements evolved before the audience asks aren't necessary. For artists participating in a new-play discussion, dramaturgs can remind the writer that repeatedly stating how new the piece is may make an audience feel less welcome to respond. It isn't that this information shouldn't be shared—it should—but it's all about how and when.

Determining Who Participates in the Post-Play Discussions

For set-text productions, talkbacks often occur well into the run, and the director and actors may choose not to participate. The dramaturg must then represent the artistic vision *and* moderate the discussion. For new plays, the dramaturg rarely fields questions alone. On occasion, however, the writer wants to hear comments but doesn't wish to be onstage. Whatever the scenario, the active dramaturg works to craft the questions from the artists with open language that invites honest responses from the audience. As the questions address specific areas or the other artists respond, the active dramaturg may also add comments.

Whether moderating a discussion for a set text or new play, the active dramaturg comes prepared with open questions to fill the gaps when the conversation lulls. These back-pocket questions can be as general as: *What ideas did you take away?* or *How did you feel at the play's end?* Or, the active dramaturg may pose more specific questions that focus on the production and interpretation, such as asking an audience to consider certain design elements in relation to the play's themes or metaphors, to keep the conversation lively and exciting.

Possibly Misleading Discussion Questions and How to Reshape Them

Since a set-text production rarely involves changing the text (the greatest exception is Shakespeare's work), the questions that can provoke defensive responses center on the thought process that leads to specific artistic decisions. A common question might be: *What was the director's thought behind a particular production decision, such as eliminating a scene?* Clearly the patron wants to know what creative process fueled a decision, but the question could sound like a challenge to the director's artistry rather than a basic inquiry. To keep the discussion on an even keel, the active dramaturg rephrases the question so that it encourages the artists to share their process. The question might become: *What inspired or led to a particular production decision?* or *What was the process that led to cutting the scene?*

Related to the above question is: *What statement is an artist making with a particular choice?* Here again, the patron voices a desire to know what political agenda or ethical construct drives an artist's creative process. If left unframed, the discussion could unravel into a debate that fuels individual agendas, provides patrons and artists with soapboxes, and does little to serve the theatre's desire (and perhaps mission) to engage audiences and artists with vigorous and respectful intellectual and artistic conversation. A few options exist to help redirect the comment. When rephrasing a comment, there is no need to adopt a schooling or pointed tone, simply restate it as if doing so further clarifies the question, which is one of the moderator's responsibilities. One option the active dramaturg might choose is to pose the question to the patron and ask: *What message did you receive from the play?* or *What ideas resonated and how do those observations impact your views?* Another option may be to ask the artists: *What themes attracted or fueled your creative process?* The responses may encourage the artists to share more.

On occasion, a patron raises an issue that calls the theatre's artistic decision-making process into question. Although the words vary, this adversarial questioner asks: *What statement is the theatre making by presenting this play?* Frankly, this question reveals a patron's desire to voice an opinion rather than engage in a dialogue. If the dramaturg is a freelance artist and other members of the theatre staff are present, an attempt to have them answer should be made. If the dramaturg is a full-time employee of the theatre or representing the theatre at the time, she should answer. To transform the situation, the active dramaturg might ask whether something about the play came across as upsetting. Also, trying to identify what the patron actually saw or responded to will help redirect the conversation. The greatest challenge in this instance, however, is to limit the patron's participation. Repeated comments can inflame rather than temper the situation, so active dramaturgs remain ready to thank the patron for the thoughts and quickly move on by fielding another question or posing one.

Provocative Audience Questions and How to Frame Them

A question that could encourage a playwright's or actor's defensive answer is when a patron asks: *Why did a character do something?* or *Why did a particular plot twist occur?* The patron rarely intends to offend, and the query's brusqueness often masks the genuine concern or confusion. An active dramaturg works to transform the bold question into one that the artist may want to answer by connecting it to the creative discussions in the rehearsal hall, either requesting the patron to describe the impetus for the question, or rephrasing the patron's question.

To return opinion-laden questions like: *Why did a character do something?* or *Why did a particular plot twist occur?* to the patron, an active dramaturg might ask: *What was it about this character's act that surprised you?* or *What was it about this moment that surprised you?*.

Asking the patron what he thinks a character should do or what he thought should happen opens the door to someone else writing the play. If, however, the writer asks the question, let the conversation roll. If the work is incomplete or the writer hasn't yet settled on a story point, consider posing the question: *What do/did you expect to happen next?* Avoid *What do you want to happen next?*, because an audience may want a happy ending although it's clear to everyone that the choice would not serve the story. These open questions make it possible for the writer or the active dramaturg to further the dialogue with 'whys' to uncover what fuels the audience's expectations. The active dramaturg leads the audience to identify specific moments to frame what cause leads to possible effect.

Another possibly defensive question is: *Why did you write this play?* To replace this awkward question, refocus the attention on the development process and simply adjust it to the open question posed to the writer during the first meeting: *What draws you to this story?*

Fielding Inappropriate Questions

At times, young-looking writers will get questions like: *How old are you?* or, writers choosing to dramatize the story of someone outside their ethnicity may be asked: *What do you know of this particular situation?* Sometimes the audience will rise in revolt to support the writer; at other times, the shock over the questioner's brashness will render everyone silent. The active dramaturg has the challenge of mitigating the damage and rephrasing the question into an appropriate inquiry.

Tackling the Question of Appropriateness

As always, answering these challenging questions head-on may inflame the situation further. To ask the patron: *Why are you concerned by age?* or *How can we limit the scope of anyone's creativity?* is not only rude, but limits the dialogue to two, maybe three people—the dramaturg, the writer and the questioner. Worse still, a direct response to a question concerning artistic freedom runs the real risk of sounding like lecture. And what if the patron merely worded the question poorly rather than crafted a purposefully offensive statement?

What to do?

One option is to begin by admitting how awkward the question is. For example, stating that a writer may appear young, but youth brings a unique perspective to historical events, which makes it possible to draw and present unexpected parallels and insights. The active dramaturg offers rephrased questions that encourage a writer's response without challenging the writer's right to create and imagine. The new question might be: *Yes, the writer looks young and this youth provides a perspective that makes it possible to see the impact of two eras (if the play deals with the past) or historical figures on one another. What ideas did you set out to explore and what discoveries did you make along the way?*

Another approach is to address the underlying issue at hand through a different lens. If the question implies the writer's ethnicity, gender, religion or sexual orientation prevents a realistic or non-stereotypical depiction of particular characters or scenarios, it's important to discover the root of the concern. A questioner who believes that a writer must, for example, be male to write male characters can be reminded that many male writers have written fabulous female characters. If, however, the patron's question suggests that certain depictions come across as inappropriate or offensive, those concerns are serious and must be addressed through further probing.

The defensive approach to the appropriateness question is to articulate everything the artistic team or writer has done to provide truthful and genuine creative access to the character. This response sounds like pandering; it suggests it's possible to know a culture, ethnicity, or sexual experience by reading about it in a book or holding an interview or two. The defensive response assumes that the artist took these steps but fails to hear or accept that something prevents an accurate picture from appearing on stage. An active dramaturg asks the audience what strikes them as untrue or disingenuous. Care must be taken to solicit only the facts and avoid inflamed comments fueled by negative passions. Then, if the writer is willing, try to pinpoint why this happened. Simply listen to the comments. It may be that the character depictions aren't off but the dramatic build wasn't clear and therefore the character's action appeared manufactured and led to stereotypical representation. It is also possible that a writer's approach purposefully inflames the audience. But if the audience reacts so violently that it tunes out, the artists need to know this, and the writer must shape this emotional journey in future drafts. An active dramaturg might rephrase the appropriateness question and help this situation with: *What specifically about this character or event gives the sense that this is unrealistic?* or, *When did you begin to feel this way and did you ever not feel this way?*

As unnerving as some post-play discussions can be, when an active dramaturg enters the discussion seeking ways to use open questions to engage the audience in a conversation, those challenging questions can lead to a deeper understanding of the play for both parties, and the conversation can unfold in a pleasant, if not fun way.

Post-Play Discussions With Young Audiences

Discussions for young people needn't unfold much differently, however they often do because these audiences (elementary, middle, or high school students) are learning how to engage in critical thinking and then transform these thoughts into responses.

In general, young people display a level of exuberance for theatre that every artist would like to bottle and offer to every adult. Young audiences identify with either the characters or the play's emotional energy and tensions immediately and fully. This makes it easy to solicit positive comments about character choices and particular dramatic moments. Remember, however, that pre-K and elementary students rarely separate the actors from the characters, which leads the students to ask questions of the characters and articulate themes through character and action only, but their interest is as genuine as the older student who has learned to separate actors from fictitious characters.

As young people mature, they begin to ask questions that lead them to understand why characters take certain actions. Dramaturgs and those who moderate these discussions with young audiences can help shape the next generation into excellent theatre-goers and participants in the development process. Sometimes it's as easy as encouraging them to identify the moments that lead to certain decisions or twists in the story. Sometimes it's more difficult because the questions active dramaturgs pose require the students to consider *why* the characters make choices by ignoring the play's ending.

For most talkbacks with young audiences, the conversation is a brief, perfunctory exercise, but playwright Laurie Brooks initiated a major change in TYA dramatic form with her Forums. Brooks created a new type of talkback—the Forum—to conclude the action and help young audiences develop their critical reasoning skills. The Forum, which first appeared as part of her play *The Wrestling Season*, allows student audiences to shape the why behind character's choice and action. Brooks found an active way to introduce ambiguity into her audience's sense of the world and mature, healthy ways to exert some control or order in the chaotic world of teen spirit. She continues to explore ways to apply this technique to set-text plays for adults and young people.

Final Thoughts

New-play development is anything but fast. There are plays that go through one workshop and then enter rehearsal for a production, while others languish in development and never see a production. The reality is that workshops are where research and development for future work occurs. In theatre, as with any business that engages in research and development, there are numerous projects that do not go forward. Among those realized projects, even fewer manage to wow the public and achieve any real success or place in history.

Success during a workshop then is relative. Sure, an audience, producer, or institution that embraces new work invigorates the spirit and validates the work, but as with most theatrical art, the mark of success is in the process: a renewed sense of connection with the play and the new artistic relationships. An active dramaturg works to help everyone involved hear the play and its questions from a variety of perspectives. In doing this, the active dramaturg presents options, not definitive solutions.

The active dramaturg must also state with clarity and sometimes great emphasis what doesn't work. These comments, no matter how tactfully delivered, run the risk of overwhelming, even devastating a writer. Any created work is personal and, as such, any comment on a work can be taken as a personal attack. If a moment doesn't work or fails to impress, it's possible for the creator to think, "what about me falls short?" In addition, rewriting or revising demands new thinking and discovering ways to reconnect with the initial inspiration. The hope is that the active dramaturg's open questions and open listening separate critique from personal attack. Sometimes, however, that cannot happen because the writer's tool bag is somewhat incomplete or the answers aren't yet ready to be discovered.

Dramaturgs should remember that their role in new-play development workshops isn't to teach writing; nor is a workshop a playwriting seminar. An active dramaturg provides a path, shares insights and shares solutions other writers have found to similar challanges, to aid in explaining an idea or opening the creative floodgates. New-play festivals and workshops provide excellent places to grow and strengthen artistic skills, but the speed at which ideas come about and the work demanded make each a place not fit for everyone.

Finally, active dramaturgs avoid judging a writer's progress and encourage the writer to avoid doing so as well. Producers might become afraid that the play hasn't moved forward quickly enough—that's their job. Dramaturgs and the other artists involved in the process, however, work to keep the writer inspired to create during the workshop and well after it ends. Because the truth is, creativity doesn't come on a schedule. If, however, the right questions have been posed using a vocabulary that serves that particular writer and play, the writer will achieve a strong rewrite, perhaps two days or two months after the workshop. With this approach, the active dramaturg eases the tension and chaos of a new-play workshop and collaborates with the writer to help the play evolve more quickly than the writer might have achieved alone.

Chapter 9

Capturing The Vision: Program Notes, Newsletter Essays, and Study Guides

Once the curtain falls on the final performance, what remains? Some photographs, an archival recording, an audience member's memories, the play itself, a review or two, and the active dramaturg's essays and writings that articulate the artistic process. Ironically, the artist most associated with the intangible artistic efforts chronicles the production's artistic vision via a most tangible and permanent means: writing.

Whether the articles and essays appear on the college department websites or in the theatre's subscriber newsletter, literary journal, playbill, or website, this is where the creative record for the production lives. Yes, newspaper reviews and feature articles exist, but these detail the actors' or audience's experience and respond to ideas that succeeded, failed, or lived somewhere in the middle. The newsletter articles and program notes—which the dramaturg often writes—provide the best insight into playwright, director, and the production's goals and vision.

The Dramaturg as Chronicler

When deciding on content for newsletters and online copy, active dramaturgs collaborate with a number of people on the theatre's staff, chief among them the marketing director, who often oversees the publications that generate interest that directly translates into ticket sales. In some instances the marketing director even assigns the newsletter articles. Such a structure may lead to creative tensions as the marketing director and dramaturg have two seemingly conflicting ways to realize their responsibilities. The marketing director has a vision for promotion and what audiences need to know to purchase tickets, and the dramaturg has a strong connection to the production and a sense of what information will provide insight into this artistic team's creative vision. The dramaturg is often responsible for writing, editing, and managing these pieces. To avoid a fractious relationship, both would do well to remember that everyone wants the same thing: people in the seats who appreciate what's on stage.

At the heart of all good communication lies a clear articulation of goals. Active dramaturgs spend considerable time developing a shared language and vision with the director, playwright, and designers; however, the collaboration with marketing directors rarely involves a vocabulary vision-building conversation. In fact, just as the marketing director learns about the season of plays after the artistic department has deliberated at length but before a final season determined, the dramaturg may learn about a newsletter's focus or connection to the advertising campaign late in the process. Although neither the artistic nor marketing office actively seeks to keep the other in the dark, the need to proceed on different schedules and attend to different agendas can place them in minor opposition.

An active dramaturg works to minimize the conflict between the departments by keeping the marketing office abreast of possible plays with synopses and casual conversations, and regularly offers ideas for newsletter and marketing campaigns. Once the season has been selected, design for the newsletter and other promotional materials begins. Just as when meeting with the director or playwright, the active dramaturg brings ideas to discuss with the marketing director, ready to listen but prepared with suggestions and observations about the play.

The Newsletter or Website Copy

In general, the newsletter[1] or online content introduces the production and artistic vision to the theatre's subscribers, donors, and potential patrons. The articles provide a behind-the-scenes look into the production and rehearsal process, allowing an audience to better appreciate the work. Just as a dramaturg cannot guarantee a positive response from a critic, the writing done for the newsletter or online content (for example, rehearsal blogs) should not purport to defend artistic choices nor guarantee a sold-out run. Even if the dramaturgy office has full editorial control over the literary pages in the newsletter, it's good form to share the ideas and articles with the theatre's staff and marketing director because good ideas

---

1   The term 'newsletter' refers to any background information or collection of articles published online or in print by the producing organization.

come from everywhere, and a sponsor or longtime subscriber might be able to add to an article.

The active dramaturg composes articles that share information to increase a patron's level of appreciation or inspire contemplation, be it of politics, society, language, history, or the significance of art in one's life. Whatever the response, the articles or blogs needn't achieve success through academic writing.

So what do strong newsletter articles and essays cover?

What Newsletters Cover

The general answer is the entire production; the more specific answer, key aspects of the artistic process. Some newsletters reflect the common misconception that background information is synonymous with historical research, which leads to a number of articles focusing on the writer, the play's production history, previous critical responses and, if appropriate, how the play contributed to the evolution of American or world drama. The urge to provide historical background for all productions, even those of new plays or world premieres, forces the articles to cover the same ground, inadvertently sapping the life out of the play, publication, and the audience's enthusiasm. Variety is the spice of life and the key to a balanced magazine, newsletter, website, blog, or social networking site.

Active dramaturgs focus on balancing historical essays or information with the artistic team's vision to allow an audience to enter a theatre with framed questions or ideas that forge a connection to the play's themes, creating an excitement for the production. By reducing the paralyzing fear of not-knowing and replacing it with ways to appreciate dramatic mystery—especially for a new work—the active dramaturg can generate an appropriate level of wonder and curiosity (and perhaps increase ticket sales). When an audience has a sense of what informs the production or play and why, applying these topics to the play becomes the lead question as the curtain rises and fodder for the discussion when the curtain falls.

A balanced newsletter includes all aspects of the production. Each issue will not have something from each designer—nor should it—but when preparing for a meeting with the marketing and artistic director, an active dramaturg considers all aspects of the production and presents the strongest ideas at the editorial meeting. There may be more of a sense of pitching rather than offering questions, but the pitch should address a few key questions:

- How will this article excite an audience?

- Will it reveal a technical or artistic innovation?
- Will it generate curiosity and mystery?
- Will it give the audience something to be proud of? (for example, is the production a world premiere or will a well-known talent work with the theatre?)
- Does this article appeal to a visual or aural theatre-goer?
- Will it address a visual design element?
- Will it address language or sound design?
- Does this article reveal a good secret?
- Will it share how effects are built or achieved?
- Will it share information only those in the field might know?
- Will it provide insight into the creative process?
- Does this article set up a way to better appreciate the play's twist or dramatic secret without giving it away?
- Does the article introduce an artist?
- And the most important editorial question: Do the newsletter articles complement each other and avoid repeating ideas or introducing secrets neither the director nor writer want revealed?

Using these questions to shape the collaborative conversation with the marketing director can help create a dynamic publication and demonstrate the dramaturg's interest to actively contribute to the theatre's promotional efforts, thereby narrowing the gap between each office. Even so, the dramaturg's essays and articles will ground themselves in facts and adopt a quieter tone, less "buy now!" and more "consider this" or "did you know?" to elevate the publication and present the theatre as a balanced artistic institution that respects rather than panders to its audience.

What to Consider When Writing a Newsletter Article

Newsletter articles and essays introduce the artistic vision and information related to the production. For example an essay might isolate aspects of the play's elements and show how they connect to the set design. The balance of essays or interviews also establishes a context for the play that leads the reader to consider how the play's ideas and themes translate in today's society.

What tone or style to consider?

A Question of Style and Tone

Each theatre's newsletter has a unique style which dictates sentence structure and vocabulary. Because newsletters appeal to a general readership, they tend to follow the basic rules governing newspapers or magazine writing. The question is, does the theatre define its readership as *US Weekly*, *USA Today* or *Time* audience or one who reads *The New York Times*, *The Wall Street Journal* or *The New Yorker*?

Given most dramaturgs' developed critical thinking and writing skills, the transition to certain magazine styles may be difficult. Numerous writing and style manuals exist to help negotiate that shift, but one way active dramaturgs can begin to retune their writing is to position the ideas as exciting news to share. Rather than reporting information or lecturing, active dramaturgs write to introduce ideas or information and bring the audience to a new place. When sharing ideas, the lecturing tone disappears because the motivation is to bring about a way to discover some new understanding rather than explain something into clarity.

Broaching ideas through a mindset of sharing also presents fewer opportunities for assumptions to exist. To share well, introduce ideas and ground them in order to present a unique perspective. True, this is a hallmark of all good writing, but introducing ideas to argue rather than present a thesis can often lead to arch language and a somewhat pedantic tone, which is too off-putting for a subscriber newsletter.

The Focus of the Literary Journal

A theatre-published literary journal includes essays closely related to the program note in style if not tone. These articles seek to identify and delve deeply into a number of the play's central questions for a patron's consideration. Because these essays must also prepare an audience for an entire season in advance, it's not unusual for the articles to exhibit a more scholarly tone and scope.

A literary-focused publication can support a somewhat more traditional scholarly approach, because a higher expectation of familiarity with the dramatic art or theatre field may exist. As such, the vocabulary and tone for these literary journals will change as will the nature of the articles. For example, the publication may restrict its content only to essays on illuminating ideas, innovations, or nuances of the play. If production values or design do enter the picture, they are often explored through an analytical or historical (past production) perspective, as these literary-journal-like newsletters often go to press before a single design meeting takes place.

The Program Note

Although a marketing director may assign newsletter articles and literary essays, or need the articles to connect to the marketing campaign, a program note is neither under the marketing director's purview nor connected to the promotional campaign. The program note, often a brief but pithy 500-1000 word essay (perhaps longer if published online), is the one creation of which a dramaturg has almost total control. Almost, because the dramaturg does share the ideas and final product with the director and artistic director and, if it's a new play, the playwright. The essay's content, however, lies completely with the dramaturg. The program note is akin to a dramaturg's set or costume design. As such, it should connect to the play and the director's vision, but, like a design, the program note enhances the production in unique ways that demonstrate the designer's artistry.

What does the program note do?

The program note neither defends the production nor explains it; its purpose is to encourage ways to think about the play's ideas and images revealing the work's immediacy and connections to a broader social context.

The challenge to writing a program note lies in finding ways to address ideas that can be read and appreciated at three key times: before the curtain rises, during intermission, or after the curtain falls. The dramaturg's note needs to engage with the production at any point without spoiling plot twists, performances or the play's final moment. The program note is an exercise in general but specific thinking and writing: general because the writing needs to have a wide and far reach; specific, in that the writing examines particular points and magnifies them in relation to the play and production.

Grounding the Program Note

To focus the program note, the active dramaturg usually explores at least one of the play's three critical elements: theme, metaphor, or language. The advantage these critical elements present to a dramaturg is an ability to help the essay connect to the larger society. Of course program notes can and do explore character and time, but these discussions often lead to comments on individual performances rather than the entire production or the play's explorations. The impact of a character-specific approach can spoil the theatrical experience or impede the essay's ability to stand on its own and address the reader who has yet to see the show. Similarly, essays on time or form/pattern run the risk of explaining or lecturing on how these critical elements direct the company's choices, again running the risk of removing a lot of the dramatic surprise. Time and form/pattern certainly can be written about in full measure, but the more common topics remain theme, metaphor and language.

Grounding the Program Note in Themes

As when discussing themes with a director, designer, or playwright, a program note avoids articulating a definitive take on a theme or how it should impact a patron. The goal of the thematic-based essay is to identify how ideas connect to, illuminate, and extend a specific dramatic theme. The dramaturgical essay explores thematic ideas in a wholly new context to provide insight and ways to connect the play to the larger world or a more personal sphere.

Take, for example, Sarah Ruhl's *Eurydice*, a modern adaptation of the timeless love between Orpheus the flute player and his beautiful bride. When we premiered this play at Madison Repertory Theatre in Madison, Wisconsin, the temptation may have been to praise the author and explain her innovations to the story, but this would have the effect of defending the play. To discuss *Eurydice* by introducing Ruhl's plot twists would drastically reduce the play's dramatic tension and mystery. But the play's other focus, the impact of family devotion on individuals and their behavior, presents fodder for a powerful essay. A dramaturg can choose to directly or obliquely mention the responsibilities family exerts on its members, clueing the audience in to the fact that this inevitable relationship either grounds the play's action or provides the invisible boundaries characters inadvertently brush up against throughout the drama. An active dramaturg acknowledges that while the essay supports and furthers the ideas on the page and the stage, it doesn't seek to explain them into sounding mundane.

A poor example of a program note for *Eurydice* might begin like this:

> It's been written about for ages, the undying love men have for women. Men like Sir Lancelot may hide their love but devote themselves to their Guineveres; the Paolos furiously pursue their Francescas, and men like Orpheus risk everything for their Eurydices. But the writers of these tales, all

men, ignore the story's distaff side for, one imagines, a more potent example of pursuit and ardent love. Sarah Ruhl's contemporary revision of the Greek myth *Eurydice* follows the silent female and reveals a magical world that is fueled by loves stronger and at times more violent than those narratives ruled by men.

Ruhl's *Eurydice* begins as the Greek tale does, with Eurydice's death following the joyous marriage to Orpheus. Ruhl does little to suggest Orpheus is anything but a boy, and although this Eurydice is young, she is somehow more mature. She's able to resist the odd temptations of the mysterious male stranger, who we later learn rules the underworld with an impish glee tempered only slightly by a boyish immaturity.

But these men, Orpheus and the Mysterious Stranger (a bit like the god Hades), are devoted to Eurydice. They may not know who she really is or care to discover any of her personal truths other than those a tour of her physical being would reveal. These are the men literary history suggests we should root for because, well, they're the only men in the story who lust after her. Ruhl turns this expected behavior on its head by adding another male, one who knows and loves Eurydice the person in all of her phases: infant, girl, woman.

In this modern *Eurydice* we meet the heroine's father who, ever the iconoclast, violates all of the underworld's rules—the greatest being an unwillingness to wash himself in the River Styx to forget language and his connection to the land of the living. Because he holds on to the past, he can reintroduce his daughter to the ways of the world by teaching her to read, write, think and speak all over again. In doing this, Ruhl reminds us that a parent is a parent at any stage, willing to repeat anything if it means their child will have a better chance. And it is only when she truly leaves her father, to begin her life as a bride, that he relinquishes his bond and parental duties to be ready to teach his daughter, which is why he chooses to finally bathe himself in the river and forget language, parenthood and a father's love.

Such devotion, such deep love rarely finds its way into these timeless love stories. This modern adaptation makes us wonder why, since, as Ruhl shows us, this is the truest love;

the purest love able to survive the rigors in the land of the living dead.

This note fails on many levels. Aside from revealing too much plot and including the play's penultimate tragic moment, the essay continuously tells us what the playwright thinks and how the reader should respond to these images and ideas. Style aside, the tone veers quite close to an academic lecture rather than a tone that shares and invites a reader into a dramatic world.

To explore the play's relationships the dramaturg may reveal some plot or a few aspects of performance. For example, it's important to know that Eurydice dies and that she encounters key figures from her past. Because this play is an adaptation of a well-known Greek myth, it's even permissible to reveal the original's ending, especially because Ruhl imagines a new one. However, the active dramaturg takes care when writing about the original story, for there is always someone who comes to the tale for the first time. It isn't that a dramaturg should avoid describing a Greek myth, but simply exercise care when assuming every patron knows the original. An active dramaturg's program note for *Eurydice* might begin something like this:

> Certain stories resist the urge to pass into oblivion. It isn't tales of love or heroism that last, but rather tales of specific people caught in certain situations defined by emotions or acts of courage that become fixtures in the literary canon. Scheherazade's bravery and brilliant imagination will only continue to grow over time, just as Orpheus' undying devotion to his new bride will never fade. But it is Orpheus' dedication to Eurydice, his willingness to risk all to realize a life with her, a life the gods saw fit to end just as it began, that has distracted us for millennia. In most adaptations of the ill-fated love, writers, composers, and poets focus on Orpheus' journey into melancholy and then to Hades. Eurydice, the woman whose name serves as the title for the myth and scores of work it inspired, remains a silent witness to a man's brave or foolish act, depending on your thoughts on love and man's ability to cheat death. Sarah Ruhl turns the tables on us with her new adaptation, leaving Orpheus to blubber and fend for himself among the living in order to follow Eurydice's travels to the world of the living dead. Here, in a world where earthly memories and language normally disappear upon entry, Eurydice encoun-

ters those from her past who preceded her in both life and death, including her father.

Throughout the essay, active dramaturgs look for ways to discuss the 'how' of the theme. How does the theme control or impact the emotional environment? How do the themes shape performance or life decisions? To articulate how demands descriptive language that attempts to distill an emotional response to tangible ideas, something the active dramaturg works to do throughout the pre-production and rehearsal process as well. The program note might continue as follows:

> In chronicling Eurydice's time between death and near resurrection, Ruhl takes us through the ages of man (or woman) as Eurydice's father introduces her to the ways of living death. Each touching act is governed by the unselfish love defined by parental devotion. So different is this love and dedication; it is slow, gentle, and kind, ruled by a passion deeper and more still than that of a lover or husband. Both Father and Orpheus demonstrate a willingness to risk all for Eurydice, but it's in how they pursue their goals that we see the difference between a father's and a husband's love.

> Another difference in this modern tale of love and loss: we're allowed to see Eurydice's struggle. She who has been voiceless for so long now has a voice, perhaps not one we expect, but an ability nevertheless to express thoughts and to discern the level of consequence her actions have, and the actions of those around her. It is this strength of character that enables this Eurydice to do more than simply fade away at the hand of someone else's act.

If appropriate, active dramaturgs use specific characters and themes to introduce other literary works or actual events that take a more extreme approach. This may help avoid ruining surprises or setting the play or production up for inappropriate comparisons. If done with care, these discussions will connect the play to the larger society without revealing too much story. For example:

> This Eurydice learns independence and self-determination in spite of a veil of secrecy. Granted, the secrets are not as sordid as those in Poe's *Fall of the House of Usher* or as murderous as those in *The Telltale Heart*, but somewhere at the

core is a level of unrest that haunts this *Eurydice*, lending an air of caution rather than pathos to the play. Where will acts of free will take her in a land that prizes prescribed behavior? And what happens when the lords of all are disobeyed? In the *Fall of the House of Usher* decay, insanity, and death are the righteous recompense for failing to honor life's codes of conduct; simply insanity for the unclean heart. But Eurydice hasn't defiled her family nor murdered her neighbor, although her behavior throughout brings the same level of scorn from those who inhabit the land of the dead.

There are, however, those who are willing to save her from her fate, whatever that may be. Orpheus, her father, and a devilish character whose attraction to Eurydice makes us think of Persephone, a girl who escapes the confines of death for six months each year. And so we have hope for this Eurydice. She can escape having to repeatedly learn how to live fully, a fate worse than death, if only for a few months if she capitulates to an imp's will. An odd bit of humor even Poe chose to avoid, but the irreverent touch reminds us why certain literary figures have remained creative fodder for so many years.

When writing program notes, the active dramaturg works to write what is. The approach closely resembles the techniques used for art history or other criticism of live performances. Dramaturgical essays differ from performance theory or performance studies writing, for the program notes focus exclusively on the active descriptions of what takes place. The direct exploration for how a play impacts an audience, or its many levels of anthropological references, rarely has a place in a dramaturgical essay; in part because space is so small (500-1000 words) but also because these approaches provide a lens through which a patron might look at or think about a work.

The final note reads as follows:

> Certain stories resist the urge to pass into oblivion. It isn't tales of love or heroism that last, but rather tales of specific people caught in certain situations defined by emotions or acts of courage that become fixtures in the literary canon. Scheherazade's bravery and brilliant imagination will only continue to grow over time, just as Orpheus' undying devotion to his new bride will never fade. But it is Orpheus' dedication to Eurydice, his willingness to risk all to realize a life with her, a life

the gods saw fit to end just as it began, that has distracted us for millennia. In most adaptations of the ill-fated love, writers, composers, and poets focus on Orpheus' journey into melancholy and then to Hades. Eurydice, the woman whose name serves as the title for the myth and scores of work it inspired, remains a silent witness to a man's brave or foolish act, depending on your thoughts on love and man's ability to cheat death. Sarah Ruhl turns the tables on us with her new adaptation, leaving Orpheus to blubber and fend for himself among the living in order to follow Eurydice's travels to the world of the living dead. Here, in a world where earthly memories and language normally disappear upon entry, Eurydice encounters those from her past who preceded her in both life and death, including her father.

In chronicling Eurydice's time between death and near resurrection, Ruhl takes us through the ages of man (or woman) as Eurydice's father introduces her to the ways of living death. Each touching act is governed by the unselfish love defined by parental devotion. So different is this love and dedication; it is slow, gentle, and kind, ruled by a passion deeper and more still than that of a lover or husband. Both Father and Orpheus demonstrate a willingness to risk all for Eurydice, but it's in how they pursue their goals that we see the difference between a father's and a husband's love.

Another difference in this modern tale of love and loss: we're allowed to see Eurydice's struggle. She who has been voiceless for so long now has a voice, perhaps not one we expect, but an ability nevertheless to express thoughts and the level of consequence her actions have, and the actions of those around her. It is this strength of character that enables this Eurydice to do more than simply fade away at the hand of someone else's act.

This Eurydice learns independence and self-determination in spite of a veil of secrecy. Granted, the secrets are not as sordid as those in Poe's *Fall of the House of Usher* or as murderous as those in *The Telltale Heart*, but somewhere at the core is a level of unrest that haunts this *Eurydice*, lending an air of caution rather than pathos to the play. Where will acts of free will take her in a land that prizes prescribed behavior? And what happens when the lords of all are disobeyed? In the *Fall of the House of Usher* decay, insanity, and death are the righteous recompense for failing to honor life's codes of conduct; simply insanity for the unclean heart. But Eurydice hasn't defiled her family nor murdered her neighbor, although her behavior throughout brings the same level of scorn from those who inhabit the land of the dead.

There are, however, those who are willing to save her from her fate, whatever that may be. Orpheus, her father, and a devilish character whose attraction to Eurydice makes us think of Persephone, a girl who escapes the confines of death for six months each year. And so we have hope for this Eurydice. She can escape having to repeatedly learn how to live fully, a fate worse than death, if only for a few months if she capitulates to an imp's will. An odd bit of humor that even Poe chose to avoid. The irreverent touch reminds us why certain literary figures have remained creative fodder for so many years.

Grounding a Program Note in Metaphor

Visual or linguistic metaphors often inform the set or costume design, and when a dramaturg opts to write about the play's metaphorical impact, the writing focuses on the external world or reality that shapes the metaphors and symbols.

Plays like Kennedy's *Funnyhouse of a Negro* are rife with images that signify certain ideas the writer regularly twists and transforms. The urge to lecture on images and their historical or societal root must be fought: yes, the satire in Kennedy's play will be lost on those unfamiliar with Queen Victoria, African-American women's struggles with hair and wigs, or the varied history of the stars and stripes; but, if a program note opts to merely define, it does little to extend anyone's responses to the play. The active dramaturg strikes a balance between introducing symbols with their possible metaphoric impact and the desire to overanalyze that significance. As the goal of the program note is to inspire thinking, writing about symbols and what they signify presents many challenges.

A poor example of a metaphorical program note might read like this:

> Kennedy's use of disembodied heads does more than remind us of revolutions where the proletariat rises in revolt against the ruling class. Although unusual, it isn't wrong to consider this Russian event with the African uprising in what may be

a French colony. No, the floating heads of Queen Victoria and those of Negro Sarah's dead mother and father tell of the figures that loom large in Negro Sarah's memory and mixed heritage. Torn between which bloodline—white or black—which history—European or the then-little studied African-American history—reigns supreme in her life, she merely sits impassive, tormented by the options and horrors both present to her.

This passage presents finite definitions and emphatic dismissals of what the writer sees as interesting, maybe even well-intuited, but nevertheless poorly researched ideas. This excerpt also adopts a lecturing or academic tone, so that it appears to explain the play rather than illuminate the drama's possibilities. An adjusted passage from an essay grounded in metaphor might read like this:

And where does Kennedy take us with the disembodied heads? They invade Negro Sarah's space from the very beginning, tormenting her just as the Headless Horseman introduced terror to that New England town. But Sarah's figures are real, or figments of actual once-living men and women, who played a crucial role in her life, not fictitious phantoms. Sarah's now dead mother and father cajoled, supported, and observed her choices. Queen Victoria rules the land that once gave rise to Negro Sarah's homeland, America, and governed the African colonies, which in the play's world are only now (in the Sixties) beginning to break free thanks to the efforts of revolutionaries like Patrice Lamumba. The floating heads may do more than remind us of ruling classes and the powerlessness of the proletariat.

Throughout the play, in the writing if not the speaking, Sarah is known as Negro Sarah, as if her connection to an ethnic group or culture is in doubt. Her connection to the Negro or African-American is so tenuous her name must ground her if her skin color, speech pattern, taste in literature, or identification with historical figures does not. With a heritage in such doubt, especially in an era preceding the time immortalized by the slogan "Black is Beautiful" (meaning the darker the skin the better), does Negro Sarah's obviously mixed bloodline and all its implications torment her through the ghost of Queen Victoria?

The dramaturg may also choose to explore the images in a way that introduces their irony, to give the essays a broader appeal. To do this means identifying what role the symbols have for a particular character or event. Take hair in *Funnyhouse*. Some of the disembodied heads that haunt Negro Sarah wear flamboyant wigs or display a pate with only a few strands of kinky hair. Considering the African-American woman's centuries-long struggle with hair care in the United States (if not Western culture), an active dramaturg might begin to associate the black woman's relationship to straight or so-called good hair and the frizzy strands that remain following the deleterious effects of using harsh chemicals in pursuit of it, as a way to discuss the ever-evolving and ever-present struggle with self-image.

Tapping into the stress *all* women with *any* type of hair feel when their hair refuses to perform or lacks the luster and thickness of her youth, changes the meaning of these oddly coiffed, floating heads and broadens the emotional impact. The significance of the floating heads remains mysterious, but now women (and men) of any culture who grapple with hair loss or those who know someone whose self-esteem suffers due to unwanted baldness can related to Negro Sarah.

Grounding a Program Note in Language

If program notes should avoid reading like analytical treatises on the play, how does a dramaturg examine the writer's use of language without creating a literary exegesis? The secret lies in avoiding tackling the problem head on. A sideways approach to language may include a discussion of what the writer doesn't include. In Myers' play *The Realm*, for example, the sounds that replace every word her character James loses are not scripted; the actor must create the symphony of substitutions during rehearsal. Documenting this discovery process alone could lead to a newsletter article that reports on actor methods and a writer's flexibility. An active dramaturg's program note might focus on encouraging readers to consider the significance of sound in their lives. In this case the aural discussion would be both thematic and metaphoric and provide a glimpse into the performer's creative process.

Grounding an essay in language may also lead a dramaturg to write about linguistic innovations. This may mean unique spellings that clearly define a character's dialect (like "yr" or "your" in *In the Blood*), or it may mean ways language sculpts silence as with Parks' spells or unwritten lines, or Pinter's pauses. To keep the essay active, the active dramaturg focuses on how these innovations inform the rehearsal process, and the characters' relationship to the play's themes or metaphors. In essence the language-based program note uses ideas similar to those that governed a number of the dramaturg's rehearsal notes to the director.

A program note could marvel at a writer's ability to craft lines that suggest one idea on the page and with a change in emphasis indicate something else entirely. A passage from an active dramaturg's language-based program note for Parks' *The America Play* might read like this:

> As much as Parks leaves room for the actor to discover character, she gives a lot of guidance when it comes to how they speak. Some writers depend on an understanding of a region through the length of characters' sentences and word choice. Tennessee Williams rarely shapes his dialogue with dialectical spellings (yer for your or nevah for never), although his dialogue is rife with regionalisms and word choices that reveal distinct patterns of thought and speech. Parks does this too, but she also adds interesting spellings and abbreviations to guide the actors to the character through language. Less literate characters tend to truncate their words, removing the vowels so they end more quickly, lessening the amount of time people have to look and listen to them. Their discomfort in the world often reveals itself in their discomfort with language.

As long as the active dramaturg can remain focused on how these innovations generate action and tension on stage the essays thrive as active explorations of language rather than staid musings on vocabulary and etymology.

In short, the program note reveals how an active dramaturg begins to inform a creative process, even if written months before the creative collaboration begins, which is why essays focused on character and time or the play's form rarely appear in a program. Exploring character would either lead to a number of performance choices this particular production didn't make or articulate the choices in a way that defines how the actor must execute them onstage. If a dramaturg chooses to define Hamlet as the misunderstood, indecisive yet devoted law-abiding son, or Blanche Dubois as the not-so-gracefully aging and sexually frustrated matron, the dramaturg has placed an undue and heavy burden on the performer and the production to realize those interpretations on stage even if the rehearsal process suggests a different creative path. Suddenly every choice *must* be informed by these points of view; suddenly the dramaturg has become the director. The active dramaturg doesn't seek to create more hurdles for a cast or more challenges for an audience.

This too may be why form/pattern or time-centered essays rarely make up a dramaturg's note. Yes, the philosophy governing how time functions often shapes the play's mystery or dramatic questions. In discussing how time shapes the action, however, the essay might spoil the punch line.

Program Notes and Theatre for Young Audiences

An active dramaturg's success as a writer involves supporting, not defending or explaining, a play, or production. Strong dramaturgical writing points to ideas to discuss and further explores the play's ideological ambiguities.

If, however, a dramatug must write a note for a Theatre for Young Audiences (TYA) production, there are a few differences. The most obvious adjustments are length (100-500 words) and the note's purpose. Notes for young people are written with an eye to developing critical thinking skills, even so, the active dramaturg avoids using educational and leaden prose. Simply write to the youths as intelligent beings with an evolving vocabulary. However, the active dramaturg must remember that sometimes parents, guardians, or teachers read these essays to or with the child. A good rule of thumb for a TYA program note is to write in a way that challenges the child but with practice or assistance the child could read the note independently.

What about writing to sculpt a critical thinker?

Many who begin writing program notes for TYA productions assume these short bits of prose require less effort than those written for adult audiences. Yes, TYA essays include a simpler vocabulary and fewer words, but they are not easier to compose. Distilling major thematic ideas into simple ideas a young person can digest, analyze and employ requires as much if not more mental focus than that used to write for adults. Writing essays or plays for young people is more exacting because clarity is crucial and ambiguity the kiss of death. Many TYA plays engage fantasy with ease, but these mystical worlds have rules and realities and children will demand to have the world defined fully and clearly. A program note also has to support this need to ground the imagination and create a framework within which to discuss it.

Organizing a Program Note for Young Audiences

An audience of young people will identify strongly with the protagonist. A program note that reinforces the protagonist's journey and struggle to help a young theatre patron learn their sense of narrative is fine. But an active dramaturg finds ways to consider the character's actions in relation to the play's theme. For adults, a note pushes the play's ambiguity by grounding ideas in, perhaps, global society, or culture; for young people, a program note encourages similar understanding by grounding the play in references in family, school, or even global communities with an emphasis on children. The active dramaturg's goal is to help the child recognize that although the play is fictional (even if it is biographical) the life lessons or observations readily connect to their daily life. Bridging the gap between a fictional world and real life without denigrating either requires skill, and when done well establishes a strong path toward critical appreciation for theatre and expansive, analytical thinking.

A poor example of a TYA program note for the play *The Highest Heaven* by José Cruz Gonzàlez might look like this:

> *The Highest Heaven* follows Huracan from his happy days with his mother, Kika, on to his adventure returning to Mexico. Mother and son are being repatriated to Mexico because they are in America illegally. They are separated in the train station and Huracan begins to search for his mother who he never finds. It's good for him that El Negro, a kind dark-skinned Mexican, takes him under his wing and teaches Huracan that family is with you whenever and wherever you go. With El Negro's help Huracan becomes a strong young man who makes peace with his past in his dreams.

This note is nothing but a plot description, and a poor one at that. The note also makes no attempt to explore a specific theme or help the young person ground some of the play's decidedly more mature themes. Many fairy tales or folktales told to young people are about young people separated from their parents temporarily or permanently. A program note shouldn't aim to minimize or reduce the play's impact. Instead, it seeks to frame a discussion between the child and parent during the car ride home.

An excerpt from an active dramaturg's program note might read like this:

> One day Huracan enjoys the freedom of playing in his back-yard and eating dinner with his mother and the next, he's forced to take a life-altering journey. During their repatriation to Mexico, Huracan and his mother, Kika, are separated. Alone and in a strange country, Huracan begins to fend

for himself and discovers how difficult it can be to find an adult willing to protect him like his parents. Independence, it seems, means more than eating candy instead of vegetables or playing instead of doing homework. To be on your own and grown up means behaving with integrity, following through on promises, and standing up to people who mistreat or lie to others. Sometimes people seek payment for these acts of kindness, and sometimes people like El Negro act kindly and ask for nothing in return.

By remaining grounded in the play's themes, it is possible for the program note to avoid sounding like a lecture or telling the young theatre patron what to think.

Program notes for more advanced learners can move toward exploring a text's ambiguity rather than simply providing the tools needed to better appreciate art or build the foundation for nuanced and critical thinking. Should tensions rise between the literary and marketing departments over newsletter and program notes, it's time for the active dramaturg to step up and negotiate clarity.

Educational Material and Dramaturgs

Because dramaturgs play such an active role in preparing a cast for a play by exploring the play's themes, images, language, character, voice, use of time and form/pattern, as well as researching aspects of the story or the play's background, dramaturgs often assist the education directors. Given the state and National (U.S.) academic standards, as well as reduced funding for field trips to theatres, all arts organizations have begun shaping guides that demonstrate how the arts connect to and enhance the academic experience.

There is nothing wrong with identifying aspects of a play that relate to topics teachers cover in a particular academic year. The danger comes when the theatre's art is seen as nothing but an educational tool, that curricular agendas and standards conscribe the art's imaginative breadth, making a trip to the theatre no more thrilling than a pop quiz in algebra.

When active dramaturgs work as or with education directors, the goal is to create materials that support the theatre-going experience in a way that reinforces the excitement of a live performance that transports its audience to a new world.

The Basic Parts of a Study Guide

Not too long ago, the average American Study Guide included a vocabulary list, a plot summary, an activity or two, and some interesting historical information if needed. Today, the most dynamic guides are designed to resemble an adult's subscriber newsletter. Study Guides include interviews with artists, rigorous discussion questions, articles that connect the play to contemporary society (regardless of the play's subject), and hints to help incorporate the play into the curriculum.

As much as the publications differ among theatres, they do tend to focus on six major areas: welcome letters to the students and teachers; a discussion of the play's basic information; themes; curriculum connections; activities; and a way to assess learning. The guides provide background for the play and information to facilitate in-class discussions before and after seeing the production. They may closely resemble Actor Packets. The greatest difference between the Actor Packet and Study Guide is that the Study Guide includes much more original material and actively articulates and defines the play's themes.

When writing thematic descriptions (or most of the guide), it may not be possible to write directly to the student, because individual copies may not be made, or the students are too young. The active dramaturg chooses how to present information either directly to the teacher who will read the information and then distill it for the class, or directly to the student. However, when writing discussion questions or directions for activities, it may not be possible to write directly to the students because the teacher may simply read these words to the class or choose to photocopy the activities. Either way, when composing the guide, it's important to choose pronouns carefully. A misplaced 'you' may suddenly return the teacher to her student days, a time she thought was long past.

After considering who the intended audience is, keep in mind the grade levels when drafting definitions and ways to analyze or understand various topics. Although dramaturgs have not always been trained as elementary, middle, or high school teachers, it is possible to ascertain the linguistic and conceptual limits for every grade. Local libraries with strong children's sections can help an active dramaturg identify appropriate grade-level writing and material. Spending a few minutes looking through a sixth grade social studies text or a first grade reader can help inspire a grade-appropriate Study Guide. Even the state academic standards may prove helpful when assembling information for a Study Guide. By researching the curricular and cognitive expectations, the active dramaturg and education director can gain a sense of what will be covered and sometimes how it will appear on the test. In Ohio, for example, fourth graders are expected to take a prose passage and turn it into a passage with dialogue using quotation marks and following the dramatic format for a play. An active dramaturg might use this information to craft an activity that relates to the play and reinforces an academic lesson. Done this way the theatre demonstrates how theatre helps the teacher in the classroom without detracting from the art.

A strong Study Guide will find ways to extend a single field trip into a year-long experience by presenting information and activities a teacher can use with a variety of lesson plans. A strong guide also helps the teacher finesse the connections; by acknowledging that teachers spend a lot of time preparing students for the performance and its themes or topics, everyone will understand that the Study Guide should assist, not hinder the teacher with many of her instructional obligations.

Parts of the Study Guide: What They Are and What They Contain

Welcome Letters

These letters convey the theatre's enthusiasm for the production and eagerness to have the students and teachers visit. The letter to the teacher introduces the Study Guide, alerting them to topics covered and interesting facts the authors included. A separate letter to the students often addresses issues pertaining to theatre etiquette. It's important to write specifically to the students; a letter makes them feel important and in turn they treat the field trip (and the theatre) with considerably more care.

About The Play

This section includes background on the play and production. Most Study Guides include the playwright's biography, a plot summary, any historical connections, and a description of the play's style and genre, and perhaps an interview with the writer or a designer.

The biography needn't be a dry account. A number of playwrights who specialize in TYA often compose a kid-friendly bio, which may include references to summer camp experiences or pets. An active dramaturg charged with writing a bio for young people may not choose to include such personal details, but should at least opt for lively sentences.

Some Study Guide authors list every character in the play separately or write a plot summary lengthy enough to contain the entire cast. The problem with a separate list is that the characters exist out of context; and a long plot summary reveals too much. The truth is most TYA plays involve a small number of characters. An active dramaturg who writes a summary that introduces a few primary figures but suggests that other characters may appear, allows for more direct and active writing with fewer opportunities to reveal too much story. (Would a plot summary for *Hamlet* include Osric?) The summary should include a short description of the significant characters, an introduction to their journey and its complication. Too often, the plot summary for TYA discloses how the play ends. Why spoil the fun? Young people can follow a story as well as an adult, sometimes better. Concluding the summary with conceptual questions the characters will deal with or ending with a cliffhanger will give the summary the punch it needs and excite the students.

An example of a poor summary for *The Wrestling Season*:

> *The Wrestling Season* follows a group of friends and their rivals. Many high school cliques and groups are represented in this play: the jocks, the cheerleaders, the nerds. Everyone's reputation stands in the balance as classmates spread rumors that drive some to do violence to themselves or others. The play is set up like a wrestling match, with a Referee character stopping the action with whistle blows and standard referee signals. In the end, the story doesn't conclude with a revelation of truths or an explanation of character actions. Instead, the characters step forward and the audience evaluates/judges their behavior and questions the characters motives. For in this play as in life, the truth cannot be known.

What makes this summary less successful is that it never provides the names of key characters (if the cast is large, every character need not be named, but the main characters should be), the play's major question or conflict. The above summary also reveals how the play ends; in fact, the final line provides a moral interpretation rather than a question for the audience to consider.

An example of a strong summary for *The Wrestling Season*:

> *Matt* and *Luke* are best friends and preparing to qualify for another season on the wrestling team. They've been friends for so long they do not think twice about helping each other make weight for team weigh-ins or pass algebra and calculus tests. Their rivals on the wrestling team are *Jolt* and *Willy*, two

young men eager to do anything to become the number one wrestler in their respective classes, including initiating the rumor that Matt and Luke are gay. There are also four young women in the play whose lives, just like Matt and Luke, are turned upside down due to rumors based on assumptions. *Kori*, Matt's closest girl friend, is described by everyone as odd and pegged as the social outcast. *Melanie* does nothing to dispel the rumor that she is the class slut. Heather dates Jolt and does anything he says because he says he loves her. *Nicole, Heather* and Melanie's friend and the only one without a boyfriend, is being pressured to become sexually active. Throughout, the *Referee* starts and stops the action and comments on what we see by using official high school wrestling signals. Each character repeats the phrase, "You think you know me, but you don't" causing us to question what's most important— knowing the truth behind a rumor or trusting our friends.

A number of TYA plays that appeal to young audiences will involve historical figures or events. Although it is possible to include background information for these figures and events within the curriculum connection section, the play may be better served if some information is included in the About The Play section. First, the facts may be crucial to understanding the play. Take, for example, the Great Depression and the plays *Boxcar Children* or *Bud Not Buddy*. To not know what a Hooverville was or not understand that the Great Depression involved money and not an emotional state prevents students from engaging fully with the play. This historical period provides the setting or backdrop for the play's action. By introducing the subject in this early section of the guide the Depression's import cannot be denied.

A brief discussion of the play's style and genre can also help improve the student's artistic vocabulary and appreciation for various artistic performances. Presenting information on theatre styles like adaptation, realism, commedia, or epic can further hone a student's artistic eye. Defining a play's genre or general theatrical category such as musical, drama, comedy or story theatre can help students and teachers differentiate structural and performance techniques.

Themes

This section introduces students and teachers to a few of the play's larger ideas. Every theatre's Study Guide has space limitations, but an active dramaturg seeks to include at minimum two themes to demonstrate that plays present a number of ideas. When writing descriptions of the themes, it's quite possible more of the play's plot will be revealed. That's fine. In fact, if the teacher or student reads the entire Study Guide before coming to the play they will probably learn the entire story. The goal isn't to hide the play's story, but it is preferable to avoid revealing the entire story on the guide's first page.

It's also worth discussing a challenging theme. If a traditional theme for a TYA play falls along the lines of friendship, trust, responsibility, or managing sibling rivalry, challenging themes might be racism and interracial relationships as in Louis Sachar's *Holes,* or a parent's death as in *The Highest Heaven* by José Cruz Gonzalez. It's important for the Study Guide to tackle these themes in ways that provide the teachers with additional tools to facilitate a discussion. Students encounter these issues in their lives and knowing that there are stories that embrace the difficult aspects of life can help them feel less lonely in their struggle and discover positive ways to negotiate these hurdles.

Themes are tough to write, and challenging themes, even tougher. The temptation is to craft a moral or lesson, however, a theme encourages the young person's critical thinking skills to expand. When tackling these challenging themes the same rules apply: try to open up the idea in a way that frames the discussion rather than directs a particular point of view. When trying to address the challenging theme, it's worth considering whether another, larger, less inflammatory idea can initiate the thematic discussion.

An example of a poor theme for *The Wrestling Season:*

> Jolt and Willy, who want a better spot on the wrestling team, try to shake Matt and Luke's confidence, so they spread the rumor that their two rivals are gay. Kori doesn't have a track record of dating and is good friends with Matt and Luke, so everyone at school begins to assume she's gay, too. Sexual orientation does not define a person; it is, like skin or hair color, one part of a person's biological make-up. The play asks, how do we value or judge the sexual choices of homosexual students verses heterosexual students?

Rather than frame the discussion, the above passage inflames the discussion of sexual orientation by defining sexual orientation as a biological truth without any information to aid the teacher. The above passage also fails to introduce the heterosexual characters and yet the thematic question includes them, potentially skewing the conversation toward the topic of homosexuality rather than promiscuity. In the end, the passage avoids the play's larger theme, which impacts character behavior and journey, in favor of exploring homosexuality, which is simply one manifestation of the larger theme: the impact of rumors on student life and behavior.

An example of a strong theme for *The Wrestling Season*:

> Much of *Wrestling Season's* action revolves around events inspired by rumors, that is, characters make decisions based on what other characters say *about* them. No matter how the characters describe themselves, the rumors often prove too powerful to dispel. Characters then make choices that react to the rumors instead of presenting themselves as they truly are. The play encourages us to examine and consider what rumors, these unsubstantiated beliefs, do to people's lives and their self-esteem.

> Movie stars, musicians, and politicians often battle rumors regarding their personal lives. Showing up at a nightclub with another musician can automatically mean you're dating; when a senator has a power-breakfast with a presidential hopeful, it's immediately assumed they will be running mates. Some members of the press then spend their time working to turn the rumors into bonafide stories, rather than working to uncover the truth. Investigative journalists look for solid proof before deeming a rumor or statement true. These journalists search for facts and other evidence before presenting an idea for their audience to consider. Many who embrace rumors over fact are interested in influencing conversations and perception, not empowering others to see and understand.

Curriculum Connections

This section connects play's topics to various academic subjects. Often teachers associate theatre with English literature and reading, but forget that the theatre embraces all academic disciplines. Sound, set and lighting designers need to understand physics, chemistry, and math. Directors and costume designers rely heavily on history and psychology, as do playwrights and dramaturgs. For example, including a science lesson that grounds itself in a theatrical experience gives the student who enjoys drama but detests science a way to connect with or develop a curiosity for both subjects. The same may be said for the math lover who recoils at the thought of reading anything longer than a story problem. A lesson that presents the theatre's spatial challenges through mathematical means will not only open a door to reading but may inspire a new hobby or career path for the student. Curriculum connections also present ways for the Study Guide to intersect with the academic standards and goals the teachers must now use to shape their lessons. Again, it's important to include more than one and since English-related curriculum is such an obvious choice, active dramaturgs know that focusing on the other subjects often strengthens the guide.

An example of a poor curriculum connection for *The Emperor's New Clothes*:

> The tailors say that they can weave the most spectacular cloth in all the land and that their clothes can help determine who is smart and who is not. Clothes cannot tell us how smart a person is, but they can tell us something about a person such as what they do for a living or what climate they live in. For example, someone wearing sandals may live in a warm climate and someone wearing fur boots may live where it's cold. Look at the images below and see if you and your classmates can tell your teacher what the characters do based on what they wear.

Although *The Emperor's New Clothes* is a play for younger children, the curriculum connection should still provide some educational content. What's more, this passage encourages students to only look at the costume, to determine a truth about a person based solely on the exterior. The curriculum connection seems to go against Hans Christian Anderson's original point.

A curriculum connection that encourages students to consider climate and the type of fabrics worn in those areas would enable students and teachers to study weather, geography and how fabric or textiles are made in various parts of the world. With a few adjustments, the curriculum connection can become a rich extension of the play and support various state or national learning standards by using the play as a reference point.

An example of a strong curriculum connection for *The Emperor's New Clothes*:

> The tailors in *The Emperor's New Clothes* say that they can weave thread or yarn into a beautiful, invisible fabric. But how is the thread or yarn made, and what is used to create it? Some

cultures use wool to create yarn that is woven into fabric and others use cotton. Some ancient civilizations in Mexico used a variety of the Agave plant and its fibers to weave into cloth. Textiles, or fabrics that are woven or knit into clothes, may be made from plant fibers, animal fibers such as wool or fur or from insects like the silk worm. When, for example, weavers begin working, they consider how the fabric will be use—as clothing or upholstery—to determine how thick or heavy it will be. Also, people who live in warm climates use light fibers and fabrics, and those who live in cold climates use a more dense weaves or animal skins to keep themselves warm. What helps a fabric feel light or heavy is the density of the weave, how tightly the fibers or threads are bound together. Below are images of the tools used to weave fibers into fabrics and pictures of weaving patterns for lightweight and heavy textiles.

Activities

Activities provide hands-on opportunities to reinforce any of the ideas presented in the Study Guide. If, for example, the play is an adaptation, an activity focused on taking a literary passage and transforming it into a dramatic scene may be ideal. Or, an arts and crafts project may be right if the production deals with masks. It's also possible to include activities that reinforce the curriculum connection. Whatever inspires the activity is fine as long as the narrative that introduces the activity connects to the play and an area in the Study Guide to reinforce the necessary context. An active dramaturg also creates original activities by searching educational texts and art texts for ideas and then expanding them to connect to the play and topic. Take care when writing the activities, however. Each step must be clearly articulated, like a recipe, and all of the equipment listed. Also, an active dramaturg remembers to adjust the steps and materials for different age groups or grades.

Considering the curriculum connections above, a poor activity would be to have students identify the profession indicated by the image. A strong activity would be to have students choose a part of the world or country and identify its climate, natural resource used for textiles and type of clothing that best suits that climate.

Pull-Out Boxes and Vocabulary

The most interesting Study Guides include pull-out boxes with cool facts about the play, the theatre, the historical period, or connection to curriculum. It's a great way to include information that just won't fit in any place else. Vocabulary words might also fit in these boxes, whether it's a word a character uses in the play or it's a theatrical term that isn't easily defined. Many guides still include vocabulary lists. However, active dramaturgs understand that creating a context for the word within the many narratives and defining it within the written thematic discussion or About the Play section brings more opportunities for the student to learn the word as well as when and how to use it.

Discussion Questions

No guide is complete without a series of questions that help the teacher lead a discussion. No set number exists for questions, although many stronger Study Guides include before-seeing-the-play questions to help the students prepare for the theatre and after-seeing-the-play questions to help them develop critical thinking skills.

Providing an Assessment Tool

In this era of testing, a number of teachers and school districts have asked theatres to include assessment tools or quizzes in the guides. These tests are actually extensions of the activity section but examine all of the ideas explored in the play and the Study Guide. Some choose to create essay questions while others fashion elaborate word searches or crossword puzzles with fill-in-the-blank questions as clues.

Blurbs and Other Bits of Writing

There are other materials the dramaturg and literary office either initiates or helps the marketing department generate, but none is more challenging to write than blurbs. Blurbs are short, snappy 50 to 100 word bits of prose that sell the play and introduce its major idea to patrons. They are neither glorified plot descriptions nor excuses to simplify a play to its most marketable ideas. Blurbs support the season's theme or marketing campaign but uphold the play's integrity. They are also everyone's first window into a play, especially world premieres or relatively new works.

Mistaking a Summary Paragraph for a Blurb

A paragraph-long summary may prove easier, but if done without care, blurbs can pigeon-hole a play and reduce rather than increase the potential audience. The truth is, these longer summaries often provide the theatre staff's first (and sometimes only) introduction to the play, since many do not read the play or, if they do, read it through the lens focused by the paragraph-long summary. And if the staff writes the blurb—or edits the dramaturg's—based on the ideas raised by the paragraph-long summary, the blurb may end up describing something completely unlike the play the theatre plans to produce. An active dramaturg works to craft focused but unbiased descriptions that articulate the plot and a major question for the character or play—without revealing the dramatic twist or resorting to using a plethora of actual interrogative statements.

What Might a Blurb Look Like?

Few dramaturgs have practice writing blurbs while in school. The ability to distill a play into dramatic, pithy prose that helps the marketing and press office introduce a play to the community is important. A poor blurb for *Hamlet* might look like this:

> What is a boy prince to do? The Queen Mum's remarried, and to your only uncle. Your girlfriend hasn't gotten the hint and her brother has taken to fighting her battles while her father, well her father's a dolt and oblivious to it all. It would be easy to deal with this if it weren't for King Dad's untimely death and his reluctance to pass quietly into the night. When rumors of the king's murder begin to surface the little order that remained quickly disappears to reveal heated drama and intrigue.

The above blurb fails to capture the true sense of Shakespeare's revenge tragedy, distilling the play's relationships to quips better suited for a ribald comedy. The story's central question (and *Hamlet* offers many) never enters the description. And then the passage abruptly ends with words that declare a level of drama and intrigue a stronger blurb would reveal throughout. Although, the tone may successfully suggest the production's vision—a play about a disaffected youth's sarcastic world view—an active dramaturg's blurb for *Hamlet* might look like this:

> Elsinore has been a happier place but for now it's blanketed in turmoil. The king has died, leaving a grief stricken son, and

newly married wife and brother who seem anything but emotionally distraught. The prince's friends who might bring him
joy, find themselves following their elders' wayward sense of
justice and protocol. As melancholy gives way to confusion
and then revenge when rumors of murder fill the air, an outside force threatens to invade and annex the crumbling em-
pire before order and justice return.

Blurbs and Cultural Identity or Gender

The dramaturg's challenge is to present plays written from a particular
ethnic or cultural perspective in ways that invite everyone to experience
and appreciate the work, for plays with specific ethnic experiences at their
core are just as affecting and impacting as those presumed to be written
from a non-ethnically specific point of view.

An added challenge with blurbs is an awareness of presenting the play
as appropriate to a specific segment of society. For example, during the
late 1980s/early 1990s, theatres began producing a number of plays by female writers. The resulting blurbs were full of descriptions that pushed
the female nature of the play over its richer, more gender-neutral themes.
The same is still done for plays written by African Americans, Latinos, or
Asian Americans. The active dramaturg works to craft blurbs and descriptions that honor the writer's vision and the play's thematic, even universal
reach, because strong dramatic works speak to all segments of society regardless of wealth, culture, or ethnicity.

Final Thoughts

Whether writing blurbs, articles, or program notes, an active dramaturg works to deepen and support the audience and the various theatre
departments' appreciation for the play and production. These few pieces of
writing remain some of the most significant ways of communicating the
artistic vision for today and posterity; their success lies solely in the active
dramturg's pen.

Choose your words carefully.
Write well.

Appendix A

A Dramaturgical Credo

The Dramaturgical Guide For Set Texts

1. First, do no harm.
2. Do not direct, rewrite, or redesign the text, doing so does harm and ignores rule #1.
3. Listen to the play's rules, wants and needs.
4. Listen to your collaborators' wants, and needs.
5. Identify when #3 and #4 work against one another.
6. Consider and discern whether that pull enhances or distracts.
7. Pose Open Questions.
8. Listen to your collaborators' responses.
9. Listen to the play's responses.
10. Keep the play's rules, need and wants at the center of all you do.
11. Help your collaborators remain connected to their passion.

Remember, you're there to help grow a production, you are not there to save it from the critics.

The Dramaturgical Guide For New Plays

1. First, do no harm.
2. Do not write the play. Doing so does harm and ignores rule #1.
3. Listen to the play's rules, wants and needs.
4. Listen to the writer's wants and needs.
5. Identify when and where #3 and #4 work against one another.
6. Consider and discern whether that pull in #5 enhances or distracts.
7. Pose Open Questions.
8. Listen to the writer's responses.
9. Listen to the play's responses.
10. Keep the play's rules, needs and wants at the center of all you do.
11. Help your collaborators remain connected to their passion.

Remember, you're there to help grow a play (and production) into being; you are not there to save it from the critics.

Appendix B

Open Questions

The Neutral Question: "Where do you see the role of women in this play?"

Where the Bias Lies	This question implies that either women aren't active, non-stereotyped agents or that the questioner has specific ideas regarding women's power in the play.
What is at the Question's Heart	The questioner seems interested in the play and how to understand the statement the play makes regarding this specific gender.
To Craft the Open Question	Recognize that to show characters or ideas in opposition both (or all) sides of the problem need to be represented—in this case male and female.

The Open Question: "How does gender influence the play?"

The Neutral Question: "How did the female characters move the play forward?"

Where the Bias Lies	The question assumes the women do not move the play's action forward. The use of 'did' suggests that the question is also a test.
What is at the Question's Heart	That women could influence action in ways equal to or greater than the male characters.
To Craft the Open Question	Women may not drive the scenes and maybe they should be exploring how the women are—or are not—involved in the play's central action.

The Open Question: "How does the play's action shape the female characters?"

The Neutral Question: "What is the significance for each color in Mariela's painting?"

Where the Bias Lies	Such a question opens the discussion to the artist and allows the artist to describe a thought process, but also places the creator in a defensive position, if the person asking the question isn't careful.
What is at the Question's Heart	Consider color choice, the thought process that accompanied it and, more than that, begin to think about the play and what the play says (or doesn't say) about color.
To Craft the Open Question	Allow a broader discussion of all characters, not just the characters who inspired the question.

The Open Question: "What or which colors represent the characters?"

The Neutral Question: "How does the play's action begin?"

Where the Bias Lies	This vague question resembles the Passover Question but refers to a context and setting rather than exploration of a single event.
What is at the Question's Heart	See above.
To Craft the Open Question	Consider ways to rephrase it so the response may be grounded in context.

The Open Question: "What is the world like before the play begins? What do the events of this play change for this world?"

The Neutral Question: "How do we connect Amanda from *The Glass Menagerie* to this world, especially if we're exploring pushing the idea of Tom as narrator?"

Where the Bias Lies	The opening phrase '*How does Amanda connect to the world*' funnels all answers through Amanda, forcing a specific and linear connection that begins and ends with her character.
What is at the Question's Heart	The questioner wants to look at Amanda, the play's entire world and the other characters who directly serve the director's vision.
To Craft the Open Question	Consider ways to rephrase so all major characters may be discussed.

The Open Question: "How do the characters (major and minor) support this play's major themes or the production's ideas?"

The Neutral Question: "What story do you wish to tell?"

Where the Bias Lies	It risks placing artists on the defensive. Certainly tone mitigates some of this, but when dissecting the words themselves it's possible for artists, especially directors and playwrights, to hear this question as a threat to or an attack on their artistic ability. Basically, the question asks, *Do you have an idea or vision or focus for this play?*
What is at the Question's Heart	The questioner wants to discover what emotional connections the writer or director has to the play.
To Craft the Open Question	Never ask it.

The Open Question: Begin with a more open question that asks how the artist connects to the story and ground these questions of story in observations regarding theme and other elements of the play's style.

The Neutral Question: "Why this play at this time?"

Where the Bias Lies	This broadly phrased question invites a number of long rambling responses ranging from today's political situation to the story of the writer's lost cat and the subsequent constant longing for companionship.
What is at the Question's Heart	To discover what specifically compels the creating artist to write or direct the story.
To Craft the Open Question	The question encourages the writer (or director) to respond in a personal and creative way. But there's an implication that a current event must connect, and if that's the wrong assumption, a lot of good will governing collaboration has been lost.

The Open Question: "What inspires you to tell this story?" or, "What draws you to this story/play?"

Appendix C

The Need For a Dramaturgical Contract

Freelance dramaturgs automatically generate a formal contract, because they have a specific job description for each project. Other dramaturgs—students or resident artists—must choose whether to propose a contract for each production. Some see this as an added step that burdens the process; others view a contract as a way to avoid unpleasant situations. The decision to adopt a formal contract or forge an oral agreement among colleagues—the dramaturg, director, and playwright—should be made well before rehearsals and meetings begin. The contract should clearly state each artist's goals for the project and the role each will play during the process.

Without question, an agreement should include the expectations surrounding the dramaturg's presence during the rehearsal. I still meet (and work with) established directors who seem surprised I'll attend rehearsals beyond the tablework phase. Active dramaturgs are a part of the company and artistic team. Period. Active dramaturgs play a vital role in realizing the production and do not need to wait to be invited. But sometimes a contract helps lessen the surprise.

In general, the dramaturg should attend all days spent at the table, a few days when specific scenes are worked, significant runs of large sections of the play or stumble-throughs, and every run-through and preview performance. If the theater has an unusually long preview process, two weeks or more, establish with the theatre, producer, and director how many performances to attend and which shows are most important. A rule of thumb would be the first preview, a matinee, a preview during the middle of this process and the final preview prior to the last rehearsal day. If it's a world premiere, everyone should plan for the dramaturg to attend a few more performances early in the preview process, if not all of them. Of course, there will be production meetings and director/dramaturg/

playwright meetings following the performance. Be prepared for some late nights.

For more information on contracts and fees, consult the Literary Managers and Dramaturgs of the Americas, www.lmda.org.

Bibliography

Ball, David. Backwards and Forwards: *A Technical Manual for Reading Plays*. Carbondale: Southern Illinois University Press, 1983.

Borreca, Art. "Dramaturging New Play Dramaturgy: The Yale and Iowa Ideals." *Dramaturgy in American Theatre: A Sourcebook*. Ed. Susan Jonas, Geoffrey S. Proehl and Michael Lupu. New York: Harcourt Brace, 1997. 56-69.

Brockett, Oscar G. "Dramaturgy in Education: Introduction." *Dramaturgy in American Theatre: A Sourcebook*. Ed. Susan Jonas, Geoffrey S. Proehl and Michael Lupu. New York: Harcourt Brace, 1997. 42-47.

Brustein, Robert. "The Future of Un-American Activity." *Dramaturgy in American Theatre: A Sourcebook*. Ed. Susan Jonas, Geoffrey S. Proehl and Michael Lupu. New York: Harcourt Brace, 1997. 33-36.

Churchill, Carol. *Cloud Nine*. New York: Theatre Communications Group, 2000.

———. *Far Away*. New York: Theatre Communications Group, 2001.

Dixon, Michael Bigelow. "The Dramaturgical Dialogue: New Play Dramaturgy at Actors Theatre of Louisville." *Dramaturgy in American Theatre: A Sourcebook*. Ed. Susan Jonas, Geoffrey S. Proehl and Michael Lupu. New York: Harcourt Brace, 1997. 412-420.

Doyle, Sir Arthur Conan. "A Scandal in Bohemia." *The Complete Adventures of Sherlock Holmes* ed. Julian Symons, London: Martin Secker & Warburg, Ltd. 1981.

Gonzalez, José Cruz. *The Highest Heaven*. Woodstock: Dramatics Publishing, 2002.

Ibsen, Heinrich. *Four Major Plays, Vol 1.: The Doll's House, The Wild Duck, Hedda Gabler, The Master Builder*. Transl. Rolf Fjelde. New York: The New American Library, 1996.

Kennedy, Adrienne. "Funnyhouse of a Negro." *The Adrienne Kennedy Reader.* Minneapolis: University of Minnesota Press, 2001.

Kennedy, Allen. "Professional Theatre in Education: Contexts for Dramaturgy." *Dramaturgy in American Theatre: A Sourcebook.* Ed. Susan Jonas, Geoffrey S. Proehl and Michael Lupu. New York: Harcourt Brace, 1997. p. 190-208.

Kramer, Larry. *The Normal Heart and The Destiny of Me: Two Plays by Larry Kramer.* New York: Grove Press, 2000.

Lerman, Liz. "Toward a Process for Critical Response." *High Performance* 64.4 (1993): 17-19.

Lerman, Liz and John Borstel. *Liz Lerman's Critical Response Process: A Method for Getting Useful Feedback from Anything you Make, from Dance to Dessert.* Takoma Park: Liz Lerman Dance Exchange, 2003.

Martin, Steve. "Studio Script Notes on 'The Passion'." *The New Yorker* (March 8, 2004): 94.

Müller, Heiner. *Hamlet-Machine and Other Texts for the Stage.* Ed./ transl. Carl Weber. New York: Performing Arts Journal Publications, 2001.

Myers, Sara L. *The Realm.* New York: Playscripts, Inc., 2007.

Parks, Suzan-Lori. "The America Play." *The America Play and Other Works.* New York: Theatre Communications Group, 1995.

———. "The Elements of Style". *The America Play and Other Works.* New York: Theatre Communications Group, 1995.

———. *Top Dog/Underdog.* New York: Theatre Communications Group, 2001.

Pettingill, Richard. "Dramaturging Education." *Dramaturgy in American Theatre: A Sourcebook.* Ed. Susan Jonas, Geoffrey S. Proehl and Michael Lupu. New York: Harcourt Brace, 1997.

Rivera, José. "Marisol." *Marisol and Other Plays.* New York: Theatre Communications Group, 1997.

Rush, David. "Talking Back: A Model for Post-performance Discussion of New Plays." Theatre Topics 10.1 (Mar. 2000): 53-63.

Schecter, Joel. "In the Beginning There Was Lessing...Then Brecht, Müller, and Other Dramaturgs." *Dramaturgy in American Theatre: A Sourcebook.* Ed. Susan Jonas, Geoffrey S. Proehl and Michael Lupu. New York: Harcourt Brace, 1997. 105-146.

Shakespeare, William. *The Arden Shakespeare: A Midsummer Night's Dream.* ed. Harold Brooks. London: Methuen & Co. 1979.

———. *The Arden Shakespeare: Richard III.* ed. Antony Hammond. New York: Methuen. 1981.

———. *The Arden Shakespeare: Hamlet.* eds. Ann Thompson and Neil Taylor London: Thomson Learning, 2006

Strindberg, August. *Plays: One. The Father; Miss Julie; The Ghost Sonata.* Transl. Michael Meyer. London: Methuen Drama. 1976.

Williams, Tennessee. *The Glass Menagerie.* Introduction by Robert Bray. New York: New Directions Publishing Co., 1999.

Plays Discussed

Laurie Brooks	*The Wrestling Season*
José Cruz Gonzalez	*The Highest Heaven*
Henrik Ibsen	*A Doll's House*
Adrienne Kennedy	*Funnyhouse of a Negro*
Sarah L. Myers	*The Realm*
Suzan-Lori Parks	*The America Play; In the Blood; Topdog/ Underdog*
José Rivera	*Boleros for the Disenchanted*
Sarah Ruhl	*Eurydice*
William Shakespeare	*Hamlet; King Lear; A Midsummer Night's Dream; Richard III*
August Strindberg	*Miss Julie*

Plays Mentioned

George Büchner	*Woyzeck*
Caryl Churchill	*Cloud Nine; Far Away*
Barbara Field (adapted by)	*Boxcar Children*
Barbara Garson	*MacBird!*
David Ives	*Philip Glass Buys a Loaf of Bread*

Reginald Andre Jackson (adapted by)	*Bud Not Buddy*
Sarah Kane	*4.48 psychosis*
Larry Kramer	*The Normal Heart*
Tony Kushner	*Angels in America; Homebody/ Kabul*
Dora Litinakes	*The Fly*
Martin McDonagh	*Pillowman*
Arthur Miller	*Finishing the Picture*
Heiner Müller	*Hamlet-machine*
Lynn Nottage	*Crumbs From the Table of Joy; Fabulation, or the Re-education of Undine; Intimate Apparel; Las Meninas*
William Shakespeare	*King Lear*
George Bernard Shaw	*Major Barbara*
Neil Simon	*Laughter on the 23rd Floor*
Stephen Sondheim	*Sunday in the Park with George*
Cheryl L. West	*Holiday Heart*
Tennessee Williams	*A Streetcar Named Desire*
Doug Wright	*I Am My Own Wife*
Karen Zacarías	*Mariela and the Desert*

Films Cited

Hamlet. Dir. Kenneth Branagh. With Kenneth Branagh, Derek Jacobi, Julie Christie, Kate Winslet, Richard Briers and Michael Maloney. Castle Rock Entertainment, 240 minutes. 1996. DVD

Hamlet. Dir. Michael Almereyda. With Ethan Hawke, Kyle MacLachlan, Diane Venora, Sam Shepard, Bill Murray, Liev Schreiber and Julia Stiles. 112 minutes. Miramax, 2000. DVD.

Richard III. Dir. Richard Loncraine. With Ian McKellen, Annette Benning, Jim Broadbent, Robert Downey Jr., Nigel Hawthorne, Kristin Scott Thomas, John Wood, and Maggie Smith. 104 minutes. MGM Home Entertainment, 2000. DVD.